Victorian Literature and Postcolonial Studies

Postcolonial Literary Studies

Series Editors: David Johnson, The Open University and Ania Loomba, University of Pennsylvania

Published titles:
Victorian Literature and Postcolonial Studies, Patrick Brantlinger
Eighteenth-century British Literature and Postcolonial Studies, Suvir Kaul

Forthcoming titles:
Medieval Literature and Postcolonial Studies, Lisa Lampert-Weissig
Renaissance Literature and Postcolonial Studies, Shankar Raman

Victorian Literature and Postcolonial Studies

Patrick Brantlinger

Edinburgh University Press

© Patrick Brantlinger, 2009

Transferred to digital print 2013

Edinburgh University Press Ltd
22 George Square, Edinburgh

Typeset in 10.5/13 Sabon
by Servis Filmsetting Ltd, Stockport, Cheshire, and
Printed and bound by CPI Group (UK) Ltd, Croydon, CR0 4YY

A CIP record for this book is available from the British Library

ISBN 978 0 7486 3303 6 (hardback)
ISBN 978 0 7486 3304 3 (paperback)

The right of Patrick Brantlinger
to be identified as author of this work
has been asserted in accordance with
the Copyright, Designs and Patents Act 1988.

Contents

Acknowledgments

I am grateful to many people for their ideas and comments. They include Todd Avery, Dan Bivona, Purnima Bose, Eva Cherniavsky, Deirdre David, Rob Fulk, Richard Higgins, Anna Johnston, Hussein Khadim, Paula Krebs, Ivan Kreilkamp, Todd Kuchta, John Kucich, Andrew Libby, Jason Lindquist, Sara Maurer, Brook Miller, Jan Nederveen Pieterse, Sylvia Pamboukian, Don Randall, Brian Rasmussen, Ranu Samantrai, Cannon Schmitt, and Janet Sorensen. I thank, too, Helen Gilbert, Chris Tiffin, and their crew of postcolonialists at Queensland University. Suk Koo Rhee, Kyung Won Lee, and their students at Yonsei University offered interesting comments about my version of postcolonial studies. Thanks, too, to Sang-Kee Park for his friendship and hospitality. Ania Loomba and David Johnson have been helpful throughout this project; I hope it meets their expectations. And Ellen Brantlinger, as always, has been supportive in innumerable ways.

Timeline

Date	Historical Events	Literary and Other Publications
1756–63	Seven Years War in North America, securing British hegemony	
1757	Battle of Plassey establishes domination of East India Company in Bengal	
1775–83	American Revolution	
1776		American *Declaration of Independence*
1786–92	French Revolution	
1787	Settlement of freed slaves in Sierra Leone	
1788	The First Fleet establishes a penal colony at Botany Bay in Australia	
1790		Edmund Burke, *Reflections on the Revolution in France.*
1791–8	Revolution in Haiti led by Toussaint Louverture	Mary Wollstonecraft, *A Vindication of the Rights of Woman*
1794	Revolutionary government in France abolishes slavery in all French territory	William Blake, *Songs of Innocence and of Experience*
1795	London Missionary Society establishes	

	missions in South Pacific; war against the maroons in Jamaica	
1798	United Irishman's Rebellion fails to liberate Ireland from Britain	Rev. Thomas Malthus, *Essay on Population*
1799	Tipu Sultan killed and Mysore brought under British control	
1800	Act of Union uniting England and Ireland	Maria Edgeworth, *Castle Rackrent*
1805	Admiral Nelson's victory over the French fleet	
1806		Sydney Owenson (Lady Morgan), *The Wild Irish Girl*
1807	Parliament outlaws the slave trade	
1812		Lord Byron, *Child Harold's Pilgrimage*
1812–14	Anglo-American War	
1813	Revoking of East India Company's trade monopoly; opening of India to British missionaries	Jane Austen, *Pride and Prejudice*
1814		Sir Walter Scott, *Waverley*
1815	Battle of Waterloo marks the end of Napoleonic Wars	
1817		James Mill, *History of British India*; Thomas Moore, *Lalla Rookh*
1819	Sir Stamford Raffles takes over Singapore	Percy Bysshe Shelley, *Prometheus Unbound*; Sir Walter Scott, *Ivanhoe*
1819–25	Revolutions against Spanish and Portuguese imperialism in Latin America	
1823	Slave rebellion in Demarara (British Guiana)	

1824–6	First Anglo-Ashanti War; British forces from India invade Burma	
1826–30	'Black War' in Tasmania between Aborigines and British settlers	
1829	Passage of Catholic Emancipation Act	
1830	France colonises Algeria; revolution in Paris and establishment of the July Monarchy; founding of Royal Geographical Society in London	
1831	Slave rebellion in Jamaica; Charles Darwin begins his round-the-world voyage on *The Beagle*	
1832	Passage of the First Reform Bill, giving the franchise to much of the British middle class	Charles Lyell, *Principles of Geology*
1833	Parliament abolishes slavery in all British territory	
1834	Passage of New Poor Law	Thomas Pringle, *African Sketches*
1835	Macaulay's 'Minute on Indian Education' advocates education in English for Indians seeking government employment	
1836	Boers begin Great Trek in South Africa, establishing the Boer republics of the Transvaal and Orange Free State	Captain Frederick Marryat, *Mr. Midshipman Easy*; Charles Dickens, *The Pickwick Papers*; Edward Lane, *The Modern Egyptians*; Catherine Parr Traill, *The Backwoods of Canada*

1837	Death of King William IV and coronation of Queen Victoria; constitutional revolts in Canada; invention of electric telegraph; founding of the Aborigines Protection Society in London	Thomas Carlyle, *The French Revolution*
1838–9	In the US, the Cherokee 'Trail of Tears' as part of removing all Indians to reservations west of the Mississippi River; South Australia founded as colony of free settlers; first indentured labourers from India arrive in the Caribbean	Charles Dickens, *Oliver Twist*
1838–48	Working-class Chartist movement advocating universal suffrage for all adult male Britons; Queen Victoria marries Prince Albert	
1839	The Durham Report recommends partial home rule for the Canadian colonies	Philip Meadows Taylor, *Confessions of a Thug*; Rev. John Williams, *Missionary Enterprises in the South Sea Islands*
1839–42	British forces wage Opium War in China and take over Hong Kong; first Afghan War	
1840	Creation of centralised Post Office; Treaty of Waitangi makes colonisation of New Zealand official	
1841		Thomas Carlyle, *Heroes and Hero Worship*

1842	Formation of Young Ireland; Chartist Plug-Plot riots	Founding of Edward Mudie's Circulating Library, which dominated novel-publishing until the 1890s; Charles Dickens, *American Notes*
1843	Natal becomes a British crown colony; conquest of Sind in India	Thomas Carlyle, *Past and Present*; Charles Rowcroft, *Tales of the Colonies*; Lady Florentia Sale, *A Journal of the First Afghan War*
1843–8	First Maori War in New Zealand	
1845		Benjamin Disraeli, *Sybil; or, the two Nations*; Frederick Douglass, *Narrative of the Life of Frederick Douglass, an American Slave*; [James Tucker,] *Ralph Rashleigh, A Penal Exile in Australia*
1845–50	Irish Famine; railway building boom in Britain; Sikh Wars and conquest of the Punjab in India	
1846	Parliament abolishes the 'corn laws' in favor of 'free trade'	
1846–8	US-Mexican War leads to the US annexation of territory from Texas to California	
1847	Parliament passes the Ten Hours Act, limiting the hours and ages children could be employed in Britain's textile factories	Charlotte Brontë, *Jane Eyre*; Emily Brontë, *Wuthering Heights*; Benjamin Disraeli, *Tancred*; William

		Carleton, *The Black Prophet*
1848	Revolutions in Paris and other continental capitals; abolition of slavery in French colonies	Marx and Engels, *The Communist Manifesto*; Charles Dickens, *Dombey and Son*; William Makepeace Thackeray, *Vanity Fair*; Elizabeth Gaskell, *Mary Barton*; beginning of the Pre-Raphaelite Brotherhood of artists and poets
1849		Charles Dickens, *David Copperfield*; Edward Bulwer-Lytton, *The Caxtons*
1850	Start of the Australian gold rush; formal colonization of the Gold Coast in West Africa.	Alfred Tennyson, *In Memoriam*; after Wordsworth's death, he becomes Poet Laureate
1850–3	Anglo-Xhosa War on eastern frontier in South Africa; Taiping Rebellion in China	
1851	Opening of the Great Exhibition in London	Herman Melville, *Moby Dick*; W. H. G. Kingston, *Peter the Whaler*
1851–60	Australian gold rush	
1852	Second Anglo-Burmese War	Harriet Beecher Stowe, *Uncle Tom's Cabin*.
1852–70	French Second Empire under Napoleon III	
1853	US 'gunboat diplomacy' opens Japan to Western trade	Charles Dickens, *Bleak House*; Robert Browning, *Men and Women*
1854–5	Crimean War pitting England and France against Russia	
1855		Walt Whitman, first edition of *Leaves of*

		Grass; Richard Burton, *Pilgrimage to Al-Madinah and Meccah*; Charles Kingsley, *Westward Ho!*
1856		Gustave Flaubert, *Madame Bovary*; Charles Reade, *It Is Never Too Late to Mend*; Elizabeth Barrett Browning, *Aurora Leigh*; Charlotte Yonge, *The Daisy Chain*
1856–60	Second Opium War against China	
1857		David Livingstone, *Missionary Travels and Researches in Africa*
1857–8	Indian Rebellion or 'Sepoy Mutiny'	
1858	India Act ends the rule of the East India Company, placing the British government directly in charge	Harriet Martineau, *British Rule in India*; Robert Ballantyne, *The Coral Island*; John Mitchel, *The Last Conquest of Ireland (Perhaps)*
1859		Charles Darwin, *The Origin of Species*; George Eliot, *Adam Bede*; Tennyson publishes four parts of *Idylls of the King*; Samuel Smiles, *Self-Help*; Henry Kingsley, *Recollections of Geoffrey Hamlyn*; John Stuart Mill, *On Liberty*
1861	Unification of Italy; Britain acquires Lagos in	Charles Dickens, *Great Expectations*; Anthony

	West Africa; death of Prince Albert	Trollope, *Castle Richmond*; Richard Burton, *The Lake Regions of Central Africa*
1861–5	American Civil War	
1862	France occupies Mexico City and installs Maximilian as emperor	Mary Elizabeth Braddon, *Lady Audley's Secret*
1863		Frederick Maning ('A Pakeha Maori'), *Old New Zealand*
1865	Jamaican rebellion suppressed by Governor Eyre	Rev. Joseph Waterhouse, *The King and People of Fiji*
1866	Atlantic cable laid for telegraph service	G.O.Trevelyan, *The Competition Wallah*
1867	Parliament passes Second Reform Bill; Fenian uprising in Ireland suppressed; discovery of diamonds in southern Africa; British North America Act creates Dominion of Canada; US purchases Alaska from Russia	Karl Marx, *Das Kapital*, vol. 1
1868	Benjamin Disraeli's first, brief term as Prime Minister; he was succeeded by William Gladstone, who was Prime Minister until 1874; British forces invade Abyssinia	Wilkie Collins, *The Moonstone*; Charles Wentworth Dilke, *Greater Britain*
1869	Opening of Suez Canal by France	John Stuart Mill, *On Representative Government*; Matthew Arnold, *Culture and Anarchy*
1870		James Bonwick, *The Last of the Tasmanians*

1870–1	Franco-Prussian War and Paris Commune; unification of Germany under Bismarck	
1871	Henry Morton Stanley 'discovers' David Livingstone in Africa; Britain annexes diamond-rich Griqualand West in southern Africa	Charles Darwin, *The Descent of Man*; Edward Bulwer-Lytton, *The Coming Race*
1872		George Eliot, *Middlemarch*; Edward Burnett Tylor, *Primitive Culture*; Sir J. R. Seeley, *The Expansion of England*; Philip Meadows Taylor, *Seeta*; Samuel Butler, *Erewhon*; Claude Monet's painting 'Impression: Sunrise' inaugurates French impressionism
1873	Britain wages war against the Ashanti in West Africa; Benjamin Disraeli becomes Prime Minister for second term	Anthony Trollope, *Australia and New Zealand*
1874	Britain annexes Fiji	
1875	Britain purchases the Suez Canal; Disraeli's 'Royal Titles' bill names Queen Victoria 'Empress of India'	Anthony Trollope, *The Way We Live Now*
1876	Death of 'Queen' Truganini, the last full-blooded Tasmanian Aborigine; Queen Victoria accepts title of 'Empress of India'	George Eliot, *Daniel Deronda*; Dadabhai Naoroji, *The Poverty of India*
1877	Britain annexes the Transvaal	

	colonizes Cuba, Puerto Rico, the Philippines, Hawaii, and Guam	
1899	British defeat the forces of the Mahdi at the Battle of Omdurman in the Sudan	Joseph Conrad, *Heart of Darkness*; Sigmund Freud, *The Interpretation of Dreams*
1899–1902	The major Anglo-Boer War	
1900	Creation of the Commonwealth of Australia; Boxer Rebellion in China	Joseph Conrad, *Lord Jim*
1901	Death of Queen Victoria	Rudyard Kipling, *Kim*; Samuel Butler, *Erewhon Revisited*
1902	Founding of Sinn Féin	J. A. Hobson, *Imperialism: A Study*; W. B. Yeats, *Cathleen Ni Houlihan*
1904		George Bernard Shaw, *John Bull's Other Island*
1907		Wilfrid Scawen Blunt, *Secret History of the English Occupation of Egypt*
1909		Gandhi writes *Hind Swaraj* ('independent India'); Vinayak Savarkar, *The Indian War of Independence, 1857*
1910	Creation of Union of South Africa	
1914		James Joyce, *Dubliners*
1914–18	World War I	
1917		V. I. Lenin, *Imperialism: The Last Stage of Capitalism*
1918		Lytton Strachey, *Eminent Victorians*

1919		Rabindranath Tagore, *The Home and the World*
1920	Establishment of League of Nations	
1922	Creation of Irish Free State	
1924		James Joyce, *Ulysses* E. M. Forster, *A Passage to India*
1938		Virginia Woolf, *The Three Guineas*

Chapter 1

Exploring the Terrain

No free country can keep another in slavery. The price they pay for it will be their own servitude.

Edmund Burke

Introduction: Nineteenth-century Literature and Imperialism

Any examination of the relationship between Victorian literature and the British Empire must assess the extent to which imperialism influenced fiction, poetry, drama, and other kinds of writing.[1] From a postcolonial standpoint, it must also examine the forms of critique and resistance to imperialism, both in the metropole and in the colonies. This chapter focuses on the first sort of assessment. It examines imperialism in a wide range of nineteenth-century writing, including works from the Romantic period (1790s–1830s) that influenced Victorian literature. Many of these, such as Sir Walter Scott's Waverley novels, were frequently reprinted and are still read today. The Romantic poets were major influences on the Victorians, and though Blake, Byron, Coleridge, Keats, and Shelley all died before the start of Queen Victoria's reign in 1837, Wordsworth lived until 1850, becoming a Victorian. Several major Victorian authors, moreover – Carlyle, Dickens, Tennyson – began their literary careers before 1837. The boundaries of literary and historical periods overlap, so this study will also deal with some writing published after the official end of the Victorian era in 1901.

Most major Victorian writers had something to say about India, Africa, Australia, or slavery, and some of them – Anthony Trollope, for example, who traveled throughout the Empire – had much to say. Further, imperialism as a hegemonic ideology emerged earlier than the Berlin Conference of 1884–5 that inaugurated the 'scramble for Africa.' Something close to 'jingoism' – a term coined in the 1870s meaning unequivocal approval of British militarism and imperial expansion – arose during the Indian Rebellion or 'Sepoy Mutiny' of 1857–8. Taking pride in the British Empire was a major aspect of Victorian patriotism and was often indistinguishable from racial chauvinism – the belief in the absolute superiority of the Anglo-Saxon race and its providential mission to rule the supposedly inferior races of the world, Rudyard Kipling's 'lesser breeds without the law' (see his poem 'Recessional').

Rather than jingoist, however, much nineteenth-century writing about the Empire was ambivalent, at once approving and disapproving. Thus, discourse about emigration often expressed criticism of the social conditions–poverty, unemployment, famine – that prompted Britons to move to the colonies or the United States. Charles Dickens, Elizabeth Gaskell, Charles Reade, George Eliot, Thomas Hardy, and many other novelists resorted to emigration as a way of rewarding deserving – sometimes undeserving – characters while underlining the social or personal problems they were leaving behind. A second issue causing anxiety, equivocation, and sometimes condemnation arose from clashes between white colonizers and indigenous peoples. 'Natives' were hindrances to colonization, but they could be displaced or exterminated even as the colonizers claimed to offer them civilization, Christianity, and Western commerce. The very appearance of indigenous peoples in imperialist discourse, no matter how fleeting or stereotypical, is at least tacit acknowledgement that colonization was no smooth path to utopia.

Throughout the Victorian era, explorers' journals excited great public interest, recounting the search for the sources of the Nile, braving the Arctic, mapping the Australian 'bush,' and depicting 'savage' customs. Countless adventure novels, many of them written for boys, followed the tracks of the explorers. Missionary publications also offered death-defying excitement, mingled with appropriately Christian sentiments. From Wordsworth to Kipling, the British Empire inspired much patriotic poetry, such as William Ernest Henley's 'England, My England' (1892):

> They call you proud and hard,
>   England, my England;
> You with worlds to watch and ward,
>   England, my own!
> You whose mailed hand keeps the keys
> Of such teeming destinies
> You could know nor dread nor ease
>   Were the Song on your bugles blown, England –
>   Round the Pit on your bugles blown!

Mother of Ships whose might,
   England, my England,
Is the fierce old Sea's delight,
   England, my own,
Chosen daughter of the Lord –

and so on (in Buckley and Woods 1965: 805). And there were innumerable plays that also celebrated imperial deeds and events, such as *Jessie Brown; or, the Relief of Lucknow* (1858), Dion Boucicault's melodrama about the Indian Rebellion of 1857–8. Even before the Great Exhibition of 1851, moreover, there were many shows and displays that recreated famous expeditions, battles, and colonial scenes from around the globe (Altick 1978: 176–83). Tea, sugar, spices, cotton, opium, wool, gold, rubber, and many other commodities arrived at British ports on a daily basis. The business of the Empire seemed to be everyone's business. Many Victorians had relatives in India or elsewhere in the colonies. Matthew Arnold's brothers emigrated to India and Australia, as did four of Dickens's sons. And George Eliot and George Henry Lewes invested in imperial ventures, including funding two of the Lewes boys to set up as farmers in Natal (Henry). Sometimes, too, Victorian writers had colonial origins: both Thackeray and Kipling were born in India, while Olive Schreiner grew up as a missionary's daughter in southern Africa before coming to London.[2]

Most Victorians believed that, because of industry, trade, and liberty, Britain and its Empire were in the vanguard of world progress. Progress also depended on science, and scientific breakthroughs including Darwin's theory of evolution were 'propelled by the needs of a growing empire,' writes Bruce Hunt, who notes that the voyage of the *Beagle*, on which Darwin sailed around the world in the 1830s, was undertaken for the Admiralty 'primarily to improve navigational charts of South America, then being drawn more closely into Britain's informal empire of commerce and investment' (Hunt 1997: 314). The Royal Geographical Society, founded in 1830, sponsored numerous voyages and exploring expeditions that by 1900 had resulted in the nearly total mapping of the world. Geography was undoubtedly the 'imperial science': the 'exploration, mapping and topographic surveying of Africa, Asia and Latin America during the eighteenth and nineteenth centuries – generally with state support – was self-evidently an exercise in imperial authority' (Bell, Butlin, and Heffernan 1995: 4).

Victorian literature in turn was profoundly influenced by scientific developments. Realism in the novel was the literary equivalent of scientific empiricism. In his great elegy 'In Memoriam' (1850), published nine years before Darwin's *Origin of Species*, Tennyson reflects despairingly on the themes of evolution and the extinction of species that he had read about in Charles Lyell's *Principles of Geology* (1830–3). And George Eliot's *Middlemarch* (1872) traces the development of her characters and of provincial society – indeed, of history itself – in evolutionary terms: novel-writing, she suggests, is akin to biological experimentation. Then, too, the subgenre of science fiction emerged in the context of the final mapping of the globe, although it was more often dystopian than utopian. H. G. Wells's *Time Machine* (1895), for example, belongs to the subgenre of imperial Gothic fiction. Although imperialism as an ideology seems to have been strongest in the 1880s and '90s, many writers including Wells utilized Gothic conventions to express anxieties about the future.

This chapter ends with a review of imperial Gothic fiction from Robert Louis Stevenson's *Dr Jekyll and Mr Hyde* (1886) to Bram Stoker's *Dracula* (1897). The second chapter examines some of the postcolonial debates that have led to new understandings of Victorian literature. First, I survey the disgreements among imperial historiography, Marxism, and postcolonialism.[3] Issues of gender and sexuality in relation to race constitute the second debate. Patriarchy and imperialism reinforced each other, encouraging hypermasculinity and 'hero-worship.' But the colonies also offered opportunities for sexual experimentation including homoeroticism. Gender and sexual issues also intersected with race and racism, including miscegenation and anxieties about racial degeneration. The third section focuses on Edward Said's *Orientalism* and its critics: what did Said leave out of his picture of Western representations – or misrepresentations – of the Middle East and India? How have later studies by his followers and critics used or misused his ideas? Fourth comes Homi Bhabha's theory of 'mimicry' in contrast to 'going native,' twin issues in many works of literature about the Empire. The colonizers did not simply impose their beliefs and values on the colonized; exchanges across cultural boundaries always involve two-way alterations in individual attitudes and behaviors. Finally, Gayatri Spivak's argument that 'the subaltern' cannot 'speak' is matched against British representations of Australian Aborigines and the ways they resisted the colonizers. Spivak's 'subaltern' is so thoroughly dominated by powerful others that 'she' is unable to represent herself. To what extent were the Aborigines in such an absolutely dominated situation?

Chapter 3 presents four case studies, allowing a closer examination of specific works of literature. First, in early versions of 'reverse coloniza-tion,' characters in Charlotte Brontë's *Jane Eyre* (1847) and Charles Dickens's *Great Expectations* (1861) return from the colonies and influence the lives of respectively, Jane and Pip. Second comes a comparison of the treatments of Celtic materials by Tennyson, particularly in *Idylls of the King*, and William Butler Yeats. Third, I examine Orientalist narratives by Benjamin Disraeli, George Eliot, Rudyard Kipling, and others. Finally, I compare explorers' journals with fiction about Africa such as Joseph Conrad's *Heart of Darkness* (1900).

Before *Orientalism* (1978), it was widely believed that Victorian authors, prior to the 1880s, were not interested in the colonies. The 1830s through the 1860s was the era of 'free-trade imperialism' (Semmel 1965), when colonies were seen as costly 'millstones around our neck,' as Benjamin Disraeli called them in 1852 (Stembridge 1965). In contrast, the period from 1880 through World War I was 'the age of empire' (Hobsbawm 1989): responding to new rivals for global power (the United States, Germany), jingoism emerged, the 'scramble for Africa' began, the 'Anglo-Saxon race' was trumpeted as superior to all other races, and the British Empire was celebrated as the triumphant production and possession of that race. According to John MacKenzie, from about 1880 to the early 1900s

> a potent mixture of patriotism, excitements in adventure and colonial warfare, reverence for the monarchy, a self-referencing approach to other peoples, admiration for military virtues (represented also by renewed interest in medieval chivalry), and a quasi-religious approach to the obligations of world-wide power, came to dominate many aspects of, especially, popular culture.

MacKenzie adds that during this period 'sporadic excitements turned patriotism into jingoism [and] ethnic self-regard often shaded into outright racism . . .' (1998: 291). The total version of 'Imperial ideology' sketched by MacKenzie may be difficult to find in any individual author prior to the 1880s, but its separate elements are all evident in Romantic and early Victorian writing. *Ivanhoe* (1819), for example, deals with the forging of 'Great Britain' through the unification of Britain's medieval 'races' – the colonized Saxons and the colonizing Normans – while expressing Scott's fascination with chivalry. If imperialism is broadly understood to include interest in such issues as emigration, the reform of British rule in India, the exploration of sub-Saharan Africa, or the causes of unrest in Ireland, then it can be found throughout Victorian literature and culture.

In *The Expansion of England* (1883), J. R. Seeley famously declared: 'We seem, as it were, to have conquered and peopled half the world in a fit of absence of mind' (1971: 12). Seeley intended *Expansion* to help overcome the lack of public awareness about the Empire. He cited Thomas Babington Macaulay, who in his 1840 essay 'Lord Clive' claimed that the British reading public, knowledgable about Spanish imperialism in the Americas, knew little or nothing about how 'a handful' of Englishmen 'subjugated in the course of a few years one of the greatest empires in the world' in India (Macaulay 1967: 306–7; Seeley 1971: 142). Both *Expansion* and 'Lord Clive' aimed to educate their readers about Britain's imperial history. However, between 1840 and the 1880s, there were many other attempts to do so, including Harriet Martineau's *British Rule in India* (1857), Robert Montgomery Martin's *The Indian Empire* (1858–60), and Edward Nolan's *Illustrated History of the British Empire in India and the East* (1860). Collectively these texts suggest that early and mid-Victorian Britons were not 'absent-minded' about the Empire; the claim of 'absent-mindedness' was a misleading cliché well before and also well after Seeley echoed it.[4]

Between 1800 and 1880, there were so many attempts to correct 'absent-mindedness' about the Empire that one wonders who could possibly have been unaware of it. At the end of the Napoleonic Wars, Patrick Colquhoun's *The Wealth, Power and Resources of the British Empire* (1815) expressed the 'feeling of national resurgence' and pride in imperial power and extension (Bayly 1989: 3). In his *History of the British Empire* (1852), John MacGregor lauded 'the advances made by the Anglo-Saxon race over the territories of the Western and Eastern world . . . [which were] unparalleled in the history of colonization and of the acquisition of dominion' (1:xx). Charles Dilke's *Greater Britain* (1868) is sometimes cited as the first Victorian survey of the entire Empire, but there were earlier accounts, including Herman Merivale's *Lectures on Colonization and Colonies, 1839–41* (1861) and Goldwin Smith's *The Empire* (1863). As an advocate of independence for the settler colonies, Smith has been dubbed an anti-imperialist. He was, however, like Dilke a believer in the Anglo-Saxon race as the glue that would hold the colonies together with Britain and the United States in any future configuration of global power (Bell 2007: 179–201).

Countless texts prior to Dilke's dealt specifically with India, or Canada, or Australia. Trollope began his series of Empire-boosting travelogues in 1859, with *The West Indies and the Spanish Main.*There were many histories of India prior to Martineau's and Nolan's.[5] Missionary accounts of India include Bishop Richard Heber's *Narrative of a Journey through the Upper Provinces of India* (1828), while Mary Sherwood's evangelical tale or 'tract,' *The History of Little Henry and His Bearer*, was immensely popular. Between 1815 and 1850 – well into the Victorian period – it went through thirty-seven editions (Dawson 1996). Orphaned in India, the English lad Henry manages, before his highly sentimentalized death, to convert his Hindu 'bearer' or manservant Boosy to Christianity. *Little Henry* contains many biblical verses, but also many Indian terms: salam, tiffin, gooroo, and so on (even a simple story like *Little Henry* exemplifies the hybridity of colonial discourse). Also before 1857, Mary Campbell, Eliza Clemons, Ann Deane, Emily Eden, Maria Graham, Julia Harvey, Sarah Lushington, Julia Maitland, Fanny Parks, Emma Roberts, and Florentia Sale all wrote journals or narratives about traveling and living in India (Raza 2006: 256–77). Besides her travelogue *Up the Country*, written much earlier but published in 1866, Eden authored *Portraits of the People and Princes of India* (1844). In 1836 Col. William Sleeman published the first of his books on Thuggee or *thāgi*, *Ramaseeana, or a Vocabulary of the Peculiar Language Used by the Thugs*, while Philip Meadows Taylor's bestselling novel *Confessions of a Thug* (1839) rendered that criminal cult of stranglers and highway robbers notorious among British readers (Majeed 1996). From the 1790s through the 1840s, writes Martine van Woerkens, 'England was swamped by a torrent of information about India' (2002: 41; see also Bayly 1996).

Besides India, debates about the future of the Canadian colonies, leading to the Durham report of 1839 and partial 'home rule,' were frequent in Parliament and the press. Prior to 1850, hundreds of books, like James Macarthur's *New South Wales* (1837), were published about Australia (Shaw 1969: 81). And abolitionist propaganda made British activities in Africa and the Americas glaringly familiar. If slavery and the slave trade constituted a major 'scandal of Empire' (Dirks 2006), their abolition was one of Britain's greatest political achievements, a humanitarian triumph underlying the widespread Victorian belief that the work of the Empire was generally benevolent, bringing civilization and Christianity to the 'dark' places of the world.[6] As a result of both scandals and triumphs, for any educated Briton, imperial affairs were inescapable before 1880. For many late Victorians and Edwardians, moreover, imperialism was virtually a secular religion, even though its scandals continued to be glaring for those who cared to notice them.

From Adam Smith forward, the debate among economists about the value of colonies focused their fledgling science on imperial issues. Thomas Malthus's *Essay on Population*, first published in 1798, spurred arguments about emigration to the colonies as a way to alleviate poverty at home. Wilmot Horton, Edward Wakefield, Charles Buller, Nassau Senior, and Robert Torrens all contributed to the debate. In his highly influential *Principles of Political Economy* (1848), John Stuart Mill declared that 'if one-tenth of the labouring people of England were transferred to the colonies, and along with them one-tenth of the circulating capital of the country, either wages, or profits, or both, would be greatly benefited by the diminished pressure of capital and population upon the fertility of the land' in England itself (1965: 3:749).

From 1837 forward, moreover, Queen Victoria's ministers kept her apprised of the most important issues affecting what her uncle, King Leopold of Belgium, called the 'colossal machinery' of 'the British Empire' (Victoria 1908: 2:19). Leopold wrote to her on 8 January 1841, just four years after her coronation: 'Your name bears glorious fruits in all climes; this globe will soon be too small for you, and something must be done to get at the other planets . . .' (Victoria 1908: 1:255–6). Victoria followed the first Opium War in China with interest, and wrote to her uncle in 1842 that Prince Albert was 'much amused at my having got the Island of Hong Kong' (1:262). A year later, she expressed horror over the debacle of the retreat from Kabul. She read portions of the journal of the Afghan 'disasters' penned by Florentia Sale, which became a bestseller (1:383). To all of her readers, Lady Sale made it clear that running an empire was a risky business demanding courage and clear-sighted leadership even from Englishwomen – perhaps especially from Englishwomen, including Victoria.[7]

On 23 November 1844, the Governor-General of India, Sir Henry Hardinge, wrote to the Queen:

> The literature of the West is the most favourite study amongst the Hindoos in their schools and colleges. They will discuss with accuracy the most important events in British History. Boys of fifteen years of age, black in colour, will recite the most favourite passages from Shakespeare . . . . They excel in mathematics, and in legal subtleties their acuteness is most extraordinary. (2:28)

Hardinge had issued a 'resolution, by which the most meritorious students will be appointed to fill the public offices which will fall vacant throughout Bengal.' He deplored the lack of well-paid 'European civil servants' available 'throughout your Majesty's immense Empire. . ... This deficiency is the great evil of British Administration'. But it could be remedied by employing 'well-educated natives throughout the provinces, under British superintendence' (2:29).

The academic study of English literature originated in Bengal (Viswanathan 1989). Even before Macaulay's famous 'Minute on Indian Education' (1835), the training of a small cadre of Bengali civil servants, fluent in English through studying Shakespeare and English literature, was a goal of the East India Company. The English-speaking 'baboos' were never expected to be more than 'mimic men,' but their discontent with their subordination was one source of Indian nationalism. 'The

British,' writes Jim Masselos, 'although they thus provided themselves with a steady stream of recruits for their administrative and judicial services, had in many ways also created a Frankenstein's monster' (1985: 50). Starting fairly early in the 1800s, Indian authors began to express nationalistic ideas in English, using English literary models. Thus, according to Rosinka Chaudhuri, Henry Derozio's poetry in English is 'the first example of a nascent pan–Indian nationalism,' although it 'defined that sense of nationhood against Islam' (2002: 45). Two of the earliest fictional narratives in English by Indian authors recount future rebellions against British rule. These are Kylas Chunder Dutt's 'A Journal of Forty-Eight Hours of the Year 1945,' which appeared in the *Calcutta Literary Gazette* in 1835, and Shoshee Chunder Dutt's 'The Republic of Orissa,' published by the *Saturday Evening Harakuru* in 1845 (M. Mukherjee 2003: 94–5).

At the time of the Indian Rebellion (1857–8), Queen Victoria responded to the massacre of women and children at Kanpur ('Cawnpore' in Victorian texts) the way most of her British subjects did: 'the horrors committed on the poor ladies – women and children – are unknown in these ages, and make one's blood run cold' (3:247). She urged her ministers to dispatch more troops as quickly as possible. In its aftermath, when it became clear that the Crown would replace the East India Company as official ruler of British India, the Queen was delighted that it was *'all . . . to be mine'* (quoted in Longford 1964: 280). She wrote to Viscount Canning, Viceroy of India, on 2 December 1858:

> It is a source of great satisfaction and pride to her to feel herself in direct communication with that enormous Empire which is so bright a jewel in her Crown, and which she would wish to see happy, contented, and peaceful. May the publication of her Proclamation be the beginning of a new era, and may it draw a veil over the sad and bloody past! (3:304)

In sum, long before 1875 when she acquired the title 'Empress of India,' Queen Victoria was well aware and very proud of the Indian 'jewel in her Crown' and of lesser jewels such as Hong Kong.

Of course, the Queen's knowledge and opinions about the Empire did not necessarily correspond to those of the British public. However, although they may not have been thoroughgoing jingoists prior to the 1880s, many Britons, perhaps of all classes, were well aware of the jewels in Victoria's crown, the colonies. While the social and political conditions of the 1840s were not conducive to imperialist sentiments, the Great Exhibition of 1851 foregrounded the Empire. Jeffrey Auerbach comments that the Exhibition, though it presented artefacts and materials from many countries around the world, placed the British 'imperial displays . . . at the very center of the Crystal Palace':

> The list of contributors was impressive, and included, as the *Official Catalogue* referred to them, 'British Possessions in Asia' (India and Ceylon), Europe (Malta, Gibraltar, and the Channel Islands), Africa (Cape of Good Hope, Mauritius, the Seychelles), the Americas (Canada, the Caribbean islands such as Barbados, the Bahamas, Bermuda, and Grenada), and Australasia (Australia and New Zealand). (1999: 100)

Though France and other countries mounted displays, those of Britain and its colonies occupied half of the Crystal Palace. The Governor of Cape Colony noted that the Exhibition helped inform potential immigrants about what to expect (Auerbach 1999: 101–2). Many later exhibitions were more exclusively imperial than the Great Exhibition, but in 1851 the British Empire was definitely on display, and it would remain so through the rest of Victoria's reign.

Slavery and Empire in Romantic and Early Victorian Literature

The American and French Revolutions, the antislavery movement, and unrest in Ireland, including the abortive United Irishmen's uprising in 1798, inspired Romantic writers to address themes of tyranny and rebellion, empire and liberty. William Blake, Lord Byron, and Percy Bysshe Shelley wrote in opposition to imperialism, which all three linked to slavery. Like Tom Paine, they were champions of freedom – in France, in the United States, in Greece (where Byron died attempting to support the struggle for Greek independence from the Ottoman Empire) – and therefore opponents of slavery and empire. Thus, in *Childe Harold's Pilgrimage*, Byron writes:

> Imperial anarchs, doubling human woes!
> GOD! was thy globe ordain'd for such to win and lose? (1980: 2:58)

Byron's eastern tales, Nigel Leask comments, express the corruption or loss of 'an aristocratic, republican, civic, humanist heritage,' not because of contact with the 'despotic' and 'barbarian' Orient, but because of 'the pernicious influence of imperialism' (1992: 24).

In *Visions of the Daughters of Albion*, *The Four Zoas*, and elsewhere, Blake links slavery and 'Universal Empire,' including the British variety:

> And slaves in myriads, in ship loads, burden the hoarse sounding deep,
> Rattling with clanking chains; the Universal Empire groans . . .
> (quoted in Makdisi 1998: 19; see also Erdman 1969: 226–42)

So, too, Shelley's accounts of history in *Queen Mab* (1813), 'The Mask of Anarchy' (1819), and other poems depict the ruins of past empires, built but also destroyed by war and slavery; the same fate, Shelley asserts, is in store for the British Empire. Imperialism produces slaves such as the English workers in 'The Mask of Anarchy,' murdered by 'Anarchy's' military slaves during the 1819 Peterloo Massacre in Manchester. Earth asks the British workers she is hoping to inspire to revolution:

> What is Freedom? – ye can tell
> That which slavery is, too well –
> For its very name has grown
> To an echo of your own. (2003: 404)

Foreshadowing the closing lines of *The Communist Manifesto*, Earth urges the workers to rebel:

> Rise like lions after slumber
> In unvanquishable number –
> Shake your chains to earth like dew
> Which in sleep had fallen on you –
> Ye are many – they are few. (2003: 411)

Blake, Byron, and Shelley believed that slavery in the Ottoman Empire, plantation slavery in the Americas and the Caribbean, and 'wage slavery' at home were linked by empire in a chain of universal bondage.

Wordsworth, Coleridge, Keats, and Robert Southey also opposed slavery, although they supported, were equivocal, or just remained silent about the British Empire. Many other writers from the 1780s through the 1830s – William Cowper, Mary Wollstonecraft, Hannah More, William Godwin, James Montgomery – condemned the slave trade and slavery. Narratives by former slaves such as Olaudah Equiano and Mary Prince also had wide circulation. The Haitian revolution (1794–1803) and slave rebellions in Barbados (1816), Demerara (the future British Guiana; 1823), and Jamaica (1831–2) made the topic inescapable. In her study of Romanticism and slavery, Debbie Lee contends that the theory of the Romantic imagination stemmed in part from 'attempts to write creatively about the complex and glaringly unequal relationships between Africans and Britons' (2002: 3–4; see also Thomas 2000).

The Romantics also sometimes viewed India as enslaved by empire. Shelley located *Prometheus Unbound* (1820), his drama of rebellion against the 'tyranny' of Jupiter and all forms of empire, in the 'Indian Caucasus' or 'vale of Cashmeer,' and wrote other poems such as 'Alastor' (1815) with the same setting. These poems, however, do not directly address the British presence in India; indeed, the Oriental setting facilitates an allegorical universality that applies to all versions of 'tyranny' and struggles for 'liberty' throughout history. For Robert Southey, moreover, it wasn't the British who were enslaving India, but Hinduism and Islam. The preface to his narrative poem *The Curse of Kehama* (1810) declares that of all religions Hinduism is 'the most monstrous in its fables and the most fatal in its effects' (quoted in Rajan 1999: 139). Balanchandra Rajan lumps Southey's poem with many other evangelical 'anti-Hindu tirades.' It is puzzling that Southey even wrote it, given his 'resounding dismissal of the very mythology on which the poem is based' (Rajan 1999: 139; see also Majeed 1992: 82; Bolton 2007).

For other Romantic writers, whether they deemed them 'superstitions' or not, Hinduism and Islam provided exotic materials for narratives that, like *The Arabian Nights*, seemed timeless, or at any rate outside the inexorable forward march of Western history. The time and space configuration or 'chronotope' of Thomas Moore's *Lalla Rookh* (1817) cannot be measured by Western clocks and milestones.[8] Moore's lush extravaganza consists of a frame narrative containing four tales told by the bridegroom, disguised as a poet, to an Indian princess traveling from Delhi to Kashmir and their wedding. The third tale, 'The Fire-Worshippers,' may be 'an allegory' of Ireland's woes, as Linda Kelly claims, but the oppression comes from 'tyrannical Moslem masters' and not from the British (Kelly 2006: 134). Moore wanted his readers to draw various parallels between India and Ireland. Nevertheless, his poem is so laden with 'lascivious,' flowery ornamentation that actual politics and religion seem beside the point; Orientalist exoticism is the point (Majeed 1992: 100–22). Moore received an advance of £3,000 from the publisher of his poem, which suggests the popularity of Oriental themes in the early 1800s (Majeed 1992: 93).

Also highly popular was *The Missionary* (1811) by Sydney Owenson (Lady Morgan).[9] In 1813, under evangelical pressure, the East India Company reluctantly agreed to allow missionaries into British India. Like Moore, however, Owenson is only indirectly interested in present-day issues. Her fanciful tale of the Portuguese missionary Hilarion's sojourn in India, preaching Christianity, opposing the Spanish Inquisition, and attempting to convert while falling in love with the beautiful Hindu priestess Luxima influenced both Shelley and Moore (Leask 1992: 115–18, 126–9). Far from condemning Hinduism as superstition, *The Missionary* is, writes Carol Hart, 'a plea for religious tolerance and a trenchant critique of institutionalized religion, particularly Catholicism.' Owenson 'draws attention to the similarities between Catholicism and Hinduism through oblique comparisons of their rituals, artifacts, and practices, a strategy that creates an ironic counterpoint to [Hilarion's] denunciations of heathen rites and beliefs and his efforts to rescue Luxima from ignorance and idolatry' (Hart 1996: 241–2).[10] Owenson emphasizes Hindu piety and Indian 'indifference to Christianity,' thereby critiquing 'the missionary enterprise in particular and cultural imperialism in general.' Love overrules religion, but religious intolerance – both Catholic and Hindu – condemns Hilarion and Luxima to death. In contrast to Southey and to evangelical writers such as Mary Sherwood, both Owenson and Moore treat India and Hinduism in largely positive albeit Orientalist terms.[11]

Appearing before Scott's Waverley novels, Owenson's tale of love and religion in India does not suggest how the past it depicts was a prelude to the present; it is in that sense ahistorical. In contrast to *The Missionary*, Shelley's poems about tyranny and freedom render history in two contrasting ways. In *The Rights of Man*, Tom Paine had argued that all governments up to the present had been forms of tyranny and unreason, based on 'force' (the aristocracy, the military) and 'fraud' ('priestcraft' or religion). Revolution would bring about, at long last, the 'government of reason,' guaranteeing liberty. For Shelley, too, history was divided between an imperial, tyrannical past, characterized by slavery for the vast majority, and a future age of liberty, marked by revolutionary time – that is, utopian time, ending in human perfection. Both present-day Britain and India deserved to be relegated to the past; the route to the future lay through scientific enlightenment (reason) and revolution, the overthrow of all forms of slavery and empire. This meant, however, that for the time being India needed British rule, which Shelley deemed preferable to the Moghul Empire (Makdisi 1998: 144–53).

The politically conservative Scott also wrote about India in *Guy Mannering* (1815) and *The Surgeon's Daughter* (1827). The narrator of the earlier novel imagines the lawyer Pleydell wondering how 'an officer of distinction' such as Colonel Mannering could have come 'from India, believed to be the seat of European violence and military oppression . . .' (Scott 2003: 210). That belief had been aroused by the scandal of the Warren Hastings trial, leading to efforts to reform the East India Company. Scott understood that British activities in India had often been morally dubious; but Mannering's upright, gentlemanly character signals his view that Britain's role in India was taking a turn for the better. Scott's depiction of Mannering gestures toward later portrayals of self-sacrificing British soldiers and administrators of the Raj, as in many of Kipling's stories.

Scott's belief in the reform of British rule in India is even more evident in *The Surgeon's Daughter*, one of the three novellas in *Chronicles of the Canongate*. After her surgeon father's death, Scotswoman Menie Grey follows her fiancé, Richard Middlemas, to Madras. Having killed his commanding officer in a duel, Middlemas deserts the East India Company, joining the service of Hyder Ali and his son Tippoo in Mysore. To gain favor with Tippoo, Middlemas plots to deliver Menie to his zenana or harem. He intends soon to rescue Menie 'from the tyrant,' so that she would be merely a 'temporary prisoner' (Scott 2000: 266). But his behavior, including going native, shows Middlemas to be even more devious and dishonorable than the Indian princes he serves. Rightly chastising Tippoo for his dishonorable actions, Hyder Ali commands Middlemas to be trampled to death by an elephant (284). He then permits Menie to be taken back to Madras by the hero, Adam Hartly, and she later returns to Scotland (without, however, marrying Hartly).

After the careful, slow domestic realism of most of *The Surgeon's Daughter* (the Scottish portions), the rush of the ending – the Indian portion – reads like a fairy tale. The story of the rescue of the white damsel from barbarous 'heathens' and 'blacks' by a stalwart Englishman recurs in many imperialist adventure tales. Adventure may not be prevalent in rural Scotland, where time moves deliberately and most people are as reliable as clockwork. But as another Englishman tells Hartly, 'we are all upon the adventure in India, more or less' (253); 'adventure,' here and elsewhere in Scott's novella, connotes dishonesty and equates empire with looting – that is, with 'European violence and military oppression.' 'It is scarce necessary to say,' comments Crystal Croftangry, the narrator of *The Surgeon's Daughter*, 'that such things could only be acted in the earlier period of our Indian settlements, when the check of the Directors [of the East India Company] was imperfect, and that of the Crown did not exist' (266). So Scott expresses the opinion that British rule in India was a self-improving affair. In contrast, the rule even of the best Indian princes is barbaric and nonprogressive. One of 'the wisest' princes 'that Hindoostan could boast,' Hyder Ali has also committed 'great crimes' (248), like his brutal execution of Middlemas without a trial.

Historical fiction emerged in the late 1700s together with two other subgenres related to the past, the Gothic 'tale of terror' and the 'national tale.' Gothic fiction hardly seems celebratory or nationalistic, yet it typically identifies the terrors it evokes with the past and with foreign places and evildoers, as in Ann Radcliffe's *The Italian* (1797). By contrast, present-day Britain appears rational and progressive (Schmitt 1997). Dealing with Britain's internal colonies of Ireland and Scotland, the national tale portrays Celtic customs and beliefs in fairly positive terms, but also identifies these with the past versus modernizing Britain, while depicting the Celts as colorful but racially or culturally inferior to the

English. As in Matthew Arnold's 'On the Study of Celtic Literature' (1866), the Celts in national tales are more emotive and poetic, but less rational and reliable than the English. It's just that their 'national character' is more virtuous than English stereotyping has made it out to be.

In Owenson's *The O'Briens and the O'Flahertys, a National Tale* (1827), after the failure of the United Irishmen's Rebellion, the protagonist Murrough O'Brien goes into exile among the peasantry. When he does so, notes Ina Ferris, he enters 'another Irish nation . . . attached to temporalities outside the cursive flow of history and the rational structures of the law . . .' (2002: 81). In many novels by Irish or Anglo-Irish authors, the peasants fail to take up the calls for insurrection made by nationalist leaders. The peasants do not belong to the 'temporality' of modernization. They occupy a chronotope that is cyclical and therefore as natural as the seasons; but it is also one that does not lead them toward the future, which for Irish nationalists would entail independence from Britain. Later Irish novels such as William Carleton's *The Black Prophet* (1847) and *The Emigrants of Ahadarra* (1848), both written during the Famine of 1845–50, address the theme of the immiserisation of Ireland in ways that are anti-imperialist, but also – because of the large-scale misery they depict – without hope for Irish independence.

In *Bardic Nationalism*, Katie Trumpener writes that the national tale about Ireland or Scotland presented readers with 'an organic national society, its history rooted in place' (1997: xii). In other words, its history, like that of the Moghul Empire, was going nowhere. This is especially evident in national tales about Ireland, including Maria Edgeworth's *Castle Rackrent, An Hibernian Tale* (1800) and Owenson's *The Wild Irish Girl* (1806). According to Barry Sloan, *Castle Rackrent* 'signals the beginning of a certain kind of Anglo-Irish literature, a literature with a distinctively national character and preoccupied with national affairs' (1987: 2). But 'national' does not exactly mean anti-imperialist: neither Edgeworth nor Owenson advocated Irish independence. The narrator of *Castle Rackrent*, Irishman Thady Quirk, seems to approve of the bad behaviors of the Rackrent landlords he serves. While clearly disapproving of those behaviors, Edgeworth creates in Thady a character that reinforces stereotypes about the Celts: Thady may be 'honest,' but he is also servile and ignorant. Suvendrini Perera notes that *Castle Rackrent* is 'the first significant English novel to speak in the voice of the colonized' (1991: 15), but Thady apparently deserves to be colonized.

Though they might be charming, invested with an antiquarian if not exactly historical interest, by the early 1800s Celtic customs and legends – and also peasants like Thady Quirk – were being modernized out of existence. National tales frequently take Englishmen or Anglo-Irish absentee landlords on tours of Ireland and their estates, and they often also end 'in a wedding that allegorically unites Britain's "national characters,"' or, to quote the title of an 1814 national tale by Christian Johnstone, *The Saxon and the Gaël*' (Trumpener 1997: 141; see also Corbett 2000). The implication is that 'national' difference will disappear with British unification – that is, with modernization. So the national tale foreshadows James Clifford's description of anthropology as a 'salvage' enterprise: 'The theme of the vanishing primitive, of the end of traditional society . . . is pervasive in ethnographic writing':

> Ethnography's disappearing object is, then, in significant degree, a rhetorical construct legitimating a representational practice: 'salvage' ethnography in its widest sense. The other is lost, in disintegrating time and space, but saved in the text. (1986: 112)

The same pattern is evident in collections of folklore and ballads, as in Scott's *Minstrelsy of the Scottish Border* (1802). Doing his 'salvage' work, the anthropologist writes texts that foreground contrasting chronotopes: the place and time of the primitive, 'rooted' or 'lost' in the past, versus the place and time of modernization, pointing into the future. The national tale, as well as narratives about India or other eastern realms, features these contrasting chronotopes: the nonprogressive domain of the 'Celtic fringe' or the Oriental world versus progressive Britain and the West.

With Scott's Waverley novels, historical fiction gained a temporal dynamism that influenced later novelists and even historians. *Waverley* (1814) portrays the forging of modern Britain through the defeat of Jacobitism in 1745 and the gradual, mostly peaceful merger of Celtic with English peoples – of Highlands with Lowlands and both of these with England. Similarly, in *Ivanhoe* (1819) Scott interprets history after the Norman Conquest as the unification of Great Britain through the fusion of the Saxon and Norman 'races.' (Scott uses the term 'race' interchangeably with 'nation' and without the invidious biological significance that it came to have in the Victorian period.) However, the dynamism does not alter the contrasting chronotopes apparent in national and Orientalist tales and in anthropological texts. The Highland culture Waverley encounters is wild, exotic, alluring, but also doomed.

Taylor's *Confessions of a Thug* portrays the clash of chronotopes in imperialist writing just as vividly and even more starkly than does *Waverley*. In the 1830s and '40s, the British campaigns against *sāti* ('suttee' or Hindu widow-burning) and *thāgi* ('thuggee' or the homicidal cult of the Thugs) were presented as evidence that British rule could benefit Indians. They were also presented as evidence that India itself – even more than the East India Company – needed reforming or civilizing. If the activities of the Company in the 1700s had often been scandalous as Scott indicates, during the Victorian era, thanks partly to Taylor's novel and later to accounts of the 1857–8 Rebellion, India in general was painted as criminal, in dire need of British rule (U. P. Mukherjee 2003).[12] Based on actual confessions made to Taylor by a jailed Thug, *Confessions* implies that all of India needs imperial policing. The romantic albeit homicidal adventures of Ameer Ali form a wildly picaresque contrast to the site of his narration – namely, prison, the iron cage of imperializing modernity.[13]

In both the Scottish Highands and Ireland, meanwhile, modernization was taking its toll. During the Irish Famine of 1845–50, approximately one million peasants died and another million and a half were driven off the land and forced to emigrate. British policy during the Famine was condemned by Karl Marx, John Stuart Mill, and many others, but it was celebrated by Anthony Trollope as the salvation of Ireland. In *Castle Richmond* (1860), Trollope writes that thanks to the mercy of God and of Lord John Russell's liberal government, Ireland has shed its surplus population: 'And now again the fields in Ireland are green, and the markets are busy, and money is chucked to and fro like a weathercock' (1989: 347). The dual plots of *Castle Richmond* – aristocratic marriage and inheritance and mass starvation – render the clash of chronotopes in nearly absolute terms: fortune and a future for the well-to-do characters; immiseration and death for the nameless peasants (Corbett 136–45).

Because of the length and severity of English and Anglo-Irish domination of Catholic Ireland, and particularly of the peasantry who were often compared to slaves (see, for example, Carlyle [1850: 49] and Duffy [1881: 120, 141]), Irish independence seemed utopian to most writers in the early 1800s. Although Daniel O'Connell's crusade to repeal the Union was hugely popular among the Irish, the defeat of the United Irishman's Rebellion crushed hopes for an independent Ireland until long after the Famine. According to Irish nationalist John Mitchel, the Famine itself was 'the last' – meaning latest – 'conquest of Ireland.' With ironic understatement, Mitchel declared:

> That an island which is said to be an integral part of the richest empire on the globe . . . should in five years lose two and a half millions of its people (more than one fourth) by hunger, and fever the consequence of hunger, and flight beyond sea to escape from hunger, – while that empire of which it is

said to be a part, was all the while advancing in wealth, prosperity, and comfort, at a faster pace than ever before, – is a matter that seems to ask elucidation. (2005: 8)

Mitchel correctly prophesied, however, that 'The passionate aspiration for Irish nationhood will outlive the British Empire' (220).

The Empire Cleans Up Its Act

In *The Scandal of Empire*, Nicholas Dirks contends that 'empire was only able to realize itself once its ignominious origins were recast, once its scandal could lead to, and make necessary, the triumph of empire itself' (2006: 5). Before 1850, various aspects of Britain's imperial expansion were more scandalous than cause for pride, including in the 1840s the first Opium War (1839–41), which Harriet Martineau called 'a national disgrace' (2004: 291); the opening disaster of the first Afghan War (1839–42); and the Irish Famine (1845–50).[14] Captain Cook's voyages and the British claim to Australia may have been triumphs of geography and imperial expansion, but New South Wales and Tasmania were at first dumping grounds for British convicts – also a 'national disgrace.' And virtually everywhere the behavior of British colonizers toward indigenous peoples, including slavery, was scandalous.

Even in the early 1800s, however, there were reasons to take pride in Britain's expanding Empire. Linda Colley notes that the end of the Napoleonic Wars in 1815, perhaps because of economic depression and unemployment, did not result in a major wave of patriotic enthusiasm (1992: 321). Yet well before the Napoleonic era, the sense of British (and not merely English) identity was growing. The Act of Union of 1800, making Ireland part of the United Kingdom, complemented the Act of Union of 1707, joining Scotland and England. Although Britain's troubles with Ireland were far from over, by the early 1800s 'British' already signified the unification of the internal colonies with England in the United Kingdom.

Through the first half of the 1800s, the 'triumph of empire' emerged gradually and unevenly as scandals were relegated to the past by reforming the East India Company, by the success of the antislavery crusade, and by missionary endeavors. Reforms in India converted the Company from a piratical operation into a governing institution supposedly serving Indians rather than Britons. In 1859, Harriet Martineau wrote: 'a vague notion exists that there is something disgraceful in our tenure of India; that the native population has been somehow sacrificed to our ambition and cupidity.' That 'vague notion,' however, has been countered by 'the

few who take an interest in the India of our own day,' and who insist that
no nation other than Britain 'presents a picture of a more virtuous devo-
tion to public duty' (2004: 55). Macaulay's equivocations in 'Lord Clive'
(1840) are instructive: though Clive had 'great faults,' he was also an
imperial hero. Macaulay says that Clive 'considered Oriental politics as
a game in which nothing was unfair' (1967: 334). His failings are a
version of going native, lowering himself to the level of the Indians: 'this
man, in the other parts of his life an honourable English gentleman and
soldier, was no sooner matched against an Indian intriguer, than he
became himself an Indian intriguer.' Clive's unethical behavior helps to
explain why India prior to 1800 was regarded as 'the seat of European
violence and military oppression,' as Scott says in *Guy Mannering*.
Nevertheless, Macaulay's essay is in large measure an exercise in imperialist hero-worship.

The other major scandal of the Empire was slavery. Like the discourse
on India before the 1850s, the discourse of the antislavery crusade was
strikingly double-edged. Until 1833, abolitionists condemned Britain for
its role in the practice of slavery. However, after Parliament abolished the
slave trade (1807) and then slavery itself in all British territories (1833),
condemnation turned into praise. Britain was now playing a vanguard
role in ridding the world of slavery. British abolitionists took aim at the
United States and other nations where slavery persisted. In this second
mode, abolitionism is often difficult to distinguish from imperialist self-
aggrandizement. The British navy patrolled the coasts of Africa in an
effort to halt the slave trade; how effective it was is unclear, but its activities contributed to Britons' pride in their Empire. In Charlotte Yonge's
The Daisy Chain (1856), Alan Ernescliffe is 'a hero' who had 'distin-
guished himself in encounters with slave ships, and in command of a
prize that he had had to conduct to Sierra Leone, he had shown great
coolness and seamanship . . .' (1876: 9–10). Abolition led also to the
founding of Sierra Leone as a location to resettle former slaves – for
Yonge, an example of imperial benevolence.

Because of abolition, reforms in India, and the spread of missions, P. J.
Marshall notes that 'confidence in Britain's ability to influence the world
for the better was probably at its height in the early nineteenth century,
even if imperial propaganda might be more strident in later periods'
(1996: 29). This is the picture of imperial benevolence offered by Yonge,
by Dilke in *Greater Britain*, by Trollope in his travelogues, and many
other Victorian authors. It is one most educated Victorians accepted. If
Ireland was in wretched shape, that was supposedly because of mismanagement and absenteeism by Anglo-Irish landlords, the fecklessness of

the Irish peasantry, and Catholicism. With the transportation of convicts drawing to an end, the Australian colonies were growing prosperous and offering hope and opportunity to free settlers; the Aborigines were a nuisance, but they were supposedly doomed to complete extinction by some obscure 'law' of nature or God (McGregor 1997).[15] The 1837 rebellions in both Lower and Upper Canada had been resolved by Lord Durham and the granting of partial home rule. Also in 1837, the Boers started their Great Trek, leading to the establishment of the Transvaal and the Orange Free State as Boer republics and to future conflicts with the British in southern Africa. But the Boers were leaving the Cape because the British authorities there were passing antislavery laws, insisting on more humane treatment of black Africans.

Starting with David Livingstone in the 1850s, combatting slavery within Africa was an avowed motive of most British explorers of central Africa (Richard Burton was an exception). The abolitionism of Livingstone, Stanley, and other explorers helped make the European 'penetration' of 'the dark continent' seem exciting and urgent, leading, albeit by devious routes, to the final 'scramble for Africa' starting in the mid-1880s. Just as the slave trade had led to the formation of European outposts and eventually colonies in Africa, so the antislavery crusade within Africa itself became a motivation for colonization. Further, in the 1830s and '40s, missionary and abolitionist discourse contributed to a general concern about how colonization in the Americas, South Africa, Australia, and New Zealand was affecting indigenous populations. An offshoot of the antislavery movement, the Aborigines Protection Society was founded in 1837; its exposés contributed to a humanitarianism that criticized some, but not all, aspects of imperialism. The typical finding of the APS was that the Colonial Office needed to exert more, not less, control over the frontiers of white settlement. It deemed official imperialism preferable to uncontrolled conquest and colonization.

The explorers were also contributors to the sciences, notably geography, anthropology, botany, and zoology. The highly publicized competition to discover the source of the Nile symbolized the growing belief that scientific knowledge, progressing hand-in-hand with both exploration and the expansion of the Empire, was triumphing over ignorance and superstition, just as Christianity was supposedly triumphing over heathenism. 'The warfare between science and religion' affected many aspects of Victorian literature and culture, but the claims of both science and religion to be flooding the world with light redounded to the credit of the Empire. Explorers, naturalists, and missionaries often also acted as 'men on the spot'; if they didn't plant the Union Jack themselves, then their activities on the frontiers of the Empire or of the known world suggested that doing so might be a good idea.

Bent on destroying 'diabolical' beliefs and customs, the missionaries nevertheless frequently – like Bartolomé de Las Casas in the 1500s – defended 'the natives' against the depredations of non-missionary invaders and colonizers. They often also urged the Colonial Office to intervene, thus encouraging further imperial expansion. In *Civilising Subjects*, Catherine Hall demonstrates that Baptist missionaries in Jamaica between the early 1800s and 1867 opposed slavery and racial barriers to the salvation and advancement of African-Jamaicans while supporting intervention from London. The slave-owning planters were, hence, 'for the most part extremely hostile to missionary activities' (2002: 88). They held the missionaries responsible for the slave rebellion of 1831 and the 1865 uprising. Unlike the Anglican clergy who sided with the plantocracy, the Baptists worked for the spiritual salvation of their black congregations, and also – covertly or overtly – for emancipation.[16] Hall writes that the missionaries, 'caught between two cultures . . . produced the dream of a third, where Africans and Englishmen would live harmoniously, in a missionary regime, a new Jamaica' (2002: 137). By the 1850s, however, Jamaica was not becoming the progressive, Christian utopia the missionaries desired. The 1865 uprising and Governor Edward Eyre's repression of it ended the missionaries' 'dream.'

During that uprising, Eyre's excessive punishment of the rebels, killing over five hundred, flogging many more, and burning down over one thousand houses, ended his career as a colonial administrator and produced a controversy in which many British writers and politicians took sides. Carlyle, Dickens, Tennyson, John Ruskin, and Charles Kingsley all defended Eyre, while John Stuart Mill, John Bright, Tom Hughes, and the Jamaica Committee sought Eyre's prosecution for murder (Semmel 1965). Members of the Committee also supported the North in the American Civil War. Like the debate over the Indian Rebellion, the Jamaican controversy raised the question of whether the Empire was generally oppressive. Eyre's actions constituted 'one of the most shameful chapters in British colonial history,' writes Denis Judd (1996: 82) – that is to say, another 'scandal of empire.'

Throughout the nineteenth century, missionaries produced an enormous amount of writing, focusing on just about every area of 'darkness' or 'heathenism' in the world (Johnston 2003). Livingstone's first book, *Missionary Travels and Researches in South Africa* (1857), is only the best-known example of a missionary bestseller. It is also a good example of 'missionary ethnography' (Stocking 1987: 87–92): before the establishment of modern anthropological procedures, missionaries often provided largely accurate and sympathetic accounts of indigenous peoples and cultures.[17] Although Livingstone made only one convert, the Bakwain chief Sechele, the great missionary-explorer was certain that his 'teaching did good to the general mind of the people by bringing new and better motives into play. Five instances are positively known to me in which, by our influence on public opinion, war was prevented . . .' (1972: 21).

Missionaries figure prominently in Victorian fiction, helping to improve and justify the Empire. Under the label of the evangelical meeting place 'Exeter Hall,' Carlyle accused missionaries and abolitionists of hypocrisy (1964: 306). Dickens, too, although making an exception of Livingstone, condemned missionaries for their 'heated visions . . . for the railroad Christianisation of Africa' (1996: 124). In *Bleak House*, Dickens satirized the 'telescopic philanthropy' of Mrs. Jellyby; her concern for Africans led her to neglect much-needed work at home, including mothering her children. Nevertheless, starting with Owenson's *The Missionary*, many novels hero-worship missionaries. Although St. John Rivers fails to persuade Jane Eyre to join him, he goes to India to convert the heathen where he perishes by disease; Charlotte Brontë views him as both a stiff-necked fanatic and a hero. Brontë appears to agree when he tells Jane: 'God had an errand for me; to bear which afar, to deliver it well, skill and strength, courage and eloquence, the best qualifications of soldier, statesman, and orator, were all needed: for these all centre in the good missionary' (1996: 404–5).

In *The Coral Island* (1858), Robert Ballantyne's trio of boy-heroes learn much about the diabolical customs of cannibals and also about the miraculous success of missionaries in converting them to Christianity. Ralph Rover exclaims: 'God bless and prosper the missionaries till they get a footing in every island of the sea!' (1990: 231). For *The Coral Island*, Ballantyne drew on such missionary texts as the Rev. John Williams's *Narrative of Missionary Enterprises in the South Sea Islands* (1837); he also acknowledged Livingstone's heroic example in *Black Ivory* (1873) and several of his other stories (Hannabus 1989: 60–2). A kindly missionary is busily converting Africans in *The Gorilla Hunters* (1861). And in *Gascoyne the Sandalwood Trader* (1864), Ballantyne celebrates missionaries as zealous 'soldiers of Christ,' while Williams, the famous missionary-martyr of the South Pacific, appears in *Jarwin and Cuffy* (1878).

Missionaries are featured in several of Charlotte Yonge's novels including *The Daisy Chain* (1856), in which Ethel May brings 'civilization' and eventually a new church to the impoverished village of Cocksmoor. Meanwhile her brother Norman decides to become a missionary in New Zealand, where an uncle already serves in that role. Still another brother enters the navy and, after a shipwreck, is rescued by ex-cannibals in the Loyalty Islands, who have been saved by 'native teachers' from Samoa. The narrator explains:

> The Samoans . . . having been converted by the Church Missionary Society, have sent out great numbers of most active and admirable teachers among the scattered islands, braving martyrdom and disease, never shrinking from their work, and, by teaching and example, preparing the way for fuller doctrine than they can yet impart. (1876: 532)

Ethel calls becoming a missionary 'the most glorious thing man can do!' (517), and many Victorians agreed.

Yonge donated the royalties from her novel *The Heir of Redcliffe* (1853) to finance the building of a mission ship, *The Southern Cross*, for her family's friend, George Augustus Selwyn, bishop of New Zealand. She used the proceeds from *The Daisy Chain* to help pay for the construction of a missionary college in New Zealand. Another friend, John Coleridge Patteson, bishop of Melanesia, sailed on *The Southern Cross* and also helped pay for the college (Schaffer 2005: 211). After his martyrdom, at his sisters' request, Yonge wrote Patteson's biography (1873). He was martyred in the New Hebrides when some of the islanders mistook him for a slave trader and clubbed him to death.

Robert Louis Stevenson's reaction to missionaries was more complicated and skeptical than Ballantyne's or Yonge's, though not so negative as the views expressed by Dickens. During his years in the South Pacific, Stevenson encountered many missionaries and befriended several of them. Although generally supportive of their work, he disliked 'the overbearing and self-righteous nature of . . . missionary culture' (Colley 2004: 24). He especially disliked the missionaries' taboos on such innocent native customs as dancing. And, unlike some of the missionaries, Stevenson recognized that native 'superstitions' often persisted after conversion:

> Fully understanding this reality, he liked to compare this duality to 'the theological Highlander [who] sneaks from under the eye of the Free Church divine to lay an offering by a sacred well.' He was . . . heartened by the fact that in Tautira the chief's sister, although 'very religious [and] a great church-goer,' privately worshipped a shark. (Colley 2004: 14)

Accounts of missionary endeavors tend to be celebratory, even triumphal: the true religion conquering paganism, evil, and slavery, while resisting the violence and corrupting influences of secular white intruders into the 'dark' places of the world. Insofar as missionary texts express or imply that spreading the gospel is an offshoot of imperial expansion (or vice-versa), then they are the religious equivalent of secular jingoism. Nevertheless, the relations between missionaries, non-Western societies, and non-missionary colonizers were frequently antagonistic. The East India Company viewed missionaries with suspicion, because contesting either Hinduism or Islam could be dangerous. But the upsurge of missionary activity around the globe from the 1790s on, coupled with the success of the anti-slavery movement and the hegemony of evangelical humanitarianism in the Colonial Office in the 1830s, made later routes to imperial expansion easier to travel.

Emigration Narratives

Colonization entails diasporas that are seldom entirely voluntary and are often coerced. Both the slave trade and the transportation of convicts are examples of the coerced displacement of people, but during the 1800s millions left Britain supposedly of their own free will, because they found it difficult or impossible to make a living there. After 1815, emigration to the colonies or the United States emerged as a partial solution to poverty, unemployment, and overpopulation. 'The Condition-of-England Question,' as Carlyle called it, raised the threat of revolution at home. Economic depression, trade unionism, Chartism, and the flood of immigrants from Ireland to England caused many Victorian writers and politicians to look to the colonies for help.

Writing about emigration was, like abolitionist discourse, Janus-faced: critical of the domestic problems that caused people to leave Britain, but grateful for the colonies and the United States as places for them potentially to thrive. In *Past and Present* (1843), Carlyle angrily rejects Malthus's theory of overpopulation with its insistence that poverty is an incurable condition. Even if overcrowding, unemployment, and poverty are facts of life in the Britain of the 1840s, people can always find greener pastures abroad:

> why should there not be an 'Emigration Service' . . . with funds, forces, idle Navy-ships, and ever-increasing apparatus; in fine an *effective system* of Emigration; so that, at length . . . every honest willing Workman who found England too strait, and the 'Organisation of Labour' not yet sufficiently advanced, might find likewise a bridge built to carry him into new Western Lands, there to 'organise' with more elbow-room some labour for himself? There to be a real blessing, raising new corn for us, purchasing new

webs and hatchets from us; leaving us at least in peace; – instead of staying here to be a Physical-Force Chartist, unblessed and no blessing! (1965: 263)

The ambivalence of emigration discourse is evident as well in Felicia Hemans' 'Song of Emigration' (1830), in which the 'man's voice' sings: 'We will shape our course by a brighter star,' followed by the chorus:

'But, alas! that we should go,'
Sang the farewell voices then,
'From the homesteads, warm and low,
By the brook and by the glen!' (1914: 292)

So, too, in Charles MacKay's 'The Emigrants,' the Canadian colonies will provide what 'mother England' cannot provide:

Here we had toil and little to reward it,
  But there shall plenty smile upon our pain,
And ours shall be the mountain and the forest,
  And boundless prairies ripe with golden grain
    Cheer, boys! cheer! for England, mother England!
  Cheer, boys! cheer! united heart and hand! –
Cheer, boys! cheer! there's wealth for honest labour –
  Cheer, boys! cheer! – in the new and happy land!
    (Brooks and Faulkner 1996: 178)

Although it gave them 'little' for their 'toil,' MacKay's 'boys' nevertheless cheer for 'mother England,' but even more enthusiastically for 'the new and happy land' to which they are sailing. The editor of *The Illustrated London News*, MacKay wrote a series of 'popular songs' on emigration (1851–5), which were among many early and mid-Victorian works promoting the colonies as a place for 'self-improvement' (Thompson 2005: 57). The 1840s and 1850s also witnessed the activities of emigration agents who traveled around Britain to recruit new colonists (Thompson 2005: 58). They helped familiarize many working and lower-middle-class Victorians with what the colonies had to offer, in contrast to what was lacking at home.

Sounding himself like an emigration agent, in the introduction to his *Tales of the Colonies*, Charles Rowcroft writes:

The increasing difficulty of maintaining a family in England, in which the competition for mere subsistence has become so keen; and the still greater difficulty of providing for children when their maturer years render it imperative on the parent to seek for some profession or calling on which they may rely for their future support, has excited among all classes a strong attention towards the colonies of Great Britain, where fertile and unclaimed lands, almost boundless in extent, await only the labour of man to produce all that man requires. (1843: 1:v)

Despite this opening, Rowcroft does not paint a rosy picture of life in Tasmania. Although his protagonist, William Thornley, establishes a farm and raises his family there, many of the episodes involve struggles against bushrangers and 'natives,' who sometimes join forces against the peaceful settlers. Thornley is often 'only just saved from being shot by the bushrangers and burnt by the natives' (2:207). Rowcroft also has to deal with 'the convict system,' which one of the settlers denounces as 'wilfully scattering abroad the seeds of moral contagion, and inoculating the new country with diseases in their rifest state. That is a bad beginning for a new empire!' (2:234). But the magistrate who explains 'the system' calls it 'a balance of evils,' adding that there is less crime in Van Diemen's Land than 'in England and Ireland' (2:34). After enumerating the provisions due to a convict servant, the magistrate says that 'the convict is well off, and . . . is removed from that temptation to crime which in the mother country is often produced by actual privations' (2:225–6). Although Thornley encounters many dangers, the colonies – even Tasmania – offer the chance for success, including the reformation of the convicts.

The Famine in Ireland made leaving that sorry portion of the Empire an urgent necessity for millions. John Stuart Mill declared that the peasants of Ireland have 'learnt to fix their eyes on a terrestrial paradise beyond the ocean, as a sure refuge both from oppression of the Saxon and from the tyranny of nature' (1965: 2:325). Throughout the 1800s, but especially during and after the Famine, Irish emigrants to the United States, Canada, Australia, and England carried aspirations for an independent Ireland with them. In many Victorian novels, emigration helps characters, whether virtuous or otherwise, out of trouble in Britain. In *Mary Barton* (1848), Elizabeth Gaskell depicts the struggles against poverty and injustice of John Barton, factory worker, and his daughter Mary. Starvation and a strike lead John to murder the son of a factory owner. After Barton's arrest and trial, Mary is united with her working-class lover, now cleared of the charge of murder, and the two emigrate to Canada.

In Charles Reade's *It Is Never Too Late to Mend* (1856), George Fielding discovers gold in Australia and overcomes the misfortunes he experienced in Britain. So, too, in Mary Elizabeth Braddon's *Lady Audley's Secret* (1862), the penniless soldier George Talboys returns from Australia with £20,000. *The Recollections of Geoffrey Hamlyn* (1859) by Henry Kingsley depicts the emigration of an entire town to Australia where, 'under the free government of Britain . . . all the oppressed of the earth have taken refuge' (1924: 409). When Mr. Micawber and his family also emigrate to Australia in Dickens's *David Copperfield* (1850), he ceases to be a ne'er-do-well and becomes a magistrate in the town of Port Middlebay. In the same novel, Dickens sends his 'fallen women' characters Martha Endell and Little Em'ly to Australia. Back in England, Mr. Peggotty tells David: 'What with sheep-farming, and what with stock-farming, and what with one thing and what with t'other, we are as well to do, as well could be. There's been kiender a blessing fell upon us . . . and we've done nowt but prosper' (1989: 867–8). Emigration in Victorian fiction does not always end in happiness and prosperity, however. The protagonist of Dickens's *Martin Chuzzlewit* (1844) emigrates to the United States but is swindled in a fraudulent land scheme – 'Eden' turns out to be a fever-inducing swamp. Yet on the whole, emigration is a positive outcome for many characters in Victorian novels.

New literatures written in the colonies typically feature emigration and settlers' experiences. Rowcroft's *Tales* is an example from early Australian literature. Canadian literature, too, begins with accounts of emigration and frontier life, including Catharine Parr Traill's *Backwoods of Canada* (1836). In her epistolary narrative, Traill writes that she 'has endeavoured to afford every possible information to the wives and daughters of emigrants of the higher class who contemplate seeking a home amid our Canadian wilds.' Her desire, she says, is to provide 'utility in preference to artificial personal refinement,' for 'the struggle up the hill of Independence is often a severe one' (1836: 1–5). But 'independence' is what the emigrant can expect if she and her husband persevere. A number of British feminists such as Maria Rye and Caroline Chisholm advocated emigration for women as a way to enhance their 'independence' (Midgley 2007: 123–46).

In 1852, Traill's sister, Susanna Moodie, published *Roughing It in the Bush, or Forest Life in Canada* (1852), which Trumpener calls 'the most influential mid-Victorian chronicle of immigrant and settler life in Upper Canada' (1997: 233). In the following apostrophe to both England and Canada, Moodie expresses 'emigrant homesickness . . . as maternal desertion' (Trumpener 1997: 235):

> Dear, dear England! why was I forced by a stern necessity to leave you? What heinous crime had I committed that I, who adored you, should be torn from your sacred bosom, to pine out my joyless existence in a foreign clime? Oh that I might be permitted to return and die upon your wave-encircled shores . . . Ah, these are vain outbursts of feeling – melancholy relapses of

the spring home-sickness! Canada! thou art a noble, free, and rising country–the great fostering mother of the orphans of civilisation. The off-spring of Britain, thou must be great and I will and do love thee . . . (quoted in Trumpener 1997: 235)

This passage is typical of emigration discourse, expressing at once a feeling of being orphaned or cast away, nostalgia for 'dear, dear England,' and hope for the future in the colonial new world.

Scotsman Thomas Pringle went for several years as a settler to the new colony of Albany; his *African Sketches* (1834) has been called 'the found-ing artwork of South African English literature' (Gray 1979: 196). Pringle followed this volume with *Narrative of a Residence in South Africa* (1835). The 1830s also saw publication of the anonymous novel *Makanna, or The Land of the Savage* (1834), Dunbar Moodie's *Ten Years in South Africa* (1835), Edward Kendall's *English Boy at the Cape: An Anglo-African Story* (1835), and *Life in the Woods* (1832), one of Harriet Martineau's 'illustrations of political economy.' Like Pringle, Martineau was an abolitionist who bemoaned the destruction of indige-nous peoples wrought by colonization. The decimation of the Bushmen by both Boers and British was, she believed, simultaneously immoral and uneconomical (for Martineau, what is immoral is uneconomical, and vice versa). When he returned to Britain, Pringle became the secretary of the Antislavery Society. After the abolition of slavery in 1833, the Society focused on the treatment of the Xhosas and other African peoples, and, with the founding of the Aborigines Protection Society in 1837, on the fate of 'natives' everywhere under the impact of white colonization.

Among major Victorian writers, no one traveled more or wrote more about the colonies than did Trollope. In his various surveys of the Empire, he often focuses on prospects for British emigrants. In 1841, Trollope went to Ireland to work as a surveyor for the post office, and his first two novels and several of his later ones such as *Castle Richmond* deal with that 'internal colony' from a Unionist standpoint: 'home rule' was anathema to him. In 1858, still working for the post office, Trollope traveled first to Egypt, where, according to his *Autobiography*, he nego-tiated a treaty with the Pasha for the delivery of mail across Egypt in twenty-four hours (1968: 106). He was thus working for the Postmaster General but also for the Empire. He traveled next to Scotland to investi-gate postal services in Glasgow, and still in 1858 to the West Indies, where he 'cleanse[d] the Augean stables of our Post Office system there' (110). Trollope declared that his account of that trip, *The West Indies and the Spanish Main* (1859), was 'the best book that has come from my pen' (111).

Trollope's later journeys resulted in *North America* (1862), *Australia and New Zealand* (1873), and *South Africa* (1878). He also wrote many letters to the press about colonial affairs (see *The Tireless Traveler*). And he penned two novels about Australia, *Harry Heathcote of Gangoil* (1874), based on his son Fred's experience as a sheep farmer, and *John Caldigate* (1879), which recounts the protagonist's experiences in the gold fields. In an earlier novel, *The Three Clerks* (1857), Alaric Tudor, after a prison term for embezzlement, emigrates to Australia with his family. In all three novels, Trollope does not paint Australia as the pastoral paradise that Bulwer-Lytton depicted in his emigration novel *The Caxtons* (1849). It is nevertheless a place where British settlers can mend their fortunes and their reputations.

According to John Davidson, Trollope's 'colonial thought passed through three phases' (1969: 327). In the first phase, Trollope viewed colonies as children of the mother country, who would and should grow up into independence. That did not mean the relationship between colony and metropole should end in revolution, as happened with the American colonies that formed the United States. Canada, Australia, New Zealand, and the Cape Colony could all achieve peaceful independence and still remain loyal to Britain. In the second phase, roughly equivalent to Benjamin Disraeli's second administration as Prime Minister (1874–1880), Trollope opposed new acquisitions by the Empire, especially in Africa and other tropical locations such as Fiji. In a letter to the *Liverpool Mercury* (October 1874), Trollope wrote:

> There is, I think, a general opinion that Great Britain possesses enough of the world . . . and that new territorial possessions must be regarded rather as increased burdens than increased strength. No doubt the power of the country and the prestige which belongs to its name are based on its colonial and Indian empire. Every Englishman sufficiently awake to be proud of England feels this; but there is at the same time a general conviction that . . . we have got all that can do us good . . . (1978: 181)

This statement could be misconstrued as anti-imperialist, but it expresses a pride in the Empire self-confident enough to forego future imperial expansion. In Trollope's view, the existing colonies together with the United States offered plenty of room for Britain's ever-expanding population.

There are many other Victorian novels that feature emigration and life in the colonies. For example, besides *Geoffrey Hamlyn*, Henry Kingsley penned *The Hillyars and the Burtons* (1865), which again focuses on Australia. In New Zealand, novel-writing begins with Major

Henry B. Stoney's *Taranaki: A Tale of the War* (1861) and Mrs. J. E. Aylmer's *Distant Homes: or the Graham Family in New Zealand* (1862). Both authors recount establishing frontier homesteads in perilous conditions, including conflict with the Maoris. In these and many other stories about emigration, the characters express gratitude for their new opportunities, while viewing Britain as home, as the center of the Empire that allows them to prosper, but also as the source of their past troubles.

The quirkiest Victorian novels dealing with emigration are undoubtedly Samuel Butler's *Erewhon* (1872) and *Erewhon Revisited* (1901), based on his time as a sheep farmer in New Zealand from 1859 to 1864. Like Alice's Wonderland, 'Erewhon' ('nowhere' backwards) inverts various British customs – punishing sickness while treating crime as an illness, for example. Butler is not satirizing colonial New Zealand, which like other settler colonies was quite British in behavior and attitudes. He is instead satirizing British customs and values. In *Erewhon Revisited*, Higgs – the protagonist of both novels – returns to the scene of his earlier adventures and discovers that he is the object of worship of a new religion, a variation on the theme of 'savages' worshipping a white man or woman as a god, as in H. Rider Haggard's *She* and Joseph Conrad's *Heart of Darkness*.

Thrilling Adventures

Novels about India and also about emigration often double as adventure stories. As Martin Green says, 'Adventure is the energizing myth of empire, and empire is to be found everywhere in the modern world' (1979: xi). Writers of imperialist adventure fiction frequently imitated either Defoe's *Robinson Crusoe* or Scott's Waverley novels – sometimes both. Like emigration narratives, adventure fiction is typically focused on the future: crossing frontiers and exploring new territories, the white heroes are pathfinders for the Empire and civilization. Almost always, civilization is equated both with the supposed superiority of the white race and with colonization by white settlers. Like James Fenimore Cooper's final Mohicans, indigenous peoples in most imperialist adventure fiction must give way to the white invaders of their territories. Though the 'dying savage' is often treated with sentimentality, his demise is typically viewed as inevitable and as making room for progress – that is, for civilization on Western terms.

Starting with Captain Frederick Marryat, much imperialist adventure fiction was written for boys, and often features juvenile heroes, like Marryat's midshipmen. Seafaring itself was an integral part of imperialist myth-making. In the 1830s, maritime novels by Marryat, Frederick Chamier, and others flourished alongside maritime melodramas, featuring the stock character Jack Tar, as in T. P. Cooke and Douglas Jerrold's play *Black-Ey'd Susan* (1829). J. S. Bratton comments that in such plays the comic-heroic Jack Tar is 'the innocent ruler of the world' (1991: 58). Marryat's young sailors also rule every roost they light upon, whether on shipboard or dry land, as in *Mr. Midshipman Easy* (1836). As with most other imperialist authors, Marryat's politics were both conservative and authoritarian: democracy and equality were anathema to him. In the West Indies, one of his eponymous sailor-heroes, Newton Foster, discovers that slavery is a benevolent institution. Like Aphra Behn's Oroonoko, the cook who sails with Midshipman Easy, Mesty (short for Mephistopheles), was once a prince in Africa, but in the British navy the role of cook is about right for him; Mesty is grateful to the navy for having rescued him from slavery and also from African savagery.

In *Masterman Ready* (1841), his version of *Robinson Crusoe*, Marryat depicts the shipwreck of the Seagrave family on a desert island. Their survival depends on the practical wisdom and experience of the title character, an older version of Jack Tar. With Ready's help the Seagraves transform their island into a model colony. When young William Seagrave asks about 'the nature of a colony,' his father responds by describing the rise of the British Empire and its victories over its Spanish, Dutch, and French rivals. Today, says Mr. Seagrave, 'the sun is said, and very truly, never to set upon . . . English possessions; for . . . the sun shines either upon one portion or another of the globe which is a colony to our country' (1841: 140). Mr. Seagrave adds, however, that when a colony becomes 'strong and powerful enough to take care of itself, it throws off the yoke of subjection, and declares itself independent; just as a son who has grown up to manhood leaves his father's house and takes up a business to gain his own livelihood' (141). He offers the United States as an illustration, and adds that even 'barbarians and savages' may one day become 'a great nation.' This prompts William to ask whether, if 'nations rise and fall,' England may one day 'fall, and be of no more importance than Portugal is now?' This will be 'the fate of our dear country,' says his father, though so far in the future that there is no need for apprehension (141).

From the 1830s on, adventure fiction for young readers became a veritable industry. While the novels of G. A. Henty are familiar late-Victorian examples, other writers including Marryat were producing such fiction well before then. Both Robert Ballantyne and W. H. G. Kingston began their writing careers in the 1840s. The first journals for boy readers, with stories featuring exploration, war, and empire, cropped up in the 1850s and '60s, starting with S. O. Beeton's *Boy's Own Magazine* (1855). Edwin Brett launched *Boys of England* in 1866; a year later, it had a circulation of 150,000, and by 1869 that figure had doubled. Edmund Routledge began the rival *Every Boy's Magazine* in 1862, a decade before Forster's Education Act established compulsory elementary schooling.[18]

Many of Kingston's works, both fictional and nonfictional, feature emigration. Starting in 1844, he edited *The Colonist*, *The Colonial Magazine*, and the *East Indian Review*. He founded and edited *Kingston's Magazine* to promote the Empire and colonization. And he served as an officer of a colonization society, while publishing several books and pamphlets on emigration, including *How to Emigrate; or, The British Colonists* (1850). In 1863 Kingston published *Our Sailors; or, Anecdotes of the Engagements and Gallant Deeds of the British Navy During the Reign of Her Majesty Queen Victoria* and also *Our Soldiers; or, Anecdotes of the Campaigns and Gallant Deeds of the British Army During the Reign of Her Majesty Queen Victoria*. He followed these patriotic tomes with *How Britannia Came to Rule the Waves* (1870).

In one of Kingston's most popular tales, *Peter the Whaler* (1851), the narrator-protagonist, banished from home because of a poaching episode, first sails on an emigrant ship bound for Quebec. The *Black Swan* is badly captained; it sinks before reaching port. The captain and crew treat the emigrants, many of whom are Irish, almost as if they were slaves on a slave ship. Because of this abuse, 'instead of friends and supporters, [the emigrants] were to be foes to England and the English – aliens of the country which should have cherished and protected them, but did not' (1906: 37). Kingston was writing just as the Irish Famine was ending. Peter says that the shipboard abuse exemplifies the deplorable conditions in Britain which have forced people to emigrate in the first place: 'When so many of our poor countrymen are leaving our shores annually to lands where they can procure work and food, we should have a far better supervision and a more organised system of emigration than now exists' (33–4). Like Carlyle, Kingston urges his readers to help establish such a system.

On most counts, however, *Peter the Whaler* is thoroughly chauvinistic. Before Peter sails, his clergyman father tells him, 'Wherever you wander, my son, remember you are a Briton, and cease not to love your native land' (21). That could be taken as the main theme in everything that Kingston wrote. Indeed, once in Quebec, Peter goes on a tour of the town and its environs. Climbing to 'the summit of the Citadel on Cape Diamond, whence one may look over the celebrated Plains of Abraham,' Peter notes that was where 'the gallant Wolf gained the victory which gave Canada to England, and where, fighting nobly, he fell in the hour of triumph' (76). *Peter the Whaler* is highly critical of how immigrants from Britain are treated, both before and during their voyages; yet there is no greater country in the world than Britain.

Captain Mayne Reid emigrated from Ireland to the United States in 1839 and was wounded at the Battle of Chapultepec during the Mexican-American War of 1846–8. After returning to Britain, he began to publish adventure fiction starting with *The Rifle Rangers* (1850) and *The Scalp Hunters; or, Romantic Adventures in Northern Mexico* (1851). Reid wrote many more adventure stories such as *The Giraffe Hunters* (1867) before his death in 1883. Ballantyne was an equally prolific author of juvenile adventure fiction; his bestselling Robinsonade, *The Coral Island*, appeared in 1858, as did also *Martin Rattler; or, A Boy's Adventure in the Forests of Brazil*. Ralph Rover and the other boy-heroes from *The Coral Island* travel to central Africa for an encore in *The Gorilla Hunters* (1861), where they merrily gun down numerous specimens of the recently discovered giant ape.

In most imperialist adventure fiction, masculinity is a problem only because it is no problem at all. Boy-heroes are forever proving their manliness through their pluck and derring-do. When female characters occasionally appear in such fiction, they are often damsels in distress, to be rescued by the boy-heroes. Marryat's midshipmen sometimes fall in love and get married at the end of their tales, but Ballantyne's stories are 'uncompromisingly hostile' toward 'the milder joys found in the company of the fair sex,' writes Eric Quayle; 'The most stirring and realistic of his adventure tales are leavened with a eunuch-like approach to any female that he apologetically allowed to intrude amongst the red-blooded boys who are busily massacring the natives and bagging their fifth rhinocerus' (1967: 132). A similar misogyny characterizes most adventure fiction aimed at boy readers.

The Coral Island, *Peter the Whaler*, and many similar adventure stories inspired Robert Louis Stevenson to pen *Treasure Island* (1882), a novel that in turn prompted H. Rider Haggard to write *King Solomon's Mines* (1885). Haggard was inspired as well by the many accounts of European explorers of sub-Saharan Africa, including Livingstone's journals. For Haggard as for Livingstone, Africans – at least, some Africans – are not subhuman. After the Zulus defeated the British at the Battle of Isandhlwana in 1879, Haggard came to respect them. In *King Solomon's*

Mines, *Allan Quatermain* (1887), and *Nada the Lily* (1892), the Zulus
are noble savages; but like savages in most imperialist writing, they are
also bloodthirsty and self-destructive. Besides, Haggard's portrayal of the
cannibalistic Amahaggers in *She* (1887) suggests that he believed other
African 'races' were distinctly inferior to the white race, or at least to the
Anglo-Saxon branch of that race.

The Amahaggers of *She* are more akin to savages in most boys' adventure fiction than are Haggard's Zulu characters. Indeed, the juvenile
heroes in many adventure tales have no compunction about shooting
savages just as easily as Ballantyne's boys gun down gorillas. Violence
between white colonizers and indigenous peoples, coupled with imported
diseases such as typhoid and smallpox, led to the rapid declines of most
nonwhite populations in the Americas, Australia, and New Zealand. For
non-Europeans everywhere, European conquest and colonization was a
catastrophe. For imperialist authors, the standard rationalization was
that the demise of at least some nonwhite races was preordained, an
inevitable consequence of providence or nature or both. The apparently
total destruction of the Tasmanian Aborigines by 1876, already seen as
inevitable in the 1830s, contributed to a discourse about the extinction
of nonwhite races that was simultaneously mournful and celebratory. In
The Last of the Tasmanians (1870), James Bonwick quotes various
experts who held that, in the words of German race scientist Theodor
Waitz, '[t]he extinction of the lower [races] is predestined by Nature; and
it would thus appear that we must not merely acknowledge the right of
the white American to destroy the Red man, but perhaps praise him that
he has constituted himself the instrument of Providence in carrying
out . . . this law of destruction' (1970: 375) – a 'law' reinforced by evolutionary theory.

Though its chronotope is typically oriented toward the future, adventure fiction often inculcates history lessons. As with most of Scott's 'historical romances,' later examples of historical narratives, whether aimed
at adults or adolescents, function as versions of 'Whig history': the conflicts and confusions of the past lead to the progressive present and
forward to an ever-improving Empire. This is evident both in Tennyson's
Idylls of the King and in such historical novels as Charles Kingsley's
Westward Ho! (1855). Kingsley celebrates the brave deeds of English
sailors during the Elizabethan era. His hero, Amyas Leigh, is 'a symbol,
though he knows it not, of brave young England longing to wing its way
out of its island prison, to discover and to traffic, to colonize and to
civilize, until no wind can sweep the earth which does not bear the
echoes of an English voice' (1941: 21). Amyas's 'Saxon' blood makes him

simultaneously a 'savage' fighting machine and a natural-born 'gentleman' (19). Led by Amyas and the other 'Saxon' heroes from Devonshire, the English victories over the Spanish villains, including the defeat of the Spanish armada in 1588, lie at the origin of the modern British Empire. Kingsley declares that his novel ought to be 'sung' to 'all true English hearts . . . as an epic,' proclaiming 'the same great message which the songs of Troy, and the Persian wars, and the trophies of Marathon and Salamis, spoke to the hearts of all true Greeks of old' (12). Like his later historical novel *Hereward the Wake* (1866), *Westward Ho!* is an expression of Kingsley's belief in the absolute superiority of the Teutonic or, more specifically, the Anglo-Saxon race, a belief that he also expressed in *The Roman and the Teuton* (1864).

Many other historical adventure stories were, like *Idylls of the King*, set in the Middle Ages. An offshoot of literary and artistic Romanticism and Scott's medieval novels such as *Ivanhoe*, the 'renewed interest in medieval chivalry' enters the Victorian era with the 1839 rain-drenched Eglinton Tournament (Giraourd 1981: 87–110), the formation of 'Young England' (one of whose members was novelist and future Prime Minister Benjamin Disraeli), the beginnings of Tennyson's Arthurian poems, and Carlyle's *Past and Present* (1843). Some versions of Victorian medievalism – William Morris's, for example – were politically radical and anti-imperialist. But Carlyle, Disraeli, and Tennyson expressed the desire, albeit in quite different ways, for a renewed aristocracy and some version of feudalism. Their conservative politics reinforced imperialism; if the aristocracy was losing ground to the bourgeoisie at home, it could be reinvented in India, in Africa, or, albeit in more limited ways, in the colonies of white settlement. Kingsley's politics were at least superficially liberal, but his emphasis on Anglo-Saxon racial supremacy makes him just as much an imperialist as, say, Tennyson. Throughout the Victorian era, imperialist adventure fiction, whether set in the past or the present, and whether aimed at adults or juvenile readers, promoted the 'manifest destiny' of the Anglo-Saxon race – supposedly nature's aristocrats, as in *Westward Ho!* – to conquer and rule or else to exterminate the nonwhite races of the world.

Race and Character

At first, the loss of the American colonies seemed scandalous, but from about the 1850s forward that loss was often interpreted as a source of national and racial pride. Thus, in his popular *Short History of the English People* (1874), J. R. Green writes:

From the moment of the Declaration of Independence it mattered little whether England counted for less or more with the nations around her. She was no longer a mere European power, no longer a mere rival of Germany or Russia or France. She was from that hour a mother of nations. In America she had begotten a great people, and her emigrant ships were still to carry on the movement of the Teutonic race from which she herself had sprung. Her work was to be colonisation. (1879: 762)

For Green, colonization is the adventure story of 'the English people,' the greatest branch of the 'Teutonic race,' not restricted to the deeds merely of those from England or Great Britain. Governments, colonies, and nation-states come and go, but the 'Teutonic race' marches boldly into the future, creating new nations along the way.

'By mid-century,' writes Jan Nederveen Pieterse, 'racist beliefs . . . were common currency and the 1850s in particular saw the publication of a spate of racist texts' (1989: 247). For many Victorian intellectuals, race was the key to history. Thus, in *The Races of Men* (1850), Dr. Robert Knox proclaimed: 'race is everything: literature, science, art, in a word, civilisation, depend on it' (1969: 90). Knox heaped scorn on his own 'race,' the Anglo-Saxons, for dominating and slaughtering weaker races. Other mid-century studies of race include Robert Latham's *The Natural History of the Varieties of Man* (1850), Frenchman Arthur de Gobineau's *The Inequality of Human Races* (1853–5), and *Types of Mankind* (1854) by the Americans J. C. Nott and G. R. Gliddon. Typically racism justi-fied, in absolute terms, the imperial subjugation of the nonwhite races of the world by Britain and the other European powers.

Even before Knox, in *Tancred* (1847), Benjamin Disraeli has the sage-like Sidonia tell the young protagonist: 'A Saxon race, protected by an insular position, has stamped its diligent and methodic character on the century. And when a superior race, with a superior idea to Work and Order, advances, its state will be progressive . . . All is race; there is no other truth' (1847: 148–9). In the second of his Young England trilogy, *Sybil* (1845), Disraeli's heroine, daughter of Chartist Walter Gerard, overcomes the class barrier to her marriage with the aristocratic hero by discovering that her ancestors were Saxon nobles.[19] Disraeli considered the modern 'Whig aristocracy' a fraud, gerrymandered during the Reformation; he claimed to look back to Anglo-Saxon times for the roots of a genuine aristocracy. It is ironic that Disraeli, though a convert from Judaism to Anglicanism, should express any version of Anglo-Saxonism or even of historical explanation in terms of race. His tactic, however, is to assert the precedence in the British context of Anglo-Saxons over what he claims is the fraudulent Norman aristocracy, while also claiming the racial superiority of the 'Semites,' including both Arabs and Jews, over all other peoples as the founders of the world's greatest religions and empires. This is the key lesson Tancred learns, both from Sidonia and from the Angel of Arabia on Mount Sinai.

Throughout the Victorian era, explanations of historical change as the result of conflict between races were far more common than Marx and Engels' contention that the major causal factor in history was class struggle. Well before Disraeli and Knox, race acquired a scientific – or pseudo-scientific – dimension, stemming from the attempts by Enlightenment naturalists to categorize the different types of mankind together with all other species of animals and plants. These efforts always arranged the races in a hierarchy, with the white, Caucasian, or Aryan race at the summit. Prior to the 1840s, most naturalists subscribed to the biblical view of humanity as a single species with a common origin. The race scientists in the two decades before Darwin, however, sometimes argued in favor of polygenesis, or the theory that the races had separate origins and that they were, therefore, separate species. Darwin and his followers reverted to monogenesis, though evolutionary theory, predicated on geological time, made huge distinctions among the races based on assumptions about their uneven development.

One of the key texts prior to Darwin's *Origin of Species* (1859) that espoused a theory of evolution was Robert Chambers's *Vestiges of the Natural History of Creation* (1844). Concerning the evolution of humans, Chambers argued that the nonwhite races were all regressions and that only the white race had progressed: 'In the Caucasian or Indo-European family alone has the primitive organisation [of the human species] been improved upon. The Mongolian, Malay, American, and Negro, comprehending perhaps five-sixths of mankind, are degenerate' (1969: 309). However, according to Chambers, the different races had all sprung from 'the original type' of humanity. The idea that all races except for 'the Caucasian or Indo-European family' were incapable of progress underwrote European imperialism for at least three centuries. In the 1800s, both pre- and post-Darwinian race scientists typically assumed that 'savagery' characterized the most inferior races – a condition that, it was held, doomed at least some races to complete extinction. Thus, 'savagery' was often viewed as a main cause of extinction, rather than either disease or the violence inflicted on them through colonization. 'The fantasy of auto-genocide or racial suicide [was] an extreme version of blaming the victim,' useful for rationalizing 'the genocidal aspects of European conquest and colonization' (Brantlinger 2003: 2).

Though the 'character' of a race or nation could be explained by environmental, historical, economic, and political factors, in much Victorian discourse 'race' and 'character' blur into a vague explanation of virtually everything, including British – or English or Anglo-Saxon or white – supremacy. According to many imperialist narratives, because of their racial superiority, the conquering and colonizing heroes have 'character,' amounting to virtues; the vanquished lack character – they are 'savages' or 'barbarians' because they are racially inferior and perhaps 'unfit' to survive. The heroes of the Empire represent Britain's 'national character' by defending it and helping to extend its reach. With Ireland in mind, Seamus Deane comments: 'Only privileged, successful versions of a local national character could claim a place in the evolutionary story of the character of nations – nations, that is, that were simultaneously particular in themselves but also universal in their global appeal.' In contrast, from the typical English standpoint, the Irish 'national character' needed reforming, even if this meant making 'the Irish indistinguishable from the English' (1997: 56).

Starting at least as early as Robert Southey's 1813 *Life of Admiral Nelson*, 'historical biography played a leading role' in promoting imperial expansion as a heroic enterprise (Bayly 1999: 55). Forming a key Victorian literary genre, there were numerous 'lives' that celebrated the Empire, such as Sir John Kaye's 1867 *Lives of the Indian Officers*. In such accounts, the 'character' of British missionaries, explorers, and military men is self-sacrificing and naturally noble; for 'natives,' however, 'character' is nonexistent or negative – cruel, superstitious, perfidious, and, if not cowardly and lazy, then cruel and bloodthirsty. As already noted, some indigenous peoples were 'noble savages' – magnificent warriors like the Zulus or the Maori. Many others were ignoble – the Bushmen, the Hottentots, or the Australian Aborigines, supposedly. So, too, the British in India were often treated as case studies in heroism, especially after the Rebellion of 1857–8; but Indians themselves were typically seen as their moral opposites (Sinha).

Though he did not identify any of his contemporaries as full-fledged heroes, 'Hero-Worship' was the religion that Thomas Carlyle espoused: 'No great man lives in vain. The History of the world is but the Biography of great men' (1964: 266). Only indirectly tied to imperialism in *Heroes and Hero-Worship* (1841) and *Past and Present* (1843), hero-worship entails an authoritarianism that underpins the racism in Carlyle's 'Occasional Discourse On the Nigger Question' (1849, 1853) and his support for Governor Eyre after Eyre's brutal suppression of the Jamaican uprising in 1865. According to Carlyle, the obverse of British character as exemplified by Eyre was the laziness and stupidity of 'Quashee,' the freed slave and stereotypically lazy native, who sat in the sun all day eating pumpkins:

> And now observe, my friends, it was not Black Quashee, or those he represents, that made those West-India Islands what they are, or can, by any hypothesis, be considered to have the right of growing pumpkins there. For countless ages . . . till the European white man first saw them . . . those Islands had produced mere jungle, savagery, poison-reptiles, and swamp-malaria . . . they were as if not yet created, – their noble elements of cinnamon, sugar, coffee, pepper black and grey, lying all asleep, waiting the white enchanter who should say to them, Awake! (1968: 325–6)

Carlyle's only mention of the indigenous West Indians is 'savagery'; he also ignores the fact that it wasn't the 'white enchanter's' magic but slavery that made 'the Islands' productive for 'the white European man.'

Among Europeans, the antitheses of heroism, in Carlyle's view, are 'flunkeyism' and democracy. Since the French Revolution, democracy has been the political order of the day in Europe and the Americas, so heroism, Carlyle argues, is difficult or impossible to come by – Napoleon was 'our last Great Man!' (1964: 467). But heroism is what the world needs: 'A whole world of Heroes; a world not of Flunkeys, where no Hero-King *can* reign; that is what we aim at!' (1965: 39). To find such a world of heroes, in *Past and Present* Carlyle turns to the Middle Ages and the story of Abbott Samson, chosen by his fellow monks to reform the monastery of St. Edmundsbury. When Carlyle deals with the present, the colonies prove to be useful as places to which unemployed, 'surplus' workers can go to forge productive lives for themselves, thus escaping the 'flunkeys' in Parliament, the Home Office, and more generally in England.

In *Unto This Last* (1860), one of Carlyle's disciples, John Ruskin, emphasizes self-sacrifice as well as heroic authority. Typical heroes of the Empire embody both leadership and a willingness to give their lives in service to God, the Empire, or the nation; many of the imperial heroes most celebrated, such as David Livingstone and General Charles Gordon, are those whose careers ended in martyrdom. John Kucich remarks that a 'striking' feature of

> British imperial culture is how often it mythologised victimisation and death as foundational events in the teleology of empire. There was, seemingly, a different crucifixion scene marking the historical gateway to each colonial theater: Captain Cook in the South Pacific, General Wolfe in Canada, General Gordon in the Sudan; or else there was mass martyrdom (the Black Hole massacre in India). (2007: 4–5)

Shouldering 'the white man's burden,' to quote the title of Kipling's notorious poem, was the first step toward heroic martyrdom or 'masochistic jingoism,' depending on one's perspective (2007: 8).

Missionary careers in the far outposts of the Empire or the world frequently ended in martyrdom. After members of the London Missionary Society set sail for the South Pacific in 1795, their apparent success in making converts in Tahiti inspired hopes for further success throughout that region. The triumphalist strain in LMS discourse reached a climax in the Rev. John Williams's 1837 *Narrative of Missionary Enterprises in the South Sea Islands*; two years later, climax became apotheosis when Williams was slain and allegedly eaten by the natives of Erromanga. Williams became an evangelical martyr-saint, eulogized in countless texts and sermons in Britain, much as Livingstone would later be mourned and sanctified well beyond the circuit of missionary discourse. In his worldwide bestseller *Self-Help* (1859), under the rubric of 'energy and courage,' Samuel Smiles declared: 'It was in the course of [Williams's] indefatigable labors that he was massacred by savages on the shore of Erromanga – none worthier than he to wear the martyr's crown' (1864: 272).

Livingstone doubled as missionary and the greatest European explorer of central Africa, 'the dark continent.' His journals, his 'discovery' by Henry Morton Stanley in 1871, and his death in Africa in 1873 made him the most famous martyr-hero for the cause of bringing civilization and Christianity to Africa. Both roles – missionary and explorer – provided models of heroism and of 'national character,' which in turn generated support for more exploration, more proselytizing, and more imperial expansion. The excitement aroused by the search for the sources of the Nile produced other heroic explorers, including Richard Burton, John Hanning Speke, Vernon Cameron, and Samuel Baker, though none of them achieved the saintly status of Livingstone, probably the most celebrated hero both of the Empire and of missionary endeavors from the Victorian era to the present.

Regarding India, those Britons who fought, suffered, and died during the 1857–8 Rebellion were viewed as collective heroes and martyrs of the Empire. In George Otto Trevelyan's 1866 epistolary novel *The Competition Wallah*, the protagonist and narrator, Henry Broughton, a young Englishman who has passed the Indian Civil Service exam (he is 'the competition wallah' or man), is writing home to a friend shortly after the Rebellion. Henry notes that 'in many an isolated station a dozen or two of the Imperial race stood at bay for months before a hundred times their number of infuriated enemies, disciplined by English skill' (1977:

38). The Rebellion was a 'blaze of Oriental fanaticism, which . . . at length yielded to the courageous perseverance, and the unconquerable energy of our race' (45). The term 'race' is here, as in many other Victorian texts, virtually a collective synonym for 'character,' understood as an immutable set of traits – in the case of 'the Imperial race,' these traits are invariably virtues.

According to *Self-Help*, published immediately after the Rebellion, self-reliance adds up to 'national character.' For Smiles, the path to success is to stand on your own two feet, without help from others. Great nations – Smiles has Britain in mind – are those with the greatest individualism and liberty; weak nations are those with little or no individualism and liberty. Such nations deserve to be ruled by ones with greater amounts of 'character.' India is a case in point. On several occasions, Smiles offers the British heroes and heroines of the Rebellion as key examples of 'self-help' at its best:

> The recent terrible struggle in India has served to bring out, perhaps more prominently than any previous event in our history, the determined energy and self-reliance of the national character. Although English officialism may often drift stupidly into gigantic blunders, the men of the nation generally contrive to work their way out of them with a heroism almost approaching the sublime. (1864: 214)

With 'gigantic blunders,' Smiles may be thinking of Tennyson's 'Charge of the Light Brigade,' honoring the soldiers who made their heroic but disastrous assault during the Crimean War – disastrous because 'someone had blundered.' It was difficult to find heroism to celebrate during the Crimean fiasco; the Indian Rebellion was a quite different story. Smiles proceeds to laud the 'handful of British soldiers, civilians, and women' besieged by the rebels at Lucknow:

> Though cut off from all communication with their friends for months, and they knew not whether India was lost or held, they never ceased to have perfect faith in the courage and devotedness of their countrymen . . . they knew that while a body of men of English race held together in India, they would not be left unheeded to perish. They never dreamed of any other issue but . . . ultimate triumph. (215)

Phrases such as 'Imperial race' and 'English race' show that racism has its positive as well as negative poles: claims of racial superiority or inferiority necessarily invoke their opposites.

Smiles begins *Self-Help* with an epigraph from John Stuart Mill: 'The worth of a State, in the long run, is the worth of the individuals composing it' (1). According to Peter Mandler, Mill inaugurated 'the quest for a true "science of national character"' (2006: 49). In his 1843 *System of Logic*, Mill writes that 'ethology,' or 'the science of character' in both its individual and national branches, was in its 'infancy,' and yet was fundamental to 'social science' in general (quoted in Mandler 2006: 51). In the 1830s, Mill asserted that 'the great influence of Race in the production of national character' could not be doubted, although for him it was not the only factor to consider. Later, Mill modified this view by rejecting any simplistic application of supposed racial variation for interpreting 'national character,' but many other Victorian intellectuals – Knox, Disraeli, Carlyle, Ruskin, Trevelyan, Smiles, Trollope, and Dilke among them – had no hesitation in believing race to be the most basic factor in national character, in imperial expansion, and, indeed, in historical causation.

Dramatizing that the amalgamation of the Saxon with the Norman 'races' led progressively to the formation of Great Britain, Scott in *Ivanhoe* presented what became a widely popular view of British history. Even as Scott's Jewish characters, Isaac and Rebecca, are forced into exile from England, Ivanhoe's reconciliation with Richard I and his marriage to Rowena presage the modern unification of the nation through the merger of races – Saxon, Norman, English, Scottish. *Ivanhoe* has been read as removing the element of class conflict from the old thesis of 'the Norman Yoke' (Hill 1954), while it also adumbrates later claims to the priority of the Anglo-Saxon racial element in modern history. Scott himself was influenced by Sharon Turner's *History of the Anglo-Saxons* (1799–1805), which initiated the race-based orientation to British historiography evident in such later works as James Anthony Froude's *History of England* (1862) and Edward Freeman's *The Norman Conquest* (1876).

According to most versions of Anglo-Saxonism, the Germanic barbarians who invaded England at the end of the Roman Empire were simultaneously a conquering or 'imperial' race and the bearers of freedom, who laid the basis for the ancient and still living English 'constitution.'[20] 'It was in the free forests of Germany,' Baron Henry Lytton Bulwer told Parliament in 1832, 'that the infant genius of our liberty was nursed. It was from the free altars of Germany that the light of our purer religion first arose' (quoted in MacDougall 1982: 91). So, too, John MacGregor's *History of the British Empire* celebrates the 'progress of the Anglo-Saxon race' over the entire globe (1852: 1:xxviii). Although MacGregor restricts his main account to the British Isles, he offers a detailed history of the race's progress from Saxon times to the present, anticipating later accounts of the entire British Empire as the outcome of Anglo-Saxon racial superiority and unity, including Dilke's *Greater Britain* (1868) and Froude's *Oceana; or England and Her Colonies* (1886).

Although in his 1848 *The Saxons in England*, John Kemble did not stress race in any clearly biological sense (that remained to be done by the pre-Darwinian race theorists of the 1850s), he nevertheless celebrated 'the great epos of the Germanic and Scandinavian races' (1876: 1:59). Toward the end of Roman times, the

> irruption of the Germanic tribes breathed into the dead bones of heathen cultivation the breath of a new life; and the individual dignity of man as a member of a family, – the deep-seated feeling of all those [Germanic] nations, – while it prepared them to become the founders of Christian states which should endure, made them the wonder of the philosophers and theologians of Rome, Greece and Africa, and an example to be held up to the degenerate races whom they had subdued. (1:231–2)

Kemble believed the 'Germanic tribes' embodied freedom; nevertheless, they were a conquering 'race' that was organized hierarchically and that worshipped kings and heroes. Like the 'thrall' Gurth in *Ivanhoe*, 'the Saxon peasant knew his position,' Kemble declares; 'it was a hard one, but he bore it: he worked early and late, but he worked cheerfully, and amidst all his toils there is no evidence of his ever having shot at his landlord from behind a stone wall or a hedge' (1:326) – presumably unlike present-day Irish peasants. In *Past and Present* (1843), Carlyle drew upon *Ivanhoe* for his depiction of 'Gurth, born thrall of Cedric,' to illustrate his views of what proper master–servant relations ought to be. The Saxon nobleman Cedric enjoys Saxon freedom, but Gurth deserves his Saxon brass collar.

Throughout his career, Carlyle expressed the view that many of the heroes of 'universal history' were Saxons, or at any rate Germans. In *Heroes and Hero-Worship*, he forecasts a time when Britain's 'Indian Empire will go' the way of all past empires (1964: 345). But the British Empire, consisting of a 'Saxondom covering great spaces of the Globe,' will not end, because it will be held together by an eternal hero, 'King Shakespeare' (345). In short, the Empire of white settlement will be united by language, culture, and race. Carlyle is, hence, a forerunner of the many Victorian commentators on the Empire who viewed the colonies, with the main exception of India, as an extended 'community' or 'family' of Anglo-Saxons whose ultimate interest lay in racial solidarity. Thus, in Froude's *Oceana*, the Anglo-Saxon 'race' and 'family' has carried 'the genius of English freedom' (1886: 2) around the globe. Froude's advocacy of an imperial federation binding Britain, Australia,

New Zealand, Canada, and South Africa together is based on the ideal of racial unity. As in Charles Kingsley's *Westward Ho!*, 'the sea is the natural home of Englishmen; the Norse blood is in us, and we rove over the waters,' founding Empires as 'we' go (Froude 1886: 18). The future prosperity and freedom of 'England' and its colonial extensions depends on maintaining 'family' – that is, racial – ties (Bell 2007: 143–9).

There were at least as many objections to Anglo-Saxonism or Teutonism, however, as there were straightforward assertions of it in accounts of Britain's imperial power and glory (MacDougall 1982: 91). Thus, Matthew Arnold objected to his father's claim, similar to Hegel's, that the German 'race' was the main agent of historical progress. Like Scott, Arnold noted the merger of 'races' in Britain over time – the various Germanic invaders, the Normans, the Celts – and advocated a blending of components, Celtic with English, Hellenic with Hebraic, that he nevertheless persisted in understanding in racial terms (Young 1995: 55–80). For Arnold history was still to be explained by racial conflicts and mergers. In *Culture and Anarchy*, he based his conceptions of 'Hebraism' and 'Hellenism' on the 'science of ethnology.' And in 'On the Study of the Celtic Element in Literature,' he regarded that 'element' as the product of a gradually expiring 'race,' whose cultural virtues – poetry, music, melancholia – he nevertheless wished to preserve.

When 'race' is treated as historical causation, it is invariably a form of circular logic. To claim, for example, that the British defeated the Indian Rebellion because of 'the unconquerable energy of our race' is tautological, because it says only that the British won because they were British. No less an authority on the Empire than Seeley objected to such racial reckonings:

> This unhistorical way of thinking, this disposition to ascribe an inherent necessity to whatever we are accustomed to, betrays itself in much that is said about the genius of the Anglo-Saxon race. That we might have been other than we are, nay that we once were other, is to us so inconceivable that we try to explain *why* we were always the same before ascertaining by an inquiry whether the fact is so. It seems to us clear that we are the great wandering, working, colonising race, descended from sea-rovers and Vikings. (1971: 66)

This 'unhistorical way of thinking,' Seeley rightly points out, explains precisely nothing. Despite this critique, Seeley later declares that the 'Spanish Empire had the fundamental defect of not being European in blood,' whereas the 'English Empire was throughout of civilised blood, except so far as it had a slave-population' (110–11). Seeley's failure to avoid historical explanations in terms of race or 'blood,' even though he criticizes them, shows just how pervasive and powerful race-thinking was in the Victorian period.

Besides circular reasoning, racism depends on a fallacious assumption of racial purity. Race 'only works when defined against potential inter-mixture,' Young notes, 'which . . . threatens to undo its calculations alto-gether' (1995: 19). Even the believers in Anglo-Saxon supremacy sometimes refer to the 'English' or 'Anglo-Saxon' race as hybrid or 'mon-grelized.' Young quotes John Crawfurd in 1861: 'At best we [English] are but hybrids, yet, probably, not the worse for that.' Also in 1861 *The London Review* declared: 'We Englishmen may be proud of the results to which a mongrel breed and a hybrid race have led us' (Young 1995: 17). In 'What Is a Nation?' Ernest Renan, who influenced Matthew Arnold among others, similarly declared: 'The truth is that there is no pure race and that to make politics depend upon ethnographic analysis is to surrender it to a chimera. The noblest countries, England, France, and Italy, are those where the blood is most mixed' (Renan in Bhaba 1990: 14).

Imperial Gothic

Reaching its apogee in the 1880s and '90s, imperialist ideology never-theless registered anxiety about the purity and permanence of its racial categories. Many late-Victorian stories and novels used Gothic elements to suggest that the Anglo-Saxon race or the Empire itself was imperiled. Citing Edmund Burke's theory of the sublime, Howard Malchow defines the Gothic broadly as 'a language of panic, of unreasoning anxiety, blind revulsion, and distancing sensationalism,' and finds it at work in most imaginings of racial others throughout nineteenth-century British culture (1996: 4). But after its efflorescence during the Romantic era, the Gothic romance gave way to domestic realism in the early and mid-Victorian decades, only to make a comeback with Robert Louis Stevenson's *Dr Jekyll and Mr Hyde* and H. Rider Haggard's *King Solomon's Mines* and *She* in the 1880s. These and many other end-of-century romances exem-plify the subgenre of imperial Gothic fiction.

Besides the threat of racial degeneration or contamination, there were many other sources of social and political anxiety that informed late-Victorian literature and that help to explain the employment by many authors, from Stevenson and Haggard to Kipling and Conrad, of the con-ventions of Gothic romance. Writers such as Yeats and Conan Doyle were intrigued by 'the Rosicrucian revival,' writes Janet Oppenheim, and also by 'cabalists, Hermeticists, and reincarnationists. . . . Palmists and astrologers abounded, while books on magic and the occult sold briskly' (1985: 160). Romance-writing toward the end of the 1800s was also in various ways compensatory, as Stephen Arata explains:

> In considering the kinds of cultural work the romance performs in this period . . . we must recognize in its aggressive optimism a desire to compensate for perceived losses: for the decline of English letters, for the degeneration through overrefinement of bourgeois society, for the 'emasculation' of the middle-class male, and so on. It is in this context that we should understand the genre's deep ideological investment in the empire as a place of renewal. Transformed into a fantasy space 'elsewhere,' the empire is imagined by romancers as a realm free from the various debilities of modernity. (1995: 94)

Imperial Gothic fiction may sometimes have seen the Empire 'as a place of renewal,' as in Haggard's adventure stories. But it just as often treated the noncivilized world as a domain in which the primitive might overwhelm the white heroes, causing them to go native, or as the source of threatened invasions of the metropole by the barbarians, as in Bram Stoker's *Dracula* (1897). What is more, along with anxiety about racial degeneration, in late Victorian culture 'the suburbs' of Britain's major cities were viewed as blurring the spatial boundaries between city and country and also between the metropole and its colonial peripheries. This 'suburban' discourse frequently registered anxiety about the decline and fall of the Empire itself. As Todd Kuchta notes, to some commentators 'suburbia was a *terra incognita* that could not be tamed' (2005: 182); it was at least a domain that threatened cultural degradation.

Evolutionary theory taught that races like species either improve on earlier generations or the reverse – growing degenerate or increasingly 'unfit' in the 'struggle for existence.' Evolution would perhaps lead to the emergence of Friedrich Nietzsche's superman, a theme explored in George Bernard Shaw's play *Man and Superman* (1905). The *übermensch* might or might not still belong to the human species, but humanity might be supplanted by an entirely new species. In *The Impressions of Theophrastus Such* (1879), George Eliot's title character speculates that 'the process of natural selection must drive men altogether out of the field,' overtaken by 'the immensely more powerful unconscious race' of machines (1994: 137–42). In Edward Bulwer-Lytton's *The Coming Race* (1871), an early instance of imperial Gothic, the protagonist discovers the underground civilization of the Vril-ya, a semi-monstrous, semi-angelic species which threatens to exterminate the human world, thus becoming the new ruling species.

Darwin and other naturalists stressed the fossil record which indicated that thousands of species had become extinct over the course of geological time. Well before Darwin, Tennyson in 'In Memoriam' (1850), recalling Lyell's *Principles of Geology*, feared that Nature was a self-destroying monster. In Tennyson's most despairing moment, Nature raves: 'A thousand types are gone: I care for nothing, all shall go' (1969: 911). No 'type' – species or race – was a permanent fixture in the universe. Further, Darwin's assertion in *The Voyage of the Beagle* that 'the varieties of man seem to act on each other in the same way as different species of animals – the stronger always extirpating the weaker' (1962: 434) was hardly confidence-boosting about the future of the Anglo-Saxon race, even if it had thus far been the strongest race. Paradoxically, as Darwin's cousin Francis Galton argued, civilization protected the 'unfit,' who by outbreeding the 'fit' threatened to undo civilization. This fear was the germ of the eugenics or racial purification movement that Galton initiated.

Besides doubts aroused by evolutionary theory, the emergence of new rivals for empire – the United States, a newly unified Germany, and to lesser extent Belgium and Italy – worried late Victorians (Bell 2007: 31–62). Britain's old rival France also participated in the new competition for colonies, during which most of Africa was carved up among the European empires. According to H. G. Wells,

> The long reign of Queen Victoria, so prosperous, progressive and effortless, had produced habits of political indolence and cheap assurance. As a people we had got out of training, and when the challenge of these new rivals became open, it took our breath away at once. We did not know how to meet it. (1934: 653)

Through his 'scientific romances' such as *The Time Machine* (1895), *The Island of Dr. Moreau* (1896), and *The War of the Worlds* (1898), Wells became a major contributor to imperial Gothic fiction.

A further issue, related both to race and to rivalry for global power, was aroused by the far East. While many 'primitive races' had been exterminated or nearly so by imperial expansion, not all nonwhite races were disappearing. Many Africans had been 'fit' enough to survive the 'middle passage' and slavery in the Americas. More importantly regarding the revival of Gothic fiction, the Chinese and Japanese constituted enormous populations, not about to disappear; immigration from Asia to Australia, Canada, and the United States and the emergence of Japan as a modern military power gave rise to the fantasy of a 'Yellow Peril,' as in M. P. Shiel's 1898 invasion novel, *The Yellow Danger*. Therein the diabolical Dr. Yen How plans to exterminate the white race by swamping the West with Asians; he is thwarted by biological warfare causing the extermination of 150 million of the 'yellow race.' The emergence of Indian nationalism also contributed to fantasies about threats from Asia. Shiel penned *The Rajah's Sapphire* (1896), in which an Indian gem haunts its possessors, while in Grant Allen's *Kalee's Shrine* (1886), Thuggee appears to be reborn in present-day Britain.

There were other, perhaps more plausible threats than the 'Yellow Peril' emanating from within Britain itself – Irish nationalism, of course, but also the spread of socialism and the growing women's movement. These internal factors, perceived as threats, suggested not just that the barbarians were outside the gates of the Empire, but that they were inside. Stevenson's *Jekyll and Hyde*, which helped inaugurate the imperial Gothic trend, is set in London rather than the colonies, but it nevertheless evokes imperial concerns. David Punter argues that 'Hyde's behaviour is an urban version of "going native."' Punter continues:

> The particular difficulties encountered by English imperialism in its decline were conditioned by the nature of the supremacy which had been asserted: not a simple racial supremacy, but one constantly seen as founded on moral superiority. If an empire based on a morality declines, what are the implications . . .? It is precisely Jekyll's 'high views' which produce morbidity in his *alter ego*. (1980: 241)

The apelike, murderous Hyde, moreover, is the stereotype of the shillelagh-wielding Irish hooligan, conjuring up fears of Fenianism.

Cannon Schmitt notes that many late-century Gothic narratives – Haggard's *She*, for example, or Stoker's *Dracula* – 'exploit the fear of an invasion of Britain by a monstrous femininity originating beyond the pale of an occidental Europe understood as normative' (1997: 19). Thus, Haggard's Ayesha or 'She Who Must Be Obeyed' announces her decision to come to Britain and usurp the throne from Queen Victoria (Haggard 2001: 255). In Stoker's *Jewel of the Seven Stars* (1903), Queen Tera, an undead mummy, also evokes mysogynistic fears of independent women and female suffrage. To its many interpreters, however, *Dracula* has come to be read as an overdetermined allegory about everything from Irish politics to the 'eastern question,' and from the New Woman to homosexuality. Its focus on 'blood' carries many associations, which can be variously interpreted – even, Joseph Valente argues, as a proto-modernist critique of anxieties about race, women, homosexuality, empire, Irish nationalism, Jews, and oriental 'others' (Dracula is Transylvanian, of course, rather than Jewish, Chinese, or Japanese, but he is nonetheless Eastern).

Along with the rise of Spiritualism and interest in the occult, the return of the Gothic was also a reaction to novelistic realism and to science, or at least to scientific materialism. Occultist romances – Marie Corelli's *A Romance of Two Worlds* (1886) or Conan Doyle's *The Mystery of Cloomber* (1897) – illustrate these trends. Corelli's potboiler about 'Chaldean mysticism and electric religion,' writes Annette Federico, was condemned as 'ridiculous' and 'pure bosh' by its 'few reviewers,' but it nevertheless 'became tremendously popular' (2000: 1). Its heroine learns the secrets of the spiritual realm from Heliobas, a Chaldean; he claims to be directly descended from one of the '"wise men of the East" . . . who, being wide awake, happened to notice the birthstar of Christ . . . before the rest of the world had so much as rubbed their sleepy eyes' (Corelli 1973: 74). *The Mystery of Cloomber* also offers an affirmative – though not exactly Christian – version of Orientalism: 'Science will tell you that there are no such powers as those claimed by the Eastern mystics. I, John Fothergill West, can confidently answer that science is wrong' (Doyle 1909: 285). In Doyle's romance, wrong too was Major-General J. B. Heatherstone, who killed the Buddhist holyman Ghoolab Shah during the first Afghan War. For forty years Heatherstone was haunted because of his crime; in a remote area of Scotland, he was finally induced to drown himself by three 'chelas' or disciples of Ghoolab Shah. They recall the three Indians who retrieve 'the Moonstone' in Wilkie Collins's novel of that name, except that Doyle's 'chelas' are 'adepts' in 'the mysteries of the Buddhist faith,' which seems to include Theosophy (203). *The Mystery of Cloomber* ends by asserting that if the skeptical European 'will look to the East, from which all great movements come, he will find there a school of philosophers and of savants, who working on different lines from his own, are many thousand years ahead of him in all the essentials of knowledge' (286).

From the 'sensation novels' of the 1860s to Wells's 'scientific romances' in the 1890s, new subgenres of fiction explored aspects of experience beyond the ken of traditional realism. Thus, sensation fiction mingled realistic with Gothic elements, foregrounding what Henry James called those 'most mysterious of mysteries, the mysteries which are at our own doors' (1865: 593). Sensation novels like Braddon's *Lady Audley's Secret* (1862) and Collins's *The Moonstone* (1868) were one source of later detective fiction such as Fergus Hume's 1886 bestseller *Mystery of a Hansom Cab*, which takes place in Melbourne, and Doyle's Sherlock Holmes stories, most of which take place in London. Perhaps because Holmes always has a materialistic explanation for any mystery, Doyle famously grew tired of writing about him. Especially after World War I, Doyle's interest in Spiritualism exceeded his interest in science.

Fantasies like *The Coming Race* and *Erewhon* anticipated Wells's 'scientific romances' and the rise of science fiction, with its Gothic ingredients and often apocalyptic, world-ending themes. Like Corelli's and Doyle's occultist romances, science fiction is frequently at odds with science. Hearking back to Victor Frankenstein, Stevenson's Dr. Jekyll has numerous mad scientist analogues in late-Victorian fiction, from Dr. Benjulia in Collins's anti-vivisection novel *Heart and Science* (1883) to Wells's Dr. Moreau and Invisible Man. Wells's inventor-explorer in *The Time-Machine* (1895) also fits this category: his contradictory explanations of what he claims to have witnessed 800,000 years in the future and beyond are perhaps lunacy. Among many apocalyptic, world-ending fantasies from Richard Jefferies' *After London* (1885) to Wells's *A Dream of Armageddon* (1903), Fred Jane's jaunty *The Violet Flame: A Story of Armageddon and After* (1899) features Professor Mirzarbeau, 'a quaint little Anglo-French scientist,' who invents a death ray with which he liquidates Waterloo Station and an entire region of China. Armed with his ray, the crazed Professor takes charge of Britain until he accidentally liquidates himself. Jane's tale parodies other doomsday stories; as Warren Wagar notes in *Terminal Visions*, between '1890 and 1914 . . . almost every sort of world's end story . . . was written, published, and accepted by a wide reading public':

> Great world wars that devastated civilisation were fought in the skies and on imaginary battlefields. . . . Fascist dictatorships led to a new Dark Age, class and race struggles plunged civilisation into Neolithic savagery, terrorists armed with super-weapons menaced global peace. Floods . . . colliding comets . . . and alien invaders laid waste to the world. (1982: 20)

Though hardly a doomsday story, Oscar Wilde's *Picture of Dorian Gray* (1991) also exemplifies imperial Gothic. If *Jekyll and Hyde* is a morality tale about the barbarian within the civilized man, so is Wilde's 'decadent' tale. Literary and aesthetic decadence in general, moreover, was avowedly a symptom of imperial decline, matching Rome's decline and fall. In *The British Barbarians* (1895), Grant Allen's 'major contribution to British science fiction' (Ruddick 1997: 13), a time-traveler from the twenty-first century returns to 1890s England to collect 'materials for a History of Taboo, from its earliest beginnings in the savage stage to the fully developed European complexity.' The time-traveler has to combat the view that 'England . . . is a civilised country, and taboos are institutions that belong to the lowest and most degraded savages.' He responds by saying that, in his future society, 'England has always been regarded with the greatest interest as the home and center of the highest and most evolved taboo development' (Allen 1975: 41–2). Unlike Allen's *Kalee's Shrine*, *The British Barbarians* is an upbeat ethnographic satire rather than a Gothic tale, but it insists that modern Britons are more barbaric than the barbarians.[21]

Like Wells, who acknowledged the older man's influence (1934: 461), Allen was a Fabian socialist and a Darwinist, and also an advocate of Home Rule for Ireland, land nationalization, women's rights, and atheism. As Richard Le Gallienne put it, Allen was 'one of those true patriots who do their country the service of differing from it on every possible occasion' (quoted in Ruddick 1997: 10). However, many of the *fin de siécle* writers most supportive of the British Empire – Conan Doyle, for instance – also wrote imperial Gothic stories. Kipling was the unofficial 'laureate of the Empire,' but he penned such Gothic tales as 'The Mark of the Beast' (1890), in which the British protagonist, after desecrating a Hindu temple, is transformed into a werewolf. Besides Doyle and Kipling, among the best writers between the 1880s and World War I – Stevenson, Conrad, Morris, Yeats, Joyce, E. M. Forster, Virginia and Leonard Woolf – conquering and ruling an empire was not something automatically to cheer about. 'The conquest of the earth,' Marlow muses in Conrad's *Heart of Darkness*, 'which mostly means the taking it away from those who have a different complexion or slightly flatter noses than ourselves, is not a pretty thing when you look into it too much' (2006: 7). In *The Break-up of Britain*, Tom Nairn declares: 'The hollowness sounds through the English imperialist mind in a thousand forms: in Rider Haggard's necrophilia, in Kipling's moments of gloomy doubt, in the self-pitying pessimism of [A. E.] Housman . . .' (1981: 265). Quoting this assertion in *The Location of Culture*, Homi Bhabha comments that 'Nairn explains this "imperial delirium" as the disproportion between the grandiose rhetoric of English imperialism and the *real* economic and political situation of late Victorian England.' Bhabha continues:

> these crucial moments in English literature are not simply crises of England's own making. They are also the signs of a discontinuous history, an estrangement of the English book. They mark the disturbance of its authoritative representations by the uncanny forces of race, sexuality, violence, cultural . . . differences which emerge in the colonial discourse as the mixed and split texts of hybridity. If the appearance of the English book is read as a production of colonial hybridity, then it no longer simply commands authority. It gives rise to a series of questions of authority . . . (1994: 113)

As this chapter indicates, questions about the authority of 'the English book' arise everywhere in Victorian writing about the colonies and the Empire, and not simply in imperial Gothic fiction.

Notes

1. 'Imperialism' in this study means the ideology – assumptions, opinions, beliefs – supportive of the British Empire. The term can also refer to the policies and actions leading to territorial expansion and rule over non-British populations. 'Colonialism' more specifically refers to those territories settled by a substantial number of British and European 'colonists.' Because of their frequent use in postcolonial studies, 'colonizer' and 'colonized' refer here to British rulers, officials, and settlers on one hand, and indigenous peoples on the other. A 'colonist' is a settler – in other words, one type of 'colonizer.'

2. A number of recent studies have also demonstrated how 'a variety of colonial "Others" circulated at the very heart of the British Empire before the twentieth century' (Burton 2003: 3). See the essay by Laura Tabili in Hall and Rose (2006). Until recently, Paul Gilroy notes, historians have typically ignored or viewed these 'Others' as 'an illegitimate intrusion into a vision of authentic national life' (1993: 7).

3. 'Postcolonialism' can have several meanings. It can refer to the era of decolonization, from the nationalist and independence movements of the nineteenth century forward, as in Robert Young's *Postcolonialism* (2001). Here I use it to refer to 'postcolonial studies' as it has emerged in academic work from the time of Edward Said's *Orientalism* (1978) forward. This in turn can refer to postcolonial cultural 'theory,' to postcolonial literary criticism, to postcolonial historical studies, and so on.

4. In the 1870s and after, J. A. Froude, the Marquis of Normanby, and many others complained about public 'indifference' to the colonies (Bell 2007: 32). The grumbling seems to have been largely a version of crying 'wolf.' In *The Absent-Minded Imperialists* (2004), Bernard Porter agrees with Seeley; but compare Andrew Thompson, *The Empire Strikes Back?* (2005) and Catherine Hall and Sonya Rose, eds, *At Home with the Empire* (2006).

5. These include Maurice Thomas, *The History of Hindostan, Sanscreet and Classical* (1800) and his *Modern History of Hindostan* (1810); Mark Wilks, *Historical Sketches of the South of India* (1817); James Mill, *History of British India* (1817); G. R. Gleig, *History of the British Empire in India* (1830–5); Edward Thornton's book of the same title (1841); Henry Spry, *Modern India* (1837); Mountstuart Elphinstone, *History of India* (1843); J. H. Stocqueler, *The Sikh Invasion of the Punjaub, or, The Wars of India* (1846); and William Erskine, *A History of India* (1854). Gleig also published biographies of Sir Thomas Munro, Governor of Madras, and Warren Hastings, while both Thornton and Stocqueler published many other volumes on India.

6. See the essays in Gilbert and Tiffin, eds, *Burden or Benefit? Imperial Benevolence and Its Legacies* (2008). The British abolition of the slave trade and slavery was not simply humanitarian, of course; it was also strategic in regard to Britain's economic interests in the Caribbean and its ongoing rivalry with France and the United States (Blackburn 1988).

7. Lady Sale's tough-mindedness hardly conforms to the 'feminine picturesque' that Sara Suleri notes in other Anglo-Indian women's journals (Suleri 1992: 75). Sale is highly critical about the mismanagement of affairs in Kabul. She details the

sufferings of both the British and the Sepoys during their retreat, including her own wounding and captivity: 'I had, fortunately, only *one* ball *in* my arm; three others passed through my poshteen [sheepskin] near the shoulder without doing me any injury,' and so on (Sale 2002: 104). Linda Colley writes: 'To the early Victorian public, Florentia Sale would indeed become a heroine, the first British woman ever to achieve nationwide fame in connection with her own contribution to military action overseas.' She was, however, something of a pest to her fellow-captives (2002: 352).

8. For the concept of the chronotope or time-space configurations in narratives, see Bakhtin (1981: 84–258).

9. Owenson based her historical romance on extensive research; both *The Missionary* and *Lalla Rookh* are larded with footnotes, which contradicts Macaulay's assertion the general reading public knew little about India before 1840. Owenson's romance and Moore's poem were highly popular.

10. The earliest novels about India – Phoebe Gibbes's *Hartly House, Calcutta* (1789) and Elizabeth Hamilton's *Letters of a Hindoo Rajah* (1792) – offer even more favorable depictions of Hindus and Hinduism.

11. Mary Sherwood, who lived in India from 1805 to 1816, gave many of her stories or religious 'tracts' Indian settings (she penned over four hundred of them).

12. Published at the outset of Victoria's reign, Taylor's bestseller was the most influential novel about India before Kipling's *Kim* (1901). The young Queen read it with great excitement, as did many other Victorians. Balanchandra Rajan comments: 'Ignorance about India [as Macaulay claimed] seems unlikely in a Europe where the Orient was in vogue, where best-selling poems and novels about India were being printed, and where Queen Victoria was sitting up at night reading the galleys of *Confessions of a Thug* because she could not wait for publication' (1999: 182). Rajan is not suggesting, however, that even a more or less documentary or realistic novel like *Confessions* provided the Victorians with an accurate picture of India to offset more exotic depictions like Owenson's *The Missionary*.

13. As to actually reforming and modernizing India, D. A. Washbrook comments: 'British rule before the Mutiny may be credited with having fundamentally changed Indian society. But this change moved against the anticipations of "modernization" and left it with a vast legacy of "backwardness" subsequently to undo' (1999: 399; and see 414, 416). Among other results, British rule reinforced rather than dismantled the caste system. Before the 1857–8 Rebellion, India is either the main setting or figures importantly in many other Victorian novels, including John William Kaye's *Peregrine Pultuney; or, Life in India* (1844); John Lang's *The Wetherbys, Father and Son; or, Sundry Chapters of Indian Experience* (1853); and William Arnold's *Oakfield; or, Fellowship in the East* (1853). India also figures peripherally in Charlotte Brontë's *Jane Eyre* (1847), Elizabeth Gaskell's *Cranford* (1853), Wilkie Collins's *The Moonstone* (1868), and in several novels and stories, including *Vanity Fair* (1848) and *The Newcomes* (1855), by Thackeray. Most of these works assert or imply that British rule is necessary for Indian progress, though they do not express the vindictive, highly racist reactions that characterize British fiction about the Rebellion. Though published a decade after the Rebellion, *The Moonstone* is an exception because the original theft of the diamond from an Indian temple by a British soldier suggests a critique of the Raj that is absent in many other mid and late Victorian novels.

14. About the Opium War, D. A. Washbrook comments: 'Company India was engaged in building . . . the world's first "narco-military" empire' (1999: 404). Have there been others? Arguably, the Iran–Contra deal during the Reagan era

was the start of its reincarnation; the American 'war on drugs' is doing very little to prevent drug trafficking, while it has allowed the CIA and the US military to infiltrate if not exactly invade Colombia and several other countries.

15. Transportation of convicts to New South Wales and Tasmania ended in 1840 and 1853, respectively. It continued to Western Australia until 1868, because of the lack of free colonists willing to go there.

16. Like joining the navy, becoming a missionary was often a poor man's way to travel abroad and lead an adventurous life, while doing so for God – that is, for the best possible motive. In any event, for the Baptists, who were often 'artisans or lower middle-class men,' serving as missionaries in Jamaica 'proved to be a great deal more exciting than working as a minister in England'; their expectant black congregations grew rapidly (Hall 2002: 89). Many of the most famous missionaries including Livingstone came from working-class backgrounds.

17. Many missionaries lived among foreign populations far longer than today's professional anthropologists doing field work. This was true, for example, of the Rev. Thomas Williams and the Rev. Joseph Waterhouse; see their books on Fiji.

18. On the flourishing of boys' adventure fiction, see Boyd (2003), Bristow (1991), Dunae (1989), James (1973), and Richards (ed. 1989).

19. In the 1830s, Disraeli joined with a number of other conservative reformers who wanted to rejuvenate the aristocracy as a ruling class that could bring prosperity and social stability to the common people. His trilogy of novels advocating Young Englandism include *Coningsby; or, The New Generation* (1844), *Sybil; or, The Two Nations* (1845), and *Tancred; or, The New Crusade* (1847).

20. Ironically, to give the 'constitution' an Anglo-Saxon origin is to see modern British freedom and the common law as rooted in 'time immemorial' and a primitive past. After the Indian Rebellion (1857–8) and the Fenian unrest in Ireland in the 1860s, Sir Henry Maine in *Village Communities* (1871) and elsewhere was one of the authorities who blamed the imperial government for overriding 'native' customary practices and law. Like England, India and Ireland would be better off if ruled by their own primitive practices: modernization was the cause of unrest. For Maine and the concept of 'time immemorial,' see Sara Maurer (2005).

21. Known today mainly as the author of the New Woman novel *The Woman Who Did* (1895), Grant Allen often combined his scientific interests with a fascination for the occult. At the outset of *Kalee's Shrine* (1886), an English girl is kidnapped for the cult of the Hindu goddess of destruction, which is also the cult of the Thugs. She is rescued, but much later, as an adult living in England, she apparently strangles a friend. Suspected by an Anglo-Indian of being a Thug, she is rescued again when her lover revives the supposedly dead friend and shows the absurdity of the Anglo-Indian's suspicion.

Chapter 2

Debates

It was an Indian girl; and yet, when he looked again – was it an Indian girl?

Charles Kingsley, *Westward Ho!*

Imperial Historiography, Marxism, and Postcolonialism

The British Empire has been divided but not conquered by many academic disciplines and interests. One major division today is between imperial historiography and postcolonialism. The former can trace its lineage back to the Victorian era and such obviously pro-Empire works as J. R. Seeley's *The Expansion of England*. Therein lies its major difficulty: how to get beyond its past investments in metropolitan, Eurocentric archives and affirmations of imperialism? Its second major difficulty is related to the first: how to incorporate and interpret evidence from and about the colonized, including both resistance and collaboration?[1] Postcolonialism is a recent development: the term is almost synonymous with decolonization since World War II. Its affinities lie with the colonized and the nationalist movements of the late nineteenth and twentieth centuries that gained independence from Britain and the other European powers. Today most imperial historians seek to move beyond Eurocentrism, and certainly beyond uncritically chauvinistic portrayals of the Empire, but their approaches can be 'traditional' and 'conservative,' adjectives Antoinette Burton applies to the 1999 *Oxford History of the British Empire* (*OHBE*) (2001: 167).[2] In contrast, for some historians, postcolonialism is both too reliant on 'theory' and politically too radical. But postcolonialism – typically represented by the triumvirate of Edward Said, Gayatri Spivak, and Homi Bhabha – is sometimes also viewed, even by postcolonialists, as a merely academic and indeed metropolitan discourse that has little of the radical energy and urgency of the anti-imperialist, decolonizing movements it is heir to (Ahmad 1992; Dirlik 1997; Young 2001).

In her review of two of the five volumes of the *OHBE*, Burton notes that several of its contributors 'caricature' postcolonialism in a 'dyspeptic and dismissive' manner (2001: 168; see also Howe 2001; Marshall 1993; Peers 2002). These contributors tend to identify postcolonialism with Edward Said's *Orientalism*, which they criticize for painting too negative and too literary a picture of Western 'discursive' constructions of 'the Orient.' They also identify Said's project with what they consider to be ahistorical 'theory.'[3] In contrast, Burton is one of a growing number of 'new imperial historians' willing to make use of the insights of Said and other postcolonialists. These include the contributors to Catherine Hall and Sonya Rose's anthology *At Home with the Empire* and also to *A New Imperial History* edited by Kathleen Wilson, who writes in the introduction that 'the 1990s saw an explosion of nuanced and cross-disciplinary studies of nation-making and empire,' including work by many 'culturalist' historians, anthropologists, and postcolonial literary critics (2004: 15). It is on such work that the 'new imperial history' is building; in contrast, the *OHBE* is notable for 'its often strident hostility to postcolonial scholars, literary critics, and other "culturalist" marauders who have laid siege to the economic and political grounds traditionally held by imperial historians' (14).

Among imperial historians who take exception to Said's *Orientalism* in particular and postcolonial studies more generally, John MacKenzie writes: 'By creating a monolithic and binary vision of the past they [postcolonialists] have too often damaged those intercultural relations which they seek to place on a more sympathetic basis for the future. In reality, Orientalism was endlessly protean, as often consumed by admiration and reverence as by denigration and depreciation' (1995: 214–15). But most postcolonialists recognize that Orientalism was and is 'protean.' Said himself acknowledged that Orientalists such as William Jones, Edward Lane, Wilfrid Scawen Blunt, and many others expressed great 'admiration' and sometimes 'reverence' for the East and its religions and cultures. For a few Britons, one version of 'going native' was to convert to Islam (Nash 2005).

If it isn't 'theory' or the radical critique of imperialism involved in postcolonial studies that some imperial historians object to, then it is the fact that postcolonial studies first took root in literature departments. And literature, it seems, is not factual enough to suit some historians. Yet a literary text is just as much a fact as a government document. It may also be a far more influential fact than a government document. It may even be epistemologically more reliable than a document, which can be just as deceptive as any other kind of text. The imperial historians charge postcolonialism with reducing everything to 'discourse,' if not literature. The postcolonialists, in common with poststructuralists, point out that histories are themselves forms of discourse. In his foreword to *Selected Subaltern Studies*, Said remarks: 'historical writing is after all writing and not reality . . .' (1988: vii). That does not mean history-writing is fiction or sheer fabrication, but neither is it merely an accumulation of facts, like a stack of bricks.

Leery of postcolonialism, some imperial historians are also leery of both new and old Marxist approaches to imperialism. Marxism entails consideration of the economic factors underlying imperial expansion and colonization. Marx and Engels themselves had much to say about imperialism in Ireland, India, and elsewhere, with capitalism as the leading cause of modern imperial expansion. Their insights influenced many twentieth-century historians, including members of the Marxist historians' group in Britain – E. P. Thompson, Victor Kiernan, and Eric Hobsbawm among them. According to recent Marxists thinkers such as Aijaz Ahmad and Arif Dirlik, neither imperial historiography nor postcolonial studies deals adequately with the economic foundations of the British Empire. Certainly when postcolonialism adopts poststructuralist approaches to the exclusion of both Marxism and empiricism, it merits criticism. Introducing *Marxism, Modernity and Postcolonial Studies*, Crystal Bartolovich writes: 'The very fact that many of the most brilliant, prominent, and effective anticolonial activists have insistently pronounced themselves Marxists should give pause to postcolonialists who stand poised to dismiss Marxism as a "European" philosophy' (2002: 11; see also Parry 2004). The ideas of Marx and Engels about Western imperialism, because focused on capitalism, were inevitably Eurocentric. Nevertheless, Bartolovich declares: 'What distinguishes a specifically Marxist critique . . . from a more general anticolonialism, is the insistence that cultural analysis of the everyday . . . is inseparable from questions of political economy, in and outside the metropole; and that the critique of colonialism . . . is inextricable from the critique of capitalism' (6).

Many Victorian writers besides Marx and Engels understood that imperialism had economic causes and consequences. As Suvendrini Perera notes, Dickens's *Dombey and Son* (1848) centers upon a business deeply implicated in 'an economy of empire' (1991: 61). Dickens writes: 'The earth was made for Dombey and Son to trade in. . . . Rivers and seas were formed to float their ships . . .' (1989: 2). Dickens describes the headquarters of Dombey and Son, in the City of London, as close to the Royal Exchange, the Bank of England, and the 'rich' East India House, 'teeming with . . . precious stuffs and stones, tigers, elephants, howdahs, hookahs, umbrellas, palm trees, panaquins, and gorgeous princes of a brown complexion sitting on carpets, with their slippers very much turned up at the toes' (32). Perera points also to the Bundelcund Bank in Thackeray's *The Newcomes* (1855). Based in India, the Bank is 'a vast multinational,' as Perera notes, with representatives in ' "Sydney, Singapore, Canton, and of course, London" '; among other sorts of business, the Bank does ' "an immense opium trade" ' with China (quoted in Perera 1991: 63). Colonel Newcome's 'redemption is possible only after the bank, like Dombey's grandiose ventures, overreaches itself, causing bankruptcy and ruin throughout the empire' (63). It was indeed the failure of an Indian invest-ment house that cost Thackeray the fortune he might have inherited. Its bankruptcy prompted him to identify Indians in general with dishonesty; all the more reason for him to support British rule in India.

Early Indian nationalists drew from Marx and Engels as well as from earlier writers including Edmund Burke the idea of the economic 'drain' of wealth from the subcontinent to Britain. This is a key theme in Dadabhai Naoroji's *Poverty of India* (1876) and *Poverty and Un-British Rule in India* (1901) and also in Romesh Chunder Dutt's *The Economic History of India under British Rule* (1902).[4] Among major Victorian writers, William Morris based his critique of British imperialism partly on Marx and Engels. The post-revolutionary, 'arts and crafts' utopia that he depicts in *News from Nowhere* (1890) has no government, possesses no colonies, and exploits no one. Old Hammond tells the narrator Guest about how in the past 'the World Market' pursued profits before every-thing else and how 'civilization (or organized misery)' dealt with 'non-civilization,' by, for example, 'the British Government deliberately [sending] blankets infected with small-pox as choice gifts to inconvenient tribes of Red-skins . . .' (Morris 2003: 140). Though he was a Ruskinian rather than a Marxist, John Hobson made economic factors central to his *Imperialism: A Study* (1902), which influenced V. I. Lenin's *Imperialism: The Last Stage of Capitalism* (1917).[5] Hobson argued that 'underconsumption' at home led inexorably to a search for new markets abroad. He also pointed out that, although imperialism was not prof-itable in general, it was so for munitions makers and other vested inter-ests. As H. N. Brailsford put it in *The War of Steel and Gold* (1914), 'Regarded as a national undertaking Imperialism does not pay. Regarded as a means of assuring unearned income to the governing class, it emphatically does pay' (quoted in Kiernan 1974: 5).[6]

Irish nationalists also saw economic exploitation as a key factor in the 'backwardness' of Ireland. Stephen Howe's claim that 'most Irish nation-alists before the 1960s did not use the colonialism/anticolonialism model in describing their situation' (2000: 43) is definitely inapplicable to

Young Ireland.[7] The contributors to Young Ireland's journal *The Nation* in the 1840s and 1850s, including John Mitchel and Gavan Duffy, presented Irish history partly in terms of imperialism and economic exploitation. In *The Last Conquest of Ireland (Perhaps)* (1858–9), Mitchel writes:

> The subjection of Ireland is now probably assured until some external shock shall break up that monstrous commercial firm, the British Empire; which, indeed, is a bankrupt firm, and trading on false credit, and embezzling the goods of others, or robbing on the highway, from Pole to Pole. . . . If any American has read this narrative . . . he will never wonder hereafter when he hears an Irishman in America curse the British Empire. So long as this hatred and horror shall last – so long as our island refuses to become, like Scotland, a contented province of her enemy, Ireland is not finally subdued. The passionate aspiration for Irish nationhood will outlive the British Empire. (2005: 220)

Mitchel blamed the Famine on deliberate misgovernment by British officials; in today's terms, it was a genocide which, as Marx also argued, facilitated the modernization of Irish agriculture by clearing the peasants off the land. In his *Jail Journal*, as he was being transported to Australia, Mitchel declared: 'The Carthaginians [British] have convict colonies everywhere: at Gibraltar, at Bermuda, in the Atlantic; at Norfolk Island, in the Pacific; besides Van Diemen's Land, and the various settlements in New South Wales; for on British felony the sun never sets' (1983: 9).

So, too, in *Young Ireland* (1881), Gavan Duffy writes that the Irish in the eighteenth century, 'whether Cromwellians or Catholics, were subject to the rule which long prevailed in all British possessions throughout the world, that the dependent state only existed for the benefit of the paramount state' (1881: 122). Noting warfare among the Normans and other non-Celtic invaders of Ireland, Duffy declares:

> English historians can recognise in resistance [to invasion], continuing through so many generations in Ireland, only a turbulence and discontent native to the Celtic race. In the case of any other country they would probably find no insuperable difficulty in understanding why the dominion of strangers was odious, or why the desire to overthrow it was regarded as honourable and praiseworthy. (87)

The Irish, he claims, have been 'taunted with the hopelessness of contending with an empire upon whose plundered dominions the sun never sets' (160).

Economic arguments against empire were not restricted to Marxists or to Indian and Irish nationalists. Ironically, capitalist economists from

Adam Smith to the Manchester School of Richard Cobden and John Bright often viewed colonies as economically retrograde (Semmel 1970; Sturgis 1969; Winch 1965). In *The Wealth of Nations* (1776), while recognizing the great benefits the discovery of the Americas brought to Europe, Smith condemns British colonial policy. Against 'colonial monopoly,' Smith advocates not just 'free trade' but the liberation of the American colonies. So far, while benefiting 'shopkeepers,' the colonies have mostly been a burden on the exchequer. Smith also condemns 'the mercantile company which oppresses and domineers in the East Indies' (1976: 1: 82). So, too, Jeremy Bentham in 1792 penned a pamphlet entitled *Emancipate Your Colonies!* Later, however, he changed his mind because he decided colonies could alleviate overpopulation at home. Donald Winch writes that by 1808 Bentham's views 'verge on jingoism' (1965: 34). The publication of James Mill's *History of British India* (1817) led to his employment by the East India Company, which later also employed his son. For both Mills, India was so 'barbarous' that it could only benefit from British rule. 'The greater part of the world has, properly speaking, no history,' writes John Stuart Mill in *On Liberty*, 'because the despotism of custom is complete. This is the case over the whole East' (1982: 136). In order to end that despotism in the subcontinent, the best tool available was the civilizing force of the (reformed) East India Company. But by 1859, when Mill published *On Liberty*, that capitalist enterprise had been replaced by the British government as the official ruler of British India.

In the 1830s, Edward Gibbon Wakefield and his allies advocated 'systematic colonisation,' promoting emigration to New Zealand and South Australia (Winch 1965: 77–89). Victorian supporters of free trade such as John Bright and Richard Cobden, however, followed Adam Smith in condemning tariffs and versions of colonial monopoly. The loss of the American colonies did not prevent the growth of trade with the United States, which indicated that colonization made no difference or even that it was an impediment to commerce. Adam Smith, writes James Sturgis, 'had also shown that there was a difference between wealth and power, and that the attempt to create the latter by empire building did not necessarily lead to wealth'. These ideas led Bright and Cobden, among others, to advocate free trade with the colonies while liberating them 'from strict home supervision so that they could manage their own affairs' (Sturgis 1969: 83). Nevertheless, for most Victorian politicians and economists, Britain's colonies represented expanding markets for British manufactures as well as 'waste lands' that British emigrants could occupy and cultivate.

Besides the economic factors which Marxists stress, the cultural factors emphasized by both postcolonialists and the 'new imperial historians' are sometimes also emphasized by historians who disapprove of postcolonialism. Thus, in *Ornamentalism*, David Cannadine seeks to counter Said's *Orientalism* by contending that 'the British Empire was at least as much (perhaps more?) about the replication of sameness and similarities originating from home as it was about the insistence on difference and dissimilarities originating from overseas' (2001: xix). Without exactly dismissing *Orientalism* and postcolonial studies, and also without exactly dismissing approaches that stress military and economic factors, Cannadine argues that the British Empire was very much about display and status. The Empire consisted largely, in his estimation, of the imperialists' clothes. Many postcolonialists would agree with Cannadine's stress on display and status and, hence, on the 'inventedness' of the Empire.[8] In passing, Cannadine refers to the older school of 'whiggish' historians such as Nicholas Mansergh who treated the Empire as evolving into the 'Commonwealth' of independent nations (xvi). From a machinery of domination and exploitation in the eighteenth century, goes this older and indeed Victorian narrative, the Empire evolved into a set of progressive institutions and processes that enabled many former colonies to gain their place in the modern world as decolonized nation-states. Victorian versions of that argument can be found in Dilke, Seeley, and Trollope, among many others.[9]

Related to 'whiggish' claims about the growing benevolence of the Empire in the Victorian era is the notion of 'Pax Britannica.' This idea was itself a Victorian invention; according to the *Oxford English Dictionary*, the London *Times* used the phrase in 1880. An article in *The Listener* (1 February 1973) offers the gist: 'In the nineteenth century, the British Navy dictated the Pax Britannica and more or less guaranteed a century of peace' (OED). But if the Navy was powerful, effective, and not exactly at peace, what about the army? There was peace within England and Scotland, but hardly anywhere else in the Empire (Judd 1996: 238). Between the Battle of Waterloo in 1815 and the end of Victoria's reign in 1901, British forces fought nine wars in Afghanistan, Burma, and India (including the Rebellion); the Crimean War (1854–6); two 'Opium Wars' with China; a war in Persia (1856–7); a conflict in Abyssinia (1867–8); the Ashanti War (1873–4); the Zulu War (1878–9); various so-called 'Kaffir wars'; the first Anglo–Boer War (1880–1); the invasion of Egypt (1882); two invasions of the Sudan, one to relieve General Gordon at Khartoum (1885) and the second avenging his death at Omdurman (1896–8); the Boxer Rebellion (1900); and the second Anglo–Boer War (1899–1902).

Seeley's claim that the 'English race' was able to expand into places 'which for the most part were so thinly peopled that our settlers took possession of them without conquest' (1971: 233) was untrue. Everywhere on colonial frontiers there were at least 'small wars,' such as the Maori Wars in New Zealand (1843–8, 1860–70), which the Maoris waged against colonial militias aided by British and Australian troops. In Australia, Aborigines engaged in countless conflicts with the white invaders of their territories, such as the 1826–30 'Black War' in Tasmania (Reynolds 1995). For good reason, Muriel Chamberlain adds a question mark to the title of her book on British foreign policy, *Pax Britannica?* 'During the long period of the so-called "Pax Britannica",' she writes, 'there was scarcely a year when the British army was not fighting somewhere.' She adds, however, that 'these wars represented no real threat to the homeland' (1988: 9), which is one reason why, during the Victorian and Edwardian periods, such conflicts could either be ignored or were dubbed 'small wars.' The military classic, Colonel C. E. Callwell's *Small Wars*, appeared in 1896. The wars were 'small' mainly because they were technologically extremely lopsided.

> Whatever happens we have got
> The Maxim gun, and they have not

as Hilaire Belloc satirically put it in *The Modern Traveller* (1970: 184). Callwell notes, however, that the savages and barbarians, unless exterminated or thoroughly defeated, tended to acquire modern weaponry.[10]

The success of the imperialist myth of 'Pax Britannica' was facilitated by the fact that no Victorian author produced a great war novel. Of the many novels written about the Indian Rebellion, only two – Philip Meadows Taylor's *Seeta* (1872) and Flora Annie Steel's *On the Face of the Waters* (1896) – are much cited today. Kipling's *The Light that Failed* (1891), partly about warfare in the Sudan, is primarily about the psychological struggles of war artist Dick Heldar. Like Thackeray's *Vanity Fair* (1848), Thomas Hardy's *Trumpet Major* (1880) is set during the Napoleonic Wars, but is less about war than about the domestic relations of John Loveday and his brother Robert. *Vanity Fair*'s cast of characters includes a number of soldiers – Rawdon Crawley, George Osborne, William Dobbin, Major O'Dowd – but it is subtitled a 'novel without a hero.' 'We do not claim to rank among the military novelists,' says the narrator, explaining why he will not depict what happens at the Battle of Waterloo. 'Our place is with the non-combatants. When the decks are cleared for action we go below and wait meekly [with] the ladies and the baggage' (1963: 282). In several of his other stories, soldiers are featured – Major Pendennis, Colonel Newcome – though again Thackeray's emphasis is on their domestic affairs in England.[11]

In many 'small wars,' most of the 'British' soldiers were Irish, or Indian 'sepoys,' or Africans. Approximately half the British troops slaughtered by the Zulus at Isandhlwana in 1879 were Africans. The East India Company maintained its own army, consisting largely of sepoys under the command of British officers. Many of the other soldiers in India were impoverished Irishmen, like Private Mulvaney in Kipling's *Soldiers Three* or Kimball O'Hara's father in *Kim*. The troops General Kitchener commanded at the Battle of Omdurman were mostly Egyptian and Sudanese. Finally, many 'small wars' were too lopsided to give much occasion for celebration by the victors. As already noted, the Opium Wars were more embarrassing than inspiring. Nevertheless, Victor Kiernan observes, 'It was always possible to think of England as on the defensive, a small nation surviving by quality and courage. . . . In the patriotic tradition of the thin red line Englishmen were always, like Macaulay's Romans, facing fearful odds' (1982: 131).

Gender, Sexuality, and Race

'If the nation is an imagined community,' writes Ania Loomba, 'that imagining is profoundly gendered' (1998: 215). She mentions the figures of Britannia and Mother India as female personifications of modern nations. Thus, Bankim Chandra Chatterjee's Bengali novel, *Anandamath* (1882), is dedicated to 'Mother India' – 'our only mother' (quoted in Boehmer 1995: 113). As Elleke Boehmer notes, it contains 'the rousing song "Bande Mataram" (Hail Mother) which was taken as an anthem by protesting Indian nationalists' (113). So, too, Loomba adds, 'gender and sexuality are central to the conceptualisation, expression and enactment of colonial relations' (1998: 215). Though nations and empires have often been personified as goddesses, and though the British monarch during most of the nineteenth century was a queen and empress, governing was supposedly men's work – an aspect of the patriarchal ideology of 'separate spheres': women presided over the private, domestic sphere, while men presided over the public sphere, including the sciences, business, politics, war, and the British Empire.

At the same time, misogyny led some imperialists, and even some imperial historians, to attribute the decline and fall of the Empire to women. 'It's . . . well-known . . . that women lost us the Empire,' Sir David Lean declared in 1985 (quoted in Strobel 1991: 1). Old-guard imperial historian Percival Spear asserted that white women were the 'ruin of empire' (quoted in Midgley 2007: 2). Before British women or 'memsahibs' came in numbers to India, male imperialists supposedly intermingled freely with Indians, often acquiring Indian mistresses and wives and creating a sizable 'Eurasian' population. According to the 'ruin of empire' narrative, the memsahibs broke up the party. If British women weren't busily installing British domesticity including increased racial segregation in the colonies, then they were supposedly busily interfering as abolitionists, missionaries, and humanitarian activists (Midgely 2007; Ware 1992). Either way, whether women were seen as enforcers of British domesticity and racial barriers or as anti-imperialist activists, male imperialists often invoked what Margaret Strobel calls 'the myth of the destructive female' (1991: 1–15; see also Knapman 1986).

The ideologies of patriarchy and imperialism reinforced each other. In *The Three Guineas* (1938), Virginia Woolf denounces 'the patriarchal system' which shut women up in 'the private house, with its nullity, its immorality, its hypocrisy, its servility,' while leaving men to rule 'the public world' with 'its possessiveness, its jealousy, its pugnacity, its greed,' including war and empire. She vows 'to take no share in patriotic demonstrations; to assent to no form of national self-praise; to make no part of any claque or audience that encourages war; to absent herself from military displays, tournaments, tattoos, prize-givings and all such ceremonies as encourage the desire to impose "our" civilisation or "our" dominion upon other people' (1966: 109). Woolf wrote her critique of patriarchy and imperialism in the 1930s, after World War I had demon-strated the dead-end of imperial rivalries. But many nineteenth-century feminists also recognized the links between patriarchy, war, and empire.

Romantic and Victorian feminists such as Mary Wollstonecraft and Harriet Martineau were often ardent abolitionists (Ferguson 1992; Midgley 2007: 41–64; Ware 1992: 49–109). The analogy between women's oppression and slavery is evident in Charlotte Brontë's *Jane Eyre* and her sister Emily's *Wuthering Heights*. Thus, Jane likens her anger toward the Reeds to that of 'the revolted slave' (1996: 22), and later imagines herself preaching 'liberty to [the] enslaved' (302). In *Beyond the Pale: White Women, Racism and History*, Vron Ware analy-ses the anti-imperialism and anti-racism of many British and American feminists such as Josephine Butler and Catherine Impey, Quaker editor of the journal *Anti-Caste*. In an 1891 issue, Impey wrote:

> While religion teaches men that God is the Father of *all*, that we are all 'brethren' . . . the 'Father of Lies' goes up and down in the world, teaching that the God of Heaven created separate races of men . . . [and] that a fair skin is always superior to a dark one, that fellowship between differing races

is contrary to man's nature, that the strong should *compel* the submission of the weak, crushing and if necessary, exterminating those who resist. From such a doctrine spring the horrors . . . from all quarters of the Globe, from Central Africa, to ice-bound Siberia, from the United States with her slaughtered Indian babes and women and her down-trodden millions of dark-hued workers, to thoughtful cultured India under the heel of British militarism. (quoted in Ware 1992: 186–7)

As part of her anti-racist and anti-imperialist activism, Impey teamed up with African-American Ida B. Wells in a crusade against the lynching of blacks in the United States. But feminists could also be imperialists: 'Feminists and particularly suffrage advocates had their own traditions of imperial rhetoric long before the formation of the Anti-Suffrage League in 1908,' writes Antoinette Burton; 'traditions that they routinely invoked to ally women's political emancipation with the health and well-being of the British Empire' (1994: 3). It would have been politically counter-productive for suffrage advocates to criticize the very institutions, including both Parliament and the Empire, in which they sought greater participation by women.

Olive Schreiner, author of *The Story of an African Farm* (1883), was a feminist and pacifist who sympathized with the Boers during the Anglo-Boer War (1899–1902). Like Impey, Martineau, and the Brontës, Schreiner recognized the similarity between women's oppression and the imperialist oppression of indigenous peoples in Africa and elsewhere. Schreiner also 'spoke out for organised labour united across "race" lines,' writes Carolyn Burdett, 'as the only means by which the mass of the population might protect itself from an exploitative capitalist system' (2001: 13). Though her sympathy for black Africans was limited by some of the racial and evolutionary assumptions common to her age, Schreiner declared that no 'white race' had ever 'dealt gently and generously with the native folks' of Africa, and that there was 'undoubtedly a score laid against us on this matter, Dutch and English South African alike; for the moment it is in abeyance; in fifty or a hundred years it will probably be presented for payment as other bills are, and the white man of Africa will have to settle it.' This would be a settling of accounts for 'the sins of our fathers' (quoted in Krebs 1999: 112).

The Story of an African Farm is usually considered the first 'New Woman novel,' a subgenre that espoused greater freedom for women and that anticipated the suffragette struggle. Burdett points out that its heroine Lyndall 'articulates, with a ferocious and diamond-like brilliance, most of the significant feminist arguments Schreiner was to elaborate and develop over the next ten or more years' (2001: 31). In South

Africa in the 1880s, however, there were no paths for an intellectually liberated woman to travel; Lyndall 'dies in a Boer cart going nowhere' (Burdett 2001: 31). Schreiner understood that many black African women suffered even greater oppression than their white counterparts. And in *Trooper Peter Halket of Mashonaland* (1897), she condemned Cecil Rhodes's ruthless, bloody takeover of what became known as 'Rhodesia.'

According to LeeAnne Richardson, New Woman fiction and imperialist adventure stories were in 'dialogical' interaction between the 1880s and early 1900s. Thus, H. Rider Haggard's *Jess* (1887) was a fictional response to *Story of an African Farm* (Richardson 2006: 3). Thus, too, the demonic, necrophiliac Ayesha in *She* is in part a response to Haggard's fear of 'wild women' both at home and abroad.[12] Ann McLintock notes 'Haggard's well-nigh pathological anxiety about female generative authority':

> Much of the fascination of Haggard's writing for male Victorians was that he played out his phantasms of patriarchal power in the arena of empire, and thus evoked the unbidden relation between male middle- and upper-middle-class power in the metropolis and control of black female labor in the colonies. (1995: 233–5)

It is a toss-up whether Ayesha is most terrifying when she indulges in necrophilia, when she magically slays any of her subjects who disobey her, when she does a voluptuous striptease before the narrator Holly, or when she threatens to usurp the throne from Queen Victoria. The self-proclaimed misogynist Holly says:

> The terrible *She* had evidently made up her mind to go to England, and it made me absolutely shudder to think what would be the result of her arrival there. . . . It might be possible to control her for a while, but her proud, ambitious spirit would be certain to break loose and avenge itself for the long centuries of its solitude. . . . In the end she would, I had little doubt, assume absolute rule over the British dominions, and probably over the whole earth . . . (Haggard 2001: 256)

As an offshoot of patriarchy, misogyny was basic in imperialist adventure fiction, and more generally in imperialist ideology. Adventure, exploration, hunting, conquest, and rule were men's activities. If women had 'adventures,' they were the sort Becky Sharp has with her male admirers in Thackeray's *Vanity Fair*. Sarah Jeanette Duncan evoked various ironic possibilities for women when she entitled an 1893 novel *The Simple Adventures of a Memsahib*, but they did not include exploration, hunting, or ruling the supposedly inferior races of the world.

Like governing, geographical exploration–'penetrating' the 'dark places' of the earth – was a male monopoly. Men could be 'explorers'; women were 'travelers' or 'tourists' who were often – like Emily Eden or Lady Anne Blunt – accompanied by men. Sara Suleri calls the standard mode in Anglo-Indian women's journals the 'feminine picturesque' (1992: 75–110). The title of Mary Kingsley's *Travels in West Africa* (1897) is an understatement; Kingsley does not present herself as an explorer or even as an anthropologist. The Royal Geographical Society, which sponsored many exploring expeditions from 1830 forward, did not admit women as 'fellows' until the twentieth century. Though opposed to women's suffrage, Lord Curzon presided over the decision to admit women to the RGS in 1913. Earlier, however, he had declared: 'We contest *in toto* the general capability of women to contribute to scientific knowledge. Their sex and training render them equally unfit for exploration' (quoted in Bell and McEwan 1996: 298). What perhaps tipped the balance was the fact that many other societies, including the Scottish Royal Geographical Society, had already admitted women as 'fellows.'

Though nineteenth-century women often traveled bravely and sometimes quite independently throughout the Empire (see, for example, Melman 1992), the 'dark places' of the world, no matter how wild or 'savage,' were typically represented as female. The treasure map in Haggard's *King Solomon's Mines* indicates that the male explorers travel over a female topography, including the twin mountains named 'the Breasts of Sheba.' Men know how to deal with women's bodies, apparently – just as they know how to deal with 'the dark continent': explore them and discover the treasures they hide (McLintock 1995: 1–4).[13] Moreover, except for noble savages like Umslopagaas, indigenous men were often represented as incapable of mastering the female terrain they and their people occupied. By century's end, Kipling believed that, however 'primitive,' 'weak,' or 'naked' Africans were, there was no longer any mystery about them; the 'law of survival' had placed the entire continent securely under the dominion of 'the white man':

> Nothing is gained by coddling weak and primitive men. The law of survival applies to races as well as to the species of animals. It is pure sentimental bosh to say that Africa belongs to a lot of naked blacks. It belongs to the race that can make the best use of it. I am for the white man and the English race. (1982: 2:256–7)

Kipling protests too much, however: nonwhite races including 'naked blacks,' women of all races, and male effeminacy all worried him.

If the Empire offered a proving ground for masculine enterprise including geographical exploration, conquest, and ruling over supposedly inferior races, it likewise offered a domain for the exploration of alternative sexual behaviors and preferences, which also worried Kipling. In contrast, in all of his travels, Richard Burton took a keen interest in the sexual customs of Eastern and African societies. In India, he responded to what he claimed was an 'indirect' order by investigating 'lupanars' or male brothels; his report almost ended his military career. Burton also hypothesized the existence of a 'Sotadic Zone' – basically the tropics – in which homosexuality was far more prevalent than in Europe (hotter climates produce hotter bodies?). Today most historians acknowledge that 'the colonies provided many possibilities of homoeroticism, homosociality, and homosexuality,' as Robert Aldrich puts it:

> The gendered nature of expansion, in which men monopolized . . . imperial activities . . . created situations congenial to intimate male bonding. The imbalance in the sex ratio between European men and women, and the limited range of sexual partners in some outposts, encouraged 'situational' homosexuality. (2003: 3; see also Hyam 1990; Lane 1995)

But while homosocial bonding in imperial settings is foregrounded in many Victorian texts, the topic of homosexuality was strictly taboo (Sedgwick 1985: 198). Behaviors that could be tacitly accepted or overlooked in imperial and foreign contexts were not tolerated in Britain or in imperialist discourse.

One of the ironies in the history of male identities is how activities that have traditionally been associated with masculinity seem frequently to have both encouraged and hidden homosexuality. Assertions of hypermasculinity like Kipling's seem to be defenses against various threats like charges of effeminacy. In this regard, imperialists were perhaps just as manly as convicts and pirates – that is, masculine but also capable of engaging in homosexual behaviors. At the same time, imperialists attribute everything from superhuman sexual prowess to effeminacy and homosexuality to indigenous peoples. Partly because Africa had apparently not been depopulated by the slave trade, Kipling's 'weak' Africans were credited with a sexual potency and a fecundity that other races did not possess (Brantlinger 2003: 70). As Dan Wylie notes, white portrayals of Shaka and the Zulus endowed them with extraordinary sexual prowess *and* sexual deviance, sometimes attributing Shaka's bloodthirstiness to his repressed homosexuality (2000: 52–3).

'Sex is at the very heart of racism,' writes Ronald Hyam (1990: 203). This is evident in the ways the metaphor of rape plays through discourse about empire. For Edmund Burke during the Warren Hastings trial, East India Company employees 'brutally violated' both Indian women and India (quoted in Suleri 1992: 60). Sara Suleri argues that 'rape as a dominant trope for the act of imperialism' is no longer 'critically liberating, particularly since it serves as a subterfuge to avoid the . . . homoeroticism of Anglo-Indian narrative' (1992: 17; Lane 1995). In any case, the meaning of rape was reversed during the Indian Rebellion. Jenny Sharpe writes that 'the idea of native men raping white women was not part of the colonial landscape in India prior to the 1857 uprisings' (1993: 4; see also Paxton 1999). Especially after the massacre of British women and children at Kanpur by Nana Sahib's men, newspapers in both Britain and India were full of accounts of the torture and rape of white women by the rebels. Even though these accounts were soon discredited, rape plays a central role in British fiction about the Rebellion and more generally about India from the 1860s forward. In *First Love and Last Love: A Tale of the Indian Mutiny* (1868), James Grant writes that 'Nana Sahib at Cawnpore [had] slain the Christian women by the hundreds and flung them into a well, because not one of them would enter his zenana' (1868: 3:232–3). This assertion follows Grant's account of the rape, torture, and bloody deaths of many 'Christian women' at Delhi (2:58–75). In various other Victorian accounts of the Rebellion such as Dion Boucicault's melodrama *Jessie Brown; or, the Relief of Lucknow* (1858), a primary motivation of the rebels is lust for white women. Long before the Indian Rebellion, however, slave rebellions in Jamaica and elsewhere had triggered the fantasy of black men raping white women.

The idea that empire involved political and economic rape, explicitly expressed by Burke, was also reversed by the campaign against *sāti* or Hindu widow-burning. In her study of that campaign, Lati Mana contends that it gave the British much cause for self-congratulation, just as did abolition and the campaign against the Thugs. She argues, however, that 'the women who burned were neither subjects nor even the primary objects of concern in the debate on its prohibition' (1998: 2). Although missionaries expressed 'concern for the widow's plight,' their resort 'to a discourse of horror . . . caricatured her suffering and dehumanised her existence' while urging 'the paramount necessity for evangelism' (191–2). Both British and Indian male voices buried 'the widows' valiant and persistent efforts at self-preservation and self-affirmation' (196). And as Gayatri Spivak argues, the outlawing of *sāti* involved an imperialist rescue fantasy in which 'White men are saving brown women from brown men' (1999: 284–5). At the same time, however, white women also campaigned against *sāti* (Midgley 2007: 64–91).

From Southey's *The Curse of Kehama* (1810) and Owenson's *The Missionary* (1811) through Mrs. Mainwaring's *The Suttee; or, The Hindoo Converts* (1830) and on to Tennyson's 1892 poem 'Akbar's Dream,' there are many references to *sāti* in British literature. In his 'Ode on the Portrait of Bishop Heber,' Robert Southey writes:

> Yea, at this hour the cry of blood
> Riseth against thee from beneath the wheels
>   Of that seven-headed Idol's car accurst;
> Against thee, from the widow's funeral pile,
>   The smoke of human sacrifice
>   Ascends even now to Heaven. (1878: 3:241)

In 'Akbar's Dream,' Deirdre David writes, 'the enlightened seventeenth-century Islamic king envisions a time when neither the "Fires of Suttee, nor the wail of baby-wife, / Or Indian widow" are heard' (1995: 92–3). Moreover, 'having become a widely accessible European symbol,' Suvendrini Perera declares, *sāti* 'could function simultaneously as an emblem of female oppression through which Western women represented their own struggles' (1991: 91). So Jane Eyre declares she will not be 'hurried away in a suttee' if Rochester's death precedes hers (Brontë 1996: 301).

A genuine rescue fantasy for both white and brown/black women might have helped during the Anglo-Boer War, when the British established concentration camps into which they herded the wives and children of their adversaries. Thousands died from harsh conditions and disease. In her study of gender, race, and empire, Paula Krebs examines the treatment of Boer and black African women and children in the concentration camps, especially as their sufferings were revealed through the exposés of British feminist Emily Hobhouse. The apologists for the camps, including some government officials and the London *Times*, tried to claim that they were intended to save the white women and children from starvation and from being exposed, as *The Times* put it, 'to outrages from the natives which would set all South Africa in a flame' (quoted in Krebs 1999: 63). Much of South Africa was already in flames, thanks to the British tactic of burning Boer farms. Meanwhile, like the victims of *sāti*, 'black women figured hardly at all in . . . writings about the camps' (Krebs 1999: 63). *The Times* claims that African men are likely to rape white women; but supposedly chivalric British men created the concentration camps to protect white women, though approximately 28,000 women and children died in them.

As Marlow and Kurtz leave the Inner Station in Conrad's *Heart of Darkness*, a 'barbarous and superb' African woman appears on shore

(2006: 67). When Marlow blows the steamer's whistle, the other Africans run away. Only the woman 'did not so much as flinch and stretched tragically her bare arms after us over the sombre and glittering river' (67). Commenting on the vagueness of Marlow's account, Marianna Torgovnick infers that Kurtz 'has apparently mated with the magnificent black woman and thus violated the British code against miscegenation':

> Marlow clearly conceives of her as a substitute for, an inversion of, Kurtz's high-minded, white 'Intended.' Like the Belgian woman, she is an impressive figure, but unlike the Intended, she is not 'high-minded': she is presented as all body and inchoate emotion . . . one woman an affianced bride, one woman, all body, surely an actual bride. (1990: 46–7)

Miscegenation 'challenges a boundary highly charged in the West, the boundary of race' (Torgovnick 1990: 147). As Robert Young argues in *Colonial Desire*, however, racism in general depends on the ideas of miscegenation and 'hybridity': racism is 'profoundly dialectical: it only works when defined against potential intermixture, which also threatens to undo its calculations altogether' (1995: 19). Against the poststructuralist concept of hybridity that Homi Bhabha offers, Young demonstrates the centrality of notions about racial mixing throughout Victorian imperialist discourse.[14]

The prospect for white men of freer, more satisfying heterosexual relations with nonwhite women was often simultaneously expressed and repressed in Victorian literature, as when the narrator of Tennyson's 'Locksley Hall' rejects his desire to mate with 'a squalid savage'. In many stories about the Empire, love affairs between British men and nonwhite women end tragically, as happens in Philip Meadows Taylor's 'Mutiny' novel *Seeta* and also in Kipling's short story 'Without Benefit of Clergy.' The tragedy almost always involves the death of the nonwhite woman, sometimes as she tries to protect the white hero from danger or death: Seeta dies by a mutineer's spear intended for Cyril Brandon, while the beautiful, light-skinned and 'refined' Foulata, attracted to Captain John Good in Haggard's *King Solomon's Mines*, is slain by the black witch Gagool. One side of Haggard's misogyny is represented by the repellent Gagool; the other, by the clinging, submissive Foulata, who, as Deirdre David says, 'possesses the sweet compliance of the *National Geographic* savage' (1995: 193). About Foulata's demise, the narrator, Allan Quatermain, remarks:

> I am bound to say that, looking at the thing from the point of view of an oldish man of the world, I consider her removal was a fortunate occurrence,

since, otherwise, complications would have been sure to ensue. The poor creature was no ordinary native girl, but a person of great, I had almost said stately, beauty, and of considerable refinement of mind. But no amount of beauty or refinement could have made an entanglement between Good and herself a desirable occurrence, for, as she herself put it, 'Can the sun mate with the darkness, or the white with the black?' (Haggard 2002: 230–1)

Despite the tragic treatment that most Victorian authors give to interracial romance, there were many interracial unions and mixed-race populations throughout the Empire. Wiltshire in Robert Louis Stevenson's 'The Beach of Falesá' ends up happily with his 'Kanaka' wife and children, but he is a rarity in fiction. Given its taboos on homosexuality, on interracial sexual relations, and on the idea of empire itself as rape, Victorian literature largely fails to represent what was actually occurring in the 'dark places' of the world.

The most famous interracial romance in Victorian literature occurs in Emily Brontë's *Wuthering Heights* (1847). Heathcliff's racial origins are, however, a mystery. Plucked off the streets of Liverpool by Mr. Earnshaw, he is wild, dark-skinned, and is often called a 'gypsy,' which may indeed indicate his race. But he could also be Irish or even African. Liverpool was Britain's major slave-trading port during the time-frame of the novel; by the 1840s, it was also a major port of entry for Irish immigrants (*Wuthering Heights* was published in the midst of the Famine). Howard Malchow speculates that Heathcliff may have been the mixed-race offspring of a British sailor and an enslaved African woman (1996: 39–40). Terry Eagleton claims that 'Heathcliff starts out as the image of the famished Irish immigrant, becomes a landless labourer set to work in the Heights, and ends up as a symbol of the constitutional nationalism of the Irish parliamentary party' (1995: 19). Given the context of the Brontë children's juvenilia, Heathcliff is a Byronic version of the colonized native or the racially oppressed person in revolt. Certainly no characters in Victorian fiction better illustrate 'colonial desire' or interracial passion than do Heathcliff and Catherine. Their love is so powerful that they declare themselves to be each other – metaphorically a vampiric, Gothic version of that hybrid figure, the doublegoer. Whatever Heathcliff's race or races, *Wuthering Heights* illustrates that 'colonial desire' could flourish even in rural, eighteenth-century Yorkshire.

Orientalism(s)

The critics of Edward Said's *Orientalism* (1978), often cited as the founding text of postcolonial studies, claim that it renders Western representations of the East (particularly of the Middle East and Islam) too monolithic and too negative. Certainly Orientalism involved much more than just a phobic reaction to the East. In his *Confessions of an English Opium Eater* as well as his articles on China and on the Indian Rebellion of 1857–8, Thomas De Quincey waxed phobic against all things Eastern (Barrell 1991). Writing in 1857 about the Chinese, De Quincey fulminated against 'this hideous degradation of human nature which has always disgraced the East. That no Asiatic state has ever debarbarised itself, is evident from the condition of woman all over Asia' (2001: 91). Concerning the Rebellion, De Quincey imagines a murdered English mother invoking her 'beloved mother,' England, to exact 'everlasting retribution . . . upon the Moloch idolatries of India' (163). De Quincey was chiming in with many other British writers responding to the Rebellion with demands for 'everlasting retribution.'[15]

On the other hand, many Britons, from William Jones in the eighteenth century to Rudyard Kipling at the end of the nineteenth century, fell in love with India and with other Eastern countries. Though perhaps only for strategic reasons, both Richard Burton and Edward Lane converted to Islam. They may not have been sincere converts, but others – novelist and Orientalist Marmaduke Pickthall at the beginning of the twentieth century, for example – did claim to be sincerely converted (Nash 2005). In *Captives* (2002), Linda Colley writes about Irish soldiers in India who absconded to live among 'the natives.' Many Anglo-Indians such as Philip Meadows Taylor spent much of their adult lives in India. Taylor was employed by the Nizam of Hyderabad, not the East India Company; and he married the granddaughter of one of the ranees of Oudh. Though his parents were Irish, Kipling's Kim can't imagine himself as anything other than Indian.

Said cites an enormous array of Western writers and texts, ranging from scientific and ethnographic works to poems and private journals. He recognizes that many Westerners – soldiers, missionaries, businessmen, diplomats – lived for years in India, Turkey, Persia, or Egypt, and often felt more at home there than in Britain. He is well aware that 'the Orient' was, for many Westerners, a region that evoked both exotic and erotic pleasure. Said also notes that 'the Orient was a place of pilgrimage' (1978: 168), and not just when Western travelers visited the 'Holy Land': Richard Burton's *Personal Narrative of a Pilgrimage to Al-Madinah and Mecca* (1855–6) is an example, and so is Lady Anne Blunt's *A Pilgrimage to Nejd* (1881). With her husband's help, she also authored *Bedouin Tribes of the Euphrates* (1878) and the posthumously published *The Authentic Arabian Horse* (Winstone 2003; Melman 1992:

276–305).[16] After she and Wilfrid separated, Lady Anne chose to spend the rest of her life in Egypt. Besides Lady Anne, many other women wrote in often highly positive terms about their travels and sometimes lengthy stays in the Middle East (Melman 1992).

The end of the Napoleonic Wars in 1815 opened the way for travel throughout Europe and to farther destinations. With the advent of the modern tourist industry in the 1830s and, '40s, the Middle East, especially Egypt and Palestine, became favorite destinations. In 1830–1, carefully following Byron's eastern travels, the young Benjamin Disraeli toured parts of the Ottoman Empire including Syria and Palestine, a journey memorialized in his semi-autobiographical novel, *Contarini Fleming* (1832), and recalled again in *Tancred; or, the New Crusade* (1847), the last of his Young England trilogy. For the religious traveler, there were guides to the Holy Land featuring scenes from the Bible, such as the Rev. Thomas Home's *The Biblical Keepsake* (1835). In *Notes of a Journey from Cornhill to Grand Cairo* (1846), Thackeray recalls reading another travelogue aboard the P&O steamer that took him East, Alexander Kinglake's *Eothen, or Traces of Travel Brought Home from the East* (1844). Kinglake in turn pays homage to Eliot Warburton, author of *The Crescent and the Cross* (1845). Thackeray's narrator, Michael Angelo Titmarsh, thinks that, during the Crusades, Saladin was 'a pearl of refinement compared to the brutal beef-eating Richard' the Lion-Hearted (1844: 166). On the other hand, the East in the 1840s is a very backward and overly 'sensual' place. The trip on the P&O steamer shows that British 'commerce' is 'stronger . . . than chivalry . . . Mahomet's crescent [will soon be] extinguished in Fulton's boiler' (137). Two years after Thackeray's book appeared, Harriet Martineau published *Eastern Life, Past and Present*, another modernizing – indeed, utilitarian – work.

There were, perhaps, as many Orientalisms as Orientalists. However, a main theme of *Orientalism* is precisely that there was no single, unified Orient, but a wide variety of societies, cultures, and even religions (not just Islam). Said's critics attack *Orientalism* for failing to recognize that wide variety; Said attacks Orientalism as a Eurocentric and imperialist discourse that unifies what has never been unified. In other words, Said isn't writing about the Orient; he is writing instead about Western representations of the Orient. At the outset of his book, Said declares: 'There were – and are – cultures and nations whose location is in the East, and their lives, histories, and customs have a brute reality obviously greater than anything that could be said about them in the West' (1978: 5). There also were and are many different types and degrees of Western (mis)representations of the East. According to Said, Orientalism is a form of 'knowledge as power' that is both inevitably reductive (knowledge often reduces the complexities of what it represents) and a reinforcement of Western authority, including imperial authority, over the East.

Said also stresses that many British and French accounts of 'the Orient' were highly positive. Among Victorian literary accounts of the East, one of the most affirmative is Disraeli's *Tancred*. The aristocratic, British hero goes on a pilgrimage – not really a 'new crusade' – to Syria and Palestine, in search of wisdom to guide his political career at home. The culmination of his journey is his visionary encounter with 'the Angel of Arabia,' who espouses 'Arabian principles' and tells Tancred: 'The thoughts of all lands come from a higher source than man, but the intellect of Arabia comes from the Most High' (Disraeli 1847: 299). For Disraeli, 'Arabian' signifies racial superiority and incorporates all Semitic peoples, including 'the Hebrews.' Throughout his career, Disraeli sought to counteract anti-Semitism with the philo-Semitism of Tancred's Jewish mentor Sidonia, who claims that 'the Jewish mind exercises a vast influence over the affairs of Europe' and the world (263–4). 'The Jewish mind' is, at least in Disraeli's account, imperializing. 'Arabian principles,' which are also Jewish principles, account for the world's greatest religions – Judaism, Christianity, Islam – but also for some of its greatest empires, such as the Mughal and Persian empires. With the 'Young Syrian' Fakredeen, Tancred hopes to establish a global empire on the basis of 'faith' (just which 'faith' seems unimportant: perhaps Judaism and Islam count equally with Christianity).

George Eliot considered *Tancred* a 'very "thin" and inferior' novel, and declared that Disraeli's 'theory of "races" . . . has not a leg to stand on' (1985: 45). Her final novel, *Daniel Deronda* (1876), is in part a response to *Tancred*. Daniel discovers his Jewish heritage and, with his Jewish bride Myrah, travels to Palestine to pursue the ideals he has partly learned from Myrah's brother Mordecai. Ironically, when Daniel tells Gwendolyn Harleth his intentions, he sounds like Tancred, hoping to found an empire–with the British Empire as model – on faith:

> 'I am going to the East to become better acquainted with the condition of my race in various countries there. . . . The idea that I am possessed with is that of restoring a political existence to my people, making them a nation again, giving them a national centre, such as the English have, though they too are scattered over the face of the globe.' (1967: 875)

Despite Daniel's use of the word 'race,' his conversion to Judaism has more to do with cultural heritage than with either race or religion. For

Eliot, Daniel's and Mordecai's Zionist views represent a rejection of both empire by conquest and English provincialism in favor of a cultural cosmopolitanism. Yet Daniel's embrace of his Jewish identity provides a grounding that preserves him from the dangers of 'cosmopolitan indifference' and mere rootlessness (Anderson 2001: 131). In contrast, Disraeli's racism is clearly biological, except that it reverses the poles: Jews and other Semites or 'Arabians,' and not Anglo-Saxons, are the greatest imperial and religious race. Eliot makes no such prejudicial judgement. *Daniel Deronda* explores Judaism (and implicitly, at least, the Orient) as an attractive cultural alternative to British insularity and racism, including Disraeli's.[17]

Nothing in *Tancred* or, for that matter, *Daniel Deronda*, contradicts Said's definition of Orientalism as 'a kind of Western projection onto and will to govern over the Orient' (1978: 95). But is Orientalism invariably an ideology or 'discursive formation' that systematically misrepresents the Middle East and Islam – or, in the case of both *Tancred* and *Daniel Deronda*, Judaism?[18] If Orientalism were merely 'imaginative geography,' as Said calls it at one point (71), then it would not have been of any practical value to Western imperialists. Popular versions of Orientalism such as *Lalla Rookh* and *Eothen* misrepresent the societies and cultures they depict in a variety of ways, although, like Disraeli's and Eliot's novels, they often do so in an affirmative mode. However, the expert, academic versions of Orientalism in which Said is most interested entail the production of 'useful knowledge' (159). In using that phrase, Said has in mind Edward Lane's influential *Manners and Customs of the Modern Egyptians* (1836), which Lane wrote for the Society for the Diffusion of Useful Knowledge. Unlike a number of the French Orientalists Said examines – Chateaubriand, Nerval, Flaubert – Lane presents himself as a neutral, scientific observer, similar to a modern anthropologist. He clearly meant his text to provide 'useful knowledge,' so to whom and how did he expect it to be 'useful'? *Modern Egyptians* is not a tourist guidebook on the model of Murray's or Baedeker's guides (these began to appear in the 1830s), but it became important reading for any Briton who had dealings with Egypt. Lane was able to write *Modern Egyptians* by learning Arabic and living for several years in Cairo, adopting Egyptian garb and customs in doing so. However, Said claims that, despite its apparent objectivity, in Lane's text 'the Orientalist ego is very much in evidence' (158). Like a number of other Western travelers in the Middle East, such as Richard Burton, Lane at least pretended to be a Muslim, which enabled him to study Islamic beliefs and practices at close quarters. But 'his identity as counterfeit believer and privileged

European,' Said writes, 'is the very essence of bad faith' (161). Moreover, the 'useful knowledge' he produced was for Europeans, not for Egyptians.

Lane 'never lets us forget' his 'ego,' Said asserts; 'the first-person pronoun moving through Egyptian customs, rituals, festivals, infancy, adulthood, and burial rights, is in reality both an Oriental masquerade and an Orientalist device for capturing and conveying valuable, otherwise inaccessible information' (160). Egoism and science, it appears, go hand-in-hand in Lane's text. But science is often trumped by what Said calls Lane's 'propensity . . . for sadomasochistic colossal tidbits' such as the glass-eating Sheik or 'the self-mutilation of dervishes' (162). Typical of Lane's 'tidbits,' in the chapter devoted to the 'character' of the Egyptians, he notes the 'great respect' they have for bread 'as the staff of life.' To illustrate this respect, Lane tells a story that he finds 'hardly credible':

> Two servants were sitting at the door of their master's house, eating their dinner, when they observed a Memlook Bey [Ottoman official], with several of his officers, riding along the street towards them. One of these servants rose, from respect to the grandee, who, regarding him with indignation, exclaimed, 'Which is the more worthy of respect, the bread that is before you, or myself?' – Without waiting for a reply, he made [a sign] with his hand; and the unintending offender was beheaded on the spot. (1963: 298–9)

This 'hardly credible' story no doubt illustrates Egyptians' respect for bread, but it also illustrates Oriental despotism at its 'sadomasochistic' worst. Lane's text contains many such stories, including ones that illustrate 'the libidinous character of the women' (Lane 1963: 305). Many others illustrate Egyptian 'superstitions,' a category that, for Lane, blurs into religion – that is, into Islam. Lane's chapter on Egyptian 'language, literature, and science' is about half as long as either of the two chapters on 'superstitions' and on 'magic, astrology, and alchymy,' and under the heading 'science' Lane emphasizes ignorance: 'Of geography, the Egyptians . . . have scarcely any knowledge,' for example (227).

Lane sometimes aligns his 'sadomasochistic colossal tidbits' with stories from *The Arabian Nights*, which he translated, as did Richard Burton. Because they suggest the changelessness of Egyptian society and culture, the references in *Modern Egyptians* to *The Arabian Nights* exemplify what Said says about 'latent' Orientalism, or the unquestioning assumption of the veracity of such-and-such a text or piece of knowledge (Lane 1963: 221–4). In his first footnote, Lane declares that if 'the English reader had possessed a close translation' of *The Arabian Nights* 'with sufficient illustrative notes, I might have spared myself the labour of the present undertaking.' That is because *Nights* 'presents most admirable pictures of the manners and customs of the Arabs, and particularly those of the Egyptians' (xxiv–xxv). The notion that 'modern' Egypt is well-represented by *The Arabian Nights* implies that historical change – at least, in the sense of progress–is foreign to it. Indeed, today's Egypt has regressed from its past condition: 'It is melancholy to contrast the present poverty of Egypt with its prosperity in ancient times' (315).

Did Lane intend *Modern Egyptians* to provide 'useful knowledge' for the promotion of British imperial interests in the Middle East? Certainly that is how Burton hoped his writings on the Middle East, Africa, and elsewhere would be used. In his *Pilgrimage to Al-Madinah and Meccah*, Burton writes: 'it requires not the ken of a prophet to foresee the day when political necessity . . . will compel us to occupy in force the fountain-head of Al-Islam' (1964: 2:231). Securing Egypt for the British Empire is even more important. Burton fears that Egypt, having wrested a semi-independence from the Ottoman Empire, will once again fall into the hands of the French, as it did under Napoleon: 'whatever European nation secures Egypt will win a treasure' (1:112). Clearly, Egypt has enormous strategic value: 'This country in western hands will command India, and by a ship-canal between Pelusium and Suez would open the whole of Eastern Africa' (1:113). In general, Burton advocated British imperial expansion, through war if need be. In *First Footsteps in East Africa* (1856), Burton declared war preferable to any 'peace policy':

> The philanthropist and the political economist may fondly hope, by outcry against 'territorial aggrandisement,' by advocating a compact frontier, by abandoning colonies . . . to retain our rank among the great nations of the world. Never! The facts of history prove nothing more conclusively than this: a race either progresses or retrogrades, either increases or diminishes. (1894: 1:xxx–xxxi)

In the conclusion to his translation of *The Arabian Nights*, Burton claims that even his explorations of Oriental and African sexual behaviors will prove useful to the British Empire: 'I . . . maintain that the free treatment of topics usually taboo'd . . . will be a national benefit to an "Empire of Opinion," whose very basis and buttresses are a thorough knowledge by the rulers of the ruled' (1886: 10:301).

In *Modern Egyptians*, Lane makes no comparable assertions about the utility of his text for the British Empire. He considers 'Late Innovations in Egypt' in an appendix; by 'innovations' he means the adoption of European values and customs throughout the Ottoman Empire and Egypt.

Western 'luxuries' such as 'the use of the knife and fork' and 'openly drinking wine' are leading to a weakening of faith and morality among 'the dominant class' which 'will doubtless spread . . . among the inferior members of the community.' This process of Europeanization, Lane supposes, is subverting 'the foundations of El-Islam,' which may in turn result in 'the overthrow of the whole fabric' (1963: 563). Unlike Burton, Lane does not explicitly advocate imperializing the Middle East; he is not even speculating about the collapse of the Ottoman Empire: the 'fabric' in question is Islam, whose authority, he believes, is being eroded by modernization – that is, by Westernization.

Lane's apparent political neutrality and Burton's aggressive imperialism are both strikingly different from the views of Wilfrid Scawen Blunt, who after the 1882 invasion of Egypt became a vigorous critic of British imperial policy. Although Said notes that, unlike most British Orientalists, Blunt did not express 'the traditional Western hostility to and fear of the Orient' (1978: 237), he does not examine Blunt's anti-imperialism. Nor does Said examine other Victorian critics of imperialism and Orientalism. Besides Blunt, these include the 'Turcophile' Scotsman David Urquhart, author of *The Spirit of the East* (1838); William Gifford Palgrave, whose travelogue on Saudi Arabia appeared in 1865, followed by his *Essays on Eastern Questions* in 1872; and Edward Browne, whose many books and essays on Persia and Islamic reform include *A Year Amongst the Persians* (1893) and *Pan-Islamism* (1902). Blunt and Browne in particular, writes Geoffrey Nash, 'were the most vociferous' critical voices championing Middle Eastern causes. 'Instead of reinforcing cultural stereotypes and re-entrenching notions of European supremacy, Blunt and Browne's espousals of Egyptian and Iranian nationalism cut across established orthodoxies concerning the East' (Nash 2005: 2).[19] Furthermore, Blunt and Browne wrote texts that were both influenced by and gave voice to Middle Eastern reformers, nationalists, and anti-imperialists. Blunt also inspired T. E. Lawrence, who in the early 1920s, albeit with British approval, helped lead the Arab nationalist rebellion against the Ottoman Empire.

Prior to Britain's invasion and crushing of Egyptian nationalism in 1882, Blunt advocated British patronage of Egypt and Arabia as these pulled away from Ottoman rule. After the invasion, however, he became a relentless critic of British imperialism (Nash 2005: 90). He saw his support of the nationalist leader Col. Arabi (or Urabi) as similar to Byron's support of Greek independence, 'the cause of freedom in the East' (Blunt 1922: 6). Both before and after the invasion, he empathized with the 'free' rulers of the Bedouin tribes of Arabia, seeing in them an approximation of the British aristocracy. Like Burton, he identified the Bedouins with 'chivalric' ideals, even while viewing their brand of tribal rule as both democratic and communal. The 1882 invasion of Egypt sharpened Blunt's sense that the British Empire, which he believed had once governed India, Ireland, and elsewhere in an honorable (aristo-cratic) fashion, had been overrun by vulgar capitalist interests.

> Oh insolence of strength! Oh boast of wisdom!
>   Oh poverty in all things truly wise!
> Thinkest thou, England, God can be outwitted
>   For ever thus by him who sells and buys?

So writes Blunt in his 1883 anti-imperialist poem, 'The Wind and the Whirlwind,' in which Britain sells 'the sad nations to their ruin' (1968: 2:232). In *Secret History of the English Occupation of Egypt* (1907) and elsewhere, Blunt condemned British misdeeds in Egypt and the Sudan. In *Ideas about India* (1884), he also criticized Britain's actions in the sub-continent. Having visited the Nizam of Hyderabad, Blunt decided India would be better off if governed by a 'revitalised' native aristocracy (Tidrick 1981: 130–1). And he took up the cause of Irish Home Rule; his political activities in Ireland landed him in jail for two months (see his *The Land War in Ireland*, 1912). Blunt's anti-imperialism had its radical implications, but it was mainly a reactionary mix of ideas and impulses that led him in old age to express a paranoid anti-Semitism.[20] He blamed capitalism for the downfall of British imperial ideals; and he blamed the Jews, including Disraeli, for capitalism (Carr 2002: 77). From Disraeli through the Rothschilds' influence on Gladstone to Lord Cromer, whom Blunt suspected of being a Jew, 'the alien gang of Jew financiers' were responsible for the decline and fall of the once-glorious British Empire (quoted in Tidrick 1981: 132).

Said contends that Orientalism supported Western imperialism by excluding voices of difference and dissent. But *Orientalism* often excludes those voices. Dissenters ranged from Blunt's partially reac-tionary but pro-Islamist stance through Liberals (Gladstone was a Home Ruler and often only a 'reluctant' imperialist) to radicals and socialists such as William Morris, Belfort Bax, Robert Blatchford, and H. M. Hyndman. Those British intellectuals who accepted versions of Auguste Comte's Positivism – Frederic Harrison and Richard Congreve foremost among them – also condemned both imperialism and racism (Claeys 2007). And there were increasing numbers of nationalists in Ireland (from Young Ireland to the IRA), India (Dadabhai Naoroji, for example, who became a member of Parliament), Egypt (Col. Arabi, whom Blunt championed), and elsewhere. To these must be added anti-imperialist feminists such as Josephine Butler and Catherine Impey. Not only does Said pay little attention to Blunt, while failing to mention Urquhart (he mentions Palgrave and Browne once each, suggesting that they were 'agents' rather than critics of imperialism), but he also overlooks the many ways even imperialist texts weave Oriental and occasionally con-testatory voices into their accounts. As Ania Loomba puts it, *Orientalism* downplays 'the self-representations of the colonised and focuses on the imposition of colonial power rather than on the resistances to it' (1998: 49). Aijaz Ahmad also writes that *Orientalism* does not make room 'for criticisms of colonial cultural domination of the kind that have been available . . . on an expanding scale, since the late nineteenth century' (1992: 174).[21]

A related criticism of *Orientalism* is that Said's sources are over-whelming Western. Thus, 'what is remarkable is that with the exception of Said's own voice, the only voices we encounter in the book are pre-cisely those of the very Western canonicity which, Said complains, has always silenced the Orient' (Ahmad 1992: 172). But if Orientalism is a Western invention and imposition on the East, inevitably Said's sources must be Western. Hence, too, in many other postcolonial literary studies (including this one), the focus is mainly on one side of the equation – that of the colonizers. This emphasis is in part an inevitable outcome of impe-rialism: most history is written by the victors, and so is most literature.

Though these and other objections to *Orientalism* may be valid, few works of cultural criticism, postcolonial or otherwise, have been more influential. However, Abdirahman Hussein remarks that 'the debate pro-voked by *Orientalism* . . . has largely been conducted in a way that . . . is . . . strangely indifferent to the contentious *present* realities of the Middle East' (2002: 230). But Orientalism as an imperialist ideology is evident in current US and British foreign policy and military blunders in Iraq, Iran, Israel–Palestine, and elsewhere. Said makes the continuities between nineteenth-century imperialism and our supposedly postcolonial world apparent in many of the works he wrote after *Orientalism*, includ-ing *Culture and Imperialism*, *Covering Islam*, *The Question of Palestine*, and *The Politics of Dispossession*. Even Said's harshest critics recognize that he challenges all Eurocentric forms of knowledge about the rest of the world, both because they involve large-scale patterns of misrepresen-tation and because those patterns have been and continue to be useful for promoting Western imperialism.

'Mimicry' versus 'Going Native'

According to Homi Bhabha, 'mimicry,' the response of the colonized seeking to emulate the colonizers, 'is at once resemblance and menace' (1994: 86). 'The *menace* of mimicry,' Bhabha adds, 'is its *double* vision which in disclosing the ambivalence of colonial discourse also disrupts its authority' (88). It does so because it reveals the inauthenticity both of the 'mimic man,' who can never completely assimilate or, in the parlance of Victorian imperialism, can never become fully civilized, and of the colonizer, whose claim to a 'civilizing mission' is his chief moral justification for undertaking the religious conversion or the education (or both) of the colonized. One criticism of Bhabha's argument is that, beyond 'menace,' he wishes to attribute an 'insurgent' agency to what amounts to a discursive contradiction. As Anne McLintock puts it, 'the question is whether it is sufficient to locate agency in the internal fissures of discourse' (1995: 63).

Bhabha is thinking in part of Macaulay's 1835 'Minute on Indian education,' which recommended that the East India Company create 'a class of interpreters between us and the millions whom we govern – a class of persons Indian in blood and colour, but English in tastes, in opinions, in morals and in intellect' (Macaulay 1967: 722). In *The Idea of India*, Sunil Khilnani writes:

> The imposition of English as the language of politics transfigured Indian public life in at least two ways: it obviously divided the British rulers from their Indian subjects; and it also divided the Indians themselves, between those who could speak English, who knew their Dicey from their Dickens, and those who did not. These often immacutely anglicised élites were also, it is essential to remember, fully bicultural, entirely comfortable with their own Marathi, Bengali or Hindustani *milieux*: it was, after all, exactly this amphibious quality which made them useful porters to the British Raj. (1998: 23)

Amphibiousness – one of 'mimicry's' results – in any complex political situation (that of the translator, for example) entails the ability to represent two or more positions, which can lead beyond 'menace' to duplicity, betrayal, and at times 'insurgency.'

According to Gauri Viswanathan, English literary studies 'had its beginnings as a strategy of containment' in India long before it became insitutionalized in British schools and universities (1989: 10). She notes that the Charter Act of 1813, rather than Macaulay's 'Minute,' was the starting point for English education in India (21). Further, the movement to 'Anglicize' Indian education, versus the 'Orientalist' advocates of training in Sanskrit and Persian, was 'spearheaded by Calcutta's foremost citizen, Rammohun Roy' (43), who insisted that, for India to enter the modern world, English education along with training in Western science and technology were essential. Macaulay wanted to produce just a small cadre of 'mimic men' as mediators between the British and the Indian masses. Roy wanted India to have the opportunity to catch up scientifically, technologically, and economically with the Europeans. In both cases, mimicry would be the result, but Macaulay did not anticipate that it would be menacing. Roy, however, probably understood that the sort of mimicry he wished for was menacing: Indian nationalism, at least in muted form, began to emerge among the first generation of English-educated Bengalis.

In every colonial context, the colonizers found it necessary to attract and utilize 'native' go-betweens as translators, guides, advisors, servants, mercenaries, and teachers. The 'mimic men' whom Bhabha sees as 'menacing' were far more than mere imitators of the colonizers. For example, the white explorers of Tasmania and the Australian 'outback' could not have traveled where they did without Aboriginal guides and interpreters (Reynolds 1982: 24–5). Nevertheless, until recently positive portrayals of Aborigines in Australian histories and literature were rare. Apart from becoming indispensable to the colonizers, the Aborigines were bad 'mimic men' and therefore all the more 'menacing': they preferred their nomadic ways to settling down, they did not want to work for anything whites had to offer, they were difficult for missionaries to convert, and they seemed to be a rapidly 'vanishing race.'[22] Bhabha does not indicate whether it is more menacing for mimicry to be, from a Western standpoint, inadequate, as was the case with the first Australians, or very skillful, as with many English-educated Indians.

According to racist stereotyping, some or perhaps all nonwhite races of the world could never be anything more than 'mimic men.' Thus, in G. A. Henty's novel *By Sheer Pluck* (1884), Mr. Goodenough declares:

> 'The intelligence of the average negro is about equal to that of a European child of ten years old. . . . They are fluent talkers, but their ideas are borrowed. They are absolutely without originality, absolutely without inventive power. Living among white men, their imitative faculties enable them to attain a considerable amount of civilisation. Left to their own devices, they retrograde into a state little above their native savagery.' (1884: 118)

If true, this would mean that Britain's civilizing mission in Africa would inevitably fail – a conclusion Henty avoids reaching. Even in twentieth-century fiction about Africa written by white authors, the Western-educated African is often treated as an inauthentic farce, as in Joyce Cary's *Mister Johnson* (1939). But what about whites who imitate Africans or, like many Australian bushrangers, the Aborigines?

Cultural exchanges affect everyone involved in them, the colonizers as well as the colonized. This is obviously the lesson Bhabha teaches by insisting on the 'hybridity' of all discursive interactions. If the imperialist civilizing mission supposedly aimed to Westernize or Anglicize all 'natives' everywhere (even though they could only be civilized with a difference, or as Bhabha puts it, 'almost but not quite'), the civilized could also regress, backslide, become 'mimic men' who emulated the natives. And in much imperialist discourse, that sort of reverse mimicry was far more menacing than the sort Bhabha has in mind. Moreover, just as the mimicry of Europeans by the natives was often coerced or involuntary, that was true also of 'going native.' In *Captives*, Linda Colley writes:

> Time and time again, British men and women taken captive in the Mediterranean, or in North America, or in India, changed their behaviour, their language, their outward appearance, and even their political and religious allegiance. Often this occurred under pressure and only temporarily; but in some cases it happened permanently and out of a measure of choice. Such adaptability in the face of other cultures was never confined merely to Britons taken captive. The cliché that Britons overseas clung to their peculiar, parochial habits . . . needs examining carefully and skeptically. (2002: 360)

By studying the many stories of captivity and Britons' 'mimicry' of dark others, Colley provides the antithesis not just to Bhabha's version of mimicry, but to the standard histories of slavery and abolition. From the Empire's violent 'underbelly' (4), she draws on 'over a hundred printed and manuscript narratives written or dictated by Britons between 1600 and the mid-nineteenth century in response to captivity in the Mediterranean and North African region, in North America, and in South and Central Asia' (13).

Everywhere imperial frontiers and cultural borders proved more 'permeable' than standard accounts have allowed (Colley 2002: 195). Between 1600 and the 1730s, as many as 18,000 'English subjects may have been captured' along the Barbary coast and 'in most cases . . . enslaved for life in North Africa and elsewhere in the Ottoman empire' (44). If many versions of going native, both coerced and willing, emerge from these early 'Barbary coast' narratives, that was also the case in North America. 'During the Seven Years War . . . desertions from among the lower ranks of British regiments based in North America to various indigenous communities proved so numerous that any redcoat discovered living alongside Indians and claiming to have been captured, risked being court-martialed' (195–6). Benjamin Franklin noted the frequency with which white captives chose to remain with their Indian captors, and Hector St. John Crèvecoeur observed that 'there must be in their social bond something singularly captivating and far superior to anything to be boasted of among us; for thousands of Europeans are Indians' (Crèvecoeur 1986: 214).

Starting with the issue of coercion versus freely chosen transformations, there were many varieties and degrees of going native, as there were also of mimicry by the colonized. From the standpoint of imperialist ideology, going native voluntarily, or the uncoerced adoption of non-British customs and cultures, was especially threatening. 'Pakeha Maori' and 'white Indians' were, writes David Thorp, 'colonial officials' worst nightmare' (2003: 1). According to Sir Harry Johnston, administrator of British Central Africa, 'I have been increasingly struck with the rapidity with which such members of the white race as are not of the best class, can throw over the restraints of civilisation and develop into savages of unbridled lust and abominable cruelty' (1906: 68). In the Canadian novel *Wacousta* (1832) by John Richardson, the title is the Indian name of a British soldier 'transformed . . . into an almost supernatural Native warrior fighting with Pontiac's forces against the British' (Goldie 2003: 44). The protagonist of James Tucker's *Ralph Rashleigh* (c. 1845) is an escaped convict who spends four and a half years as a 'white blackfellow,' initiated into a tribe of Aborigines. According to Kathryn Tidrick, in Sarawak under 'Rajah' James Brooke, his nephew, and his grandnephew, the 'administrative service became a sort of Lost Legion, gone permanently native, and indeed appeared in Kipling's poem of that name, written to celebrate the unsung path-breakers of empire. . . . They took native mistresses, tattooed themselves *à la* Dyak . . . and avoided other Europeans' (1990: 39). Bayly calls James Brooke 'a colourful example of freelance imperialism'; he 'created his own kingdom from the fief of jungle and mangrove in Sarawak . . . which the Sultan of Brunei had assigned him in 1841, as recompense for help in the suppression' of Dyak piracy (1989a: 104).

The 'nabobs' of the East India Company are also examples of going native in a voluntary mode. In his essay on Clive, Macaulay says that, though an English gentleman, Clive stooped to the level of the Indians, adopting their immoral ways of commerce, politics, and warfare. Many nabobs besides Clive, while enriching themselves in India, acquired Indian tastes, manners, mistresses, and wives; with their wealth and their oriental ways, those who returned to Britain menaced – or at least aroused anxiety and envy among – ordinary citizens. In his 1772 poem 'Tea and Sugar: or the Nabob and the Native,' Timothy Touchstone writes that the nabobs are 'my country's shame and poor Hindustan's curse' (quoted in Juneja 1992: 185). With reforms of the East India Company, the image of the nabob perhaps grew less menacing. But in 1860, free trader and anti-imperialist Richard Cobden wondered if the possession of its Indian Empire might ruin Britain itself: 'Is it not just possible that we may become corrupted at home by the reaction of arbitrary political maxims in the East upon our domestic politics, just as Greece and Rome were demoralised by their contact with Asia?' (quoted in Armitage 2000: 11).

Merely living in India or elsewhere in the tropics, it was widely believed, was demoralizing and could alter a European for the worse. 'A great many of the [British] men here have lived in the jungles for years,' writes Emily Eden in her Indian journal, 'and their poor dear manners are utterly gone – jungled out of them' (1937: 70). There were many Britons in India – Anglo-Indians, as they were called – who did not become wealthy nabobs, but who pursued careers as bureaucrats, soldiers, traders, or missionaries, and who grew into – or 'mimicked,' partly from choice and partly from necessity – Indian lifestyles. This was the case with Philip Meadows Taylor, author of *Confessions of a Thug*, who after the failure of his father's business in Liverpool was sent to India to work in a relative's firm, but instead became a military officer and police official in the service of the Nizam of Hyderabad, one of the ostensibly independent 'native princes.' Taylor married one of the 'Eurasian' daughters of William Palmer, chief banker to the Nizam; Palmer had himself married a princess of Oudh.

Like Frederick Maning, many of the early British settlers in New Zealand became 'pakeha Maoris.' Maning recounts his early years there in *Old New Zealand: A Tale of the Good Old Times* (1863). As a white trader, he 'belonged' to a chief of the Ngapuhi tribe, purchased two hundred acres from the tribe, married a Maori woman, and helped raise their four children. At the end of his narrative, he forecasts more warfare between the Maoris and the colonists, while refusing to take sides:

> I am a loyal subject to Queen Victoria, but I am also a member of a Maori tribe; and I hope I may never see this country so enslaved and tamed that a single rascally policeman, with nothing but a bit of paper in his hand, can come and take a *rangatira* [chief] away from the middle of his *hapu* [clan], and have him hanged for something of no consequence at all, except that it is against the law. (1906: 216)

In 1865 Maning became a Justice of the Peace and a Judge for the Native Lands' Court. By all accounts, he was an outstanding citizen of the new colony.

Byron Farwell notes that, like Taylor, many British soldiers and sailors wound up in the service of non-British societies: 'Britons did not hesitate to exchange their bowlers for turbans, tarbushes or mandarin caps if only they were given men whom they could lead into battle. Lawrence of Arabia was a wonder and a curiosity in [the twentieth] century, but there were hundreds of his countrymen like him who performed similar exploits in the previous century' (1972: 3). General Charles Gordon, the famous martyr of Khartoum, became known as 'Chinese' Gordon after leading the forces of the Emperor of China against the Taiping rebels. He was one of many Britons who seemed happiest the farther away from Britain and civilization he could get. 'I dwell on the joy of never seeing Great Britain again, with its horrid, wearisome dinner-parties and miseries,' Gordon declared; 'How we can put up with those things, passes my imagination! It is a perfect bondage. . . . I would sooner live like a Dervish with the Mahdi, than go out to dinner every night in London'. Gordon also averred: 'I hate Her Majesty's Government for their leaving the Sudan after having caused all its troubles' (quoted in Strachey 1988: 182–3). Even more significantly, Gordon disobeyed orders, leading to his martyrdom and his acclaim by the British press as 'the Hero of Heroes' (Strachey 1988: 192). He wasn't particularly patriotic, he was insubordinate, he caused a crisis in imperial affairs – in short, he might almost have been 'a Dervish with the Mahdi.'[23]

Once David Livingstone began trekking through southern and central Africa, he also clearly preferred remaining there rather than returning to Britain. It seems likely that he did not want to be 'found' by Henry Morton Stanley in 1871 (besides, he wasn't lost). Many other missionaries shipped out to Polynesia, India, Canada, and elsewhere, with little expectation that they would return soon (if ever) to Britain, but with every expectation that, even as they strove to Christianize and civilize the 'natives,' they would learn native languages, eat native food, and in general behave very much like the natives, while condemning and trying to eradicate 'unspeakable' customs such as infanticide and cannibalism. In Robert Louis Stevenson's 'The Beach of Falesá' (1893), Wiltshire complains that missionaries 'look down upon' traders like himself; 'and besides, they're partly Kanakaised, and suck up with natives instead of with other white men like themselves' (1996: 34). Similarly, concerning the 'Bishop of Rum-Ti-Foo,' W. S. Gilbert writes:

His people – twenty-three in sum –
They played the eloquent tum-tum
And lived on scalps served up in rum –
   The only sauce they knew.
When first good BISHOP PETER came
(For PETER was that Bishop's name),
To humor them, he did the same
   As they of Rum-ti-Foo. (in Buckley and Woods 1965: 752)

Besides 'unspeakable' episodes vividly depicting infanticide and cannibalism, the Rev. Joseph Waterhouse's 1865 book *The King and People of
Fiji* is remarkable for several reasons, not least because he was 'the first
Englishman . . . permitted to reside in [Bau,] the city of Thakombau, the
titular King of Fiji' and perhaps the most famous cannibal in history
(Waterhouse 1865: 'Preface'; Brantlinger 2006). Waterhouse became a
fluent speaker of Fijian and lived in Fiji for fourteen years before publishing his account – much longer than the time spent by most modern
anthropologists doing fieldwork. And the Rev. Thomas Williams's
1859 *Fiji and the Fijians* is equally interesting. George Stocking and
Christopher Herbert both credit Williams with being an excellent 'missionary ethnographer.' Herbert declares that, among all the 'early
Polynesianists,' Williams, having lived thirteen years in Fiji, 'explored
most daringly the issue of the possible transformation of the "civilised"
Christian through contact with barbarous heathens' (Herbert 1991: 175;
Stocking 1987: 87–92). Despite the cannibalism and infanticide that he
witnessed, Williams praised many aspects of Fijian culture and society,
including their hospitality and etiquette.

Toward the end of his account, which is largely a biography of
Thakombau, Waterhouse comments, or perhaps confesses: 'In some
degree, I was one of themselves' (1865: 241–2). So was Williams. If they
and the other Wesleyan missionaries in Fiji had 'in some degree' gone
native, that was the price they paid for transforming Thakombau and
other Fijians 'in some degree' into peaceable Methodists. In Fiji, both
missionaries and (ex)cannibals practiced mimicry; they both underwent,
to varying degrees, cultural conversions. For the Fijians, their transformations included religious conversions. There were many reasons for the
conversion of the Fijians. Perhaps the three principal motives were the
desire to escape from the ongoing warfare among the different tribes and
islands of the archipelago, the desire for Western goods (including
weapons), and the desire for knowledge of the world beyond the islands.

The most famous literary example of going native, Mr. Kurtz in Joseph
Conrad's *Heart of Darkness* (1899), appears to be summarizing his own

demoralization in his dying words: 'The horror, the horror!' (2006: 69).
Yet for many Britons, both men and women such as Lady Anne Blunt,
going native had its attractions. The disgruntled narrator of Tennyson's
'Locksley Hall' dreams of bursting 'all links of habit . . . to wander
far away,/ On from island unto island at the gateways of the day.' On
some island 'of Eden lying in dark-purple spheres of sea' he will find
fulfillment:

> There methinks would be enjoyment more than in this march of mind,
> In the steamship, in the railway, in the thoughts that shake mankind.
>
> There the passions cramped no longer shall have scope and breathing space;
> I will take some savage woman, she shall rear my dusky race.
>
> Iron jointed, supple-sinewed, they shall dive, and they shall run,
> Catch the wild goat by the hair, and hurl their lances in the sun;
>
> Whistle back the parrot's call, and leap the rainbows of the brooks,
> Not with blinded eyesight poring over miserable books . . .

Immediately, however, horrified by the thought of betraying progress,
civilization, and the white race, he rejects this vision of life in a tropical
paradise:

> Fool, again the dream, the fancy! but I *know* my words are wild,
> But I count the gray barbarian lower than the Christian child.
>
> I, to herd with narrow foreheads, vacant of our glorious gains,
> Like a beast with lower pleasures, like a beast with lower pains!
>
> Mated with a squalid savage – what to me were sun or clime?
> I the heir of all the ages, in the foremost files of time . . . (1969: 698–9)

In contrast to the narrator of 'Locksley Hall,' H. Rider Haggard's
Allan Quatermain, like General Gordon, prefers living in Africa among
savages to living in Britain among its supposedly civilized populace. In
the 'introduction' to the novel that bears his name, Quatermain declares:
'The thirst for the wilderness was on me; I could tolerate [England] no
more; I would go and die as I had lived, among the wild game and the
savages':

> no man who has for forty years lived the life I have, can with impunity go
> coop himself in this prim English country, with its trim hedgerows and cul-
> tivated fields, its stiff formal manners, and its well-dressed crowds. He
> begins to long – ah, how he longs! – for the keen breath of the desert air; he

dreams of the sight of Zulu impis breaking on their foes like surf upon the rocks, and his heart arises in rebellion against the strict limits of the civilised life. (1951: 419)

After all, Quatermain asks, what is civilization? It is 'only savagery silver-gilt. A vainglory is it, and, like a northern light, comes but to fade and leave the sky more dark. Out of the soil of barbarism it has grown like a tree, and, as I believe, into the soil like a tree, sooner or later, it will once more fall again' (420).

If in Mr. Kurtz's case going native means falling into an abyss of 'horror' from which he cannot extricate himself, just the opposite happens in Conrad's *Lord Jim* (1900). Marlowe helps the disgraced Jim find a new life and, indeed, redemption in the remote Malaysian domain of Patusan. There, his love for Jewel and his friendship with Dain Waris are not demoralizing, but the reverse. All would end happily for him were it not for the intrusion of 'latter-day buccaneer' Gentleman Brown and his gang (Conrad 1989: 303). Before that happens, Jim merges his life into those of the Patusans and becomes their 'Tuan,' their 'Lord.' Marlowe comments:

> But do you notice how, three hundred miles beyond the end of telegraph cables and mail-boat lines, the haggard utilitarian lies of our civilisation wither and die, to be replaced by charm, and sometimes the deep hidden truthfulness, of works of art? Romance had singled Jim out for its own – and that was the true part of the story, which otherwise was all wrong. (251)

Jim goes native, but he also dies for 'a shadowy ideal of conduct' (351) that Conrad identifies as perhaps the only saving factor in Western imperialism and civilization.

And then there is Kipling's Kim, an Irish boy who is more Indian than the Indians, and whose uncanny ability to maneuver through the subcontinent's many languages and cultures helps to preserve India from the meddling of the Russians and the French. In Kim's case, going native is not just redemptive for him, but for the British Empire.

Can Subalterns Speak?

Major Bagstock in Dickens's *Dombey and Son* has returned from India with an oriental servant. Referred to only as 'the Native,' he 'had no particular name, but answered to any vituperative epithet' from the 'choleric' Major such as 'villain' (1989: 273). Dickens frowns on the Major's abusive behavior, yet treats 'the Native' as an object of slapstick. Apart from being a laughing stock and someone for the Major to kick around, 'the Native' never says a word and is never characterized as an object of sympathetic identification on a par with any of the English characters. The speechless 'Native' appears to be in the position of absolute subalternity: he cannot speak; he must be spoken for, which Dickens fails to do.[24]

In her often-cited essay, 'Can the Subaltern Speak?' Gayatri Spivak invokes Marx's claim about the 'small peasants' in France: 'They cannot represent themselves, they must be represented' (Marx 1972: 608; Spivak 1988a: 276). Marx continues: 'Their representative must at the same time appear as their master, as an authority over them, as an unlimited governmental power that protects them against the other classes and sends them the rain and the sunshine from above' (608). In the relationship between the colonized and the colonizer, Spivak argues, the most abject or dominated version of the former cannot represent herself; she can only be represented by someone with more power and authority. This means in turn: 'The subaltern cannot speak,' but must be spoken for, either by her colonial master or by 'the female intellectual' such as Spivak whose 'circumscribed task' is providing a mode of representation that does not simply reinforce the oppression of 'the subaltern subject' (1998a: 308).

In a more recent essay, Spivak renders the subaltern even more speechless, if that is possible: 'Subalternity is where social lines of mobility, being elsewhere, do not permit the formation of a recognisable basis of action' (2005: 476). To be subaltern is 'to be removed from all lines of social mobility' (475). Further, 'No one can say "I am a subaltern" in whatever language'. Thus, it seems, 'Subalternity is a position without identity' (476). Ergo, once subalterns rebel or resist oppression, they cease to be subalterns. They derive their public or historical identity, at any rate, from their resistance. Spivak's argument raises the question of whether there have ever been any individuals or groups so oppressed that they have not in some manner resisted the oppression?

If indeed 'the subaltern cannot speak,' how does Spivak position herself with regard to *Subaltern Studies* and the group of historians who contribute to that journal? Her introduction to *Selected Subaltern Studies* offers a poststructuralist critique of their project. The historians seek to recover the voices of the subaltern classes in India, but, Spivak contends, they can only produce written representations of what those classes are supposed to have uttered, acted, and intended. As a version of 'history from below' (similar to that practiced by E. P. Thompson and other labor historians in the British context), the *Subaltern Studies* collective's main purpose is to demonstrate the agency of Indian peasants in the shaping of the colonial and postcolonial history of the subcontinent (Chandavarkar). Insofar as the peasantry has engaged in resistance and rebellion against both the British and their Indian overlords, to that extent they have been able to represent themselves. They have exercised a degree of historical agency, though that agency is unacknowledged in 'elite' historiography, whether written by Indian nationalists or by British historians.

Frantz Fanon was thinking along similar lines when he wrote: 'Now, the *fellah*, the unemployed man, the starving native do not lay a claim to the truth, for they *are* the truth' (1991: 49). His assertion differs from Spivak's argument, however, because he invokes an epistemological essentialism or authenticity that she rejects. If the subaltern has no identity and cannot even say she is subaltern, she cannot be the locus of a concealed truth that any investigations by nonsubalterns – historians, postcolonialists, novelists – can reveal. But what of the voices emerging from subalternity, resisting oppression, rebelling against slavery, creating movements for decolonization, demanding women's rights and the rights of labor? For Fanon, these voices are those of the truth of social and historical justice. They are also the voices of truth for the *Subaltern Studies* historians and, at a poststructuralist distance, for Spivak.

'To the extent that the ideological legitimation of colonialism took the forms of a denigration of "native" cultures and a silencing of "native" voices,' writes Neil Lazarus, 'the responses of the colonized to colonialism included, centrally, an ideological dimension, in which colonial representations were contested and the validity and integrity of "native" cultures reclaimed' (2004: 7). Spivak stresses that a full reclamation of 'native' cultures is an impossibility. Yet for postcolonial critics, her argument serves as an injunction to look for the ways individual texts and, indeed, entire literatures fail to represent subalterns and in particular the colonized. This is not simply a matter of declaring that a novel or poem does not depict 'natives,' which the author never intended to do in the first place. It is instead a necessary aspect of analyzing how any literature or individual literary text relates to the nexus of power and subordination in which it has been produced and consumed. Indeed, it is possible that literature as such fails to represent the most subjugated and speechless social positions and even classes – the ones Spivak labels 'subaltern.' But those social positions will then be the very ones that most require representation, and it is the moral obligation of the historian or postcolonialist to try to represent them.

Various colonial novels from Maria Edgeworth's *Castle Rackrent* (1800) to H. Rider Haggard's *Nada the Lily* (1892) are narrated by colonized characters. However, no more than the imprisoned Ameer Ali in *Confessions of a Thug* do these narrators represent in any demonstrably authentic way the thoughts and values of the colonized. Edgeworth's Thady Quirk satisfies many of the stereotypic notions of the Irish held by English readers. Ameer Ali is a serial murderer and highway robber. And Mopo, the narrator of *Nada the Lily*, 'is a proxy of white colonial Victorian values,' as Laura Chrisman says (2000: 110). Yet these texts have some degree of ethnographic credibility, if not demonstrable authenticity (from a poststructuralist perspective like Spivak's, authenticity cannot be demonstrated, any more than the subaltern can speak).

Among the many indigenous populations conquered and colonized by Europeans, few of them have been more speechless – or more under- and misrepresented – by white authors than the Australian Aborigines. In contrast, African slaves received much sympathetic representation during and after the abolitionist crusade. The publication of hundreds of slave narratives gave the slaves a large measure of self-representation. Though most slave narratives were collaboratively authored – escaped slaves telling their stories to white abolitionists who transcribed and published them – some, such as Frederick Douglass's narratives, were self-written. Unitarian minister Theodore Parker said of 'the Lives of Fugitive Slaves' that 'all the original romance of America is in them, not in the white man's novels' (quoted in Baker 1982: 12–13). Nothing equivalent to slave narratives emerged from nineteenth-century white–Aboriginal relations.[25]

Several of the early European explorers considered the Australian Aborigines, as William Dampier put it, 'the miserablest people in the world' (without being able to ask who the Aborigines considered 'the miserablest people in the world'). But Captain Cook declared 'they are far more happier than we Europeans' (without being able to ask if they were indeed 'far more happier' than Europeans) (quoted in Webb and Enstice 1998: 22, 27). A few explorers of the 'outback' – Edward Eyre and George Grey, for example – portrayed them fairly sympathetically.[26] But until the second half of the twentieth century, the representation of Aborigines by white authors did not improve much on Dampier and Cook. It is only with the emergence of literature by Aboriginal authors after World War II that the situation has begun to change.

During the nineteenth century, the idea that Australia was *terra nullius* or a land that, prior to the arrival of the First Fleet in 1788, belonged to nobody became the legal doctrine that helped dispossess the Aborigines of the entire continent. *Terra nullius* remained in force until 1992, when the Australian Supreme Court struck it down in the Eddie Mabo land rights case (Reynolds 1992). A key way the colonizers represented the Aborigines, *terra nullius* rendered them as completely subaltern as any legal fiction could possibly do: assuming the Aborigines even existed, they possessed nothing, because they had no conception of property or territory; thus, Australia belonged to the colonizers.

In nineteenth-century writing about the Australian colonies, the Aborigines make fleeting appearances as both pathetic and hostile savages who deserve to be chased away or slaughtered; they are members of a 'doomed race,' whose 'vanishing' was often sentimentally mourned (McGregor 1997). The Aborigines in Charles Rowcroft's *Tales of the Colonies* (1843) are just as dangerous to peaceful white settlers as the bushrangers, but the bushrangers are at least white. In Bulwer-Lytton's emigration novel *The Caxtons* (1849), 'Sisty' and his colonizing friends are 'lords of the land' – there is no hint that the Aborigines were once in that position. The white characters are also 'lords' of a rough, Arcadian 'health which an antediluvian might have envied, and of nerves so seasoned with horse-breaking, cattle-driving, fighting with wild blacks – chases from them and after them, for life and for death – that if any passion vex the breast of those kings of the Bushland, fear at least is erased from the list' (1849: 122). The 'wild blacks' are, it seems, on a par with cattle and wild horses. So, too, in Henry Kingsley's *The Recollections of Geoffrey Hamlyn* (1859), 'the blacks' are dangerous nuisances; Hamlyn expresses the common attitude toward them when he says, 'I had fully made up my mind to fire on the first black who showed himself, but I did not get the opportunity' (1924: 243).

On the sentimental side, Henry Kendall's poems 'Aboriginal Death Song' and 'The Last of His Tribe' are typical of the genre of proleptic elegy – mourning the demise of an indigenous population before it has actually expired (Brantlinger 2003). In the latter poem, published in 1864, a lone Aborigine

> . . . dreams of the hunts of yore,
> And of foes that he sought, and of fights that he fought
>   With those who will battle no more:
>   Who will go to the battle no more. (1966: 91)

The 'fights that he fought' were apparently with other Aborigines; in Kendall's poems about doomed and dying Aborigines, there is no hint that violence by whites is the cause of their demise. Instead, savagery exterminates savagery, as in 'Urara' (1861):

> And we'll cry in the dark for the foot-falls still,
> And the tracks which are fading away!

Let them yell to their lubras, the Bulginbah dogs,
And say how our brothers were slain,
We shall wipe out our grief in the blood of their chief,
And twenty more dead on the plain –
On the blood-spattered spurs of the plain! (1996: 24)

Despite blaming the Aborigines for the extermination of the Aborigines, Kendall at least attributes a humanity and a subjectivity to his dying hunters and warriors, which is more than Bulwer-Lytton, Henry Kingsley, or many other Victorian writers do when they mention Aborigines. An 1847 poem by 'Auster,' 'The Tasmanian Aborigine's Lament and Remonstrance When in Sight of His Native Land from Flinders Island,' is another example of proleptic elegy:

Our race is fast decaying. . . .
Oh! Let us die where our forefathers died,
That we may mix our wretched dust with theirs.
(Quoted in Webb and Enstice 1998: 62)

There are many similar poems, including William Sharp's 'The Last Aboriginal' (1884): 'And in his eyes I dimly trace/ The memory of a vanished race' (in Buckley and Woods 1965: 831).

In these poems, the white authors represent – or misrepresent – the speech of Aborigines who lament their extirpation, portrayed as savagery killing off savagery, conveniently enough for the white settlers the authors more faithfully represent. It was a struggle to get some white Australians to believe that the 'living fossils' – the Aborigines – could even talk, much less represent their own interests. Some colonists opposed allowing Aborigines to testify in legal proceedings, because their testimony would make no more sense than 'the chatterings of the ourang-outang' (quoted in Webb and Enstice 1998: 67). Missionary Launcelot Threlkeld, who made the first systematic attempt to learn and codify Aboriginal languages, rejected the common view that the Aborigines were both apelike and unable to utter anything more rational than 'the mere chatter of baboons' (quoted in Brantlinger 2003: 130).

Very few nineteenth-century novels, whether written in Britain or Australia, treat Aborigines as something more than subhuman nuisances. An exception is Jacky in Charles Reade's *It Is Never Too Late to Mend* (1856). When George Fielding rescues Jacky from a shark (Reade 1904: 216–18), he acquires a faithful, English-speaking friend (Jacky has spent some time in Sydney) who helps him out of numerous scrapes. Apparently dying of fever, George tells Jacky that although 'I don't care for your black skin . . . I feel we are brothers, and you have been one to me' (231–2). Jacky is overwhelmed by grief. George survives, however, and, reunited with Jacky and the reformed thief Tom Robinson, they strike it rich prospecting for gold. Jacky gives his share of the gold to George in exchange for sheep. Jacky is, no doubt, 'a stage darky with a boomerang,' as Wayne Burns puts it (1961: 146), but he is nevertheless a sympathetic character who can speak his mind.

In James Tucker's perhaps autobiographical *Ralph Rashleigh* (c. 1845), the title character escapes from prison, travels with bushrangers, and joins a tribe of Aborigines. Rashleigh lives with them for over four years, in conditions that are only a little less terrible than those of his imprisonment. But he 'was well content' with his lot, 'convinced as he was that it was safer and better than what awaited him if he returned to live among white men' (1929: 295). He is given a 'djinn' or wife by his adoptive 'father,' chief of the tribe; she 'was the first woman who had ever given him affection' (314). Like many other nonwhite lovers of white heroes in nineteenth-century novels, Lorra dies trying to protect her man from an attack by two treacherous Aborigines. Mostly, however, 'during the four years which he spent in this state of contented barbarism his life was steady and uneventful' (295).

Rosa Praed also creates sympathetic Aboriginal characters in some of her novels – for example, Kombo in *Fugitive Anne* (1902; see Healy 1989: 66–7). And in John Boyle O'Reilly's *Moondyne* (1880), the title character, an Irish convict who gets rich from a secret gold mine, learns to speak an Aboriginal language and acquires a clever 'black' servant, Ngarra-jil. When Moondyne returns to Britain incognito to take up the cause of prison reform, Ngarra-jil adapts 'with ease to his role' in that strange land (Clancy 1992: 40). Ngarra-jil may be a servant to a white man, but unlike Major Bagstock's speechless 'Native,' he can express himself in English as well as in an Aboriginal language.

The Aborigines were not entirely powerless or speechless, lacking agency, or without identity – that was the Western stereotype. Nevertheless, the Aborigines were frequently represented as doomed to complete extinction. Between the 1830s and 1876, when 'Queen' Trugannini, apparently the last full-blooded Tasmanian Aborigine, died, the total extinction of that 'primitive race' aroused much humanitarian and scientific interest.[27] It scandalized the evangelical, humanitarian officials in the Colonial Office in London in the 1830s; and it was of great scientific interest to Darwin in his consideration of the fate of 'primitive races' in *The Descent of Man* (1872). Even more than 'the Native' in *Dombey and Son*, and even more than the mainland Aborigines, the first Tasmanians seem to have been completely silenced by their total liquidation. James Bonwick tells their tragic story in sympathetic detail in *The Last of the Tasmanians* (1870; see also Reynolds 1995).

In *Aborigines of Tasmania* (1890), H. Ling Roth, who never visited that island (McDougall 2007), examined the evidence for and against Mrs. Fanny Cochrane Smith, who had been identified by another anthropologist as 'the last living aboriginal of Tasmania.' There is a photograph of Fanny Smith speaking into the gigantic tube of a phonograph, recording her voice, while a white anthropologist supervises. Uttering perhaps the last words ever spoken in her Tasmanian dialect, what she said has been lost – there is only the ghostly image of her speechless speech-act. Roth rules her out as the last Tasmanian because, on the basis of her photographs, he concludes she was a racial hybrid. So in a sense – according to Roth – she had no authentic identity. Roth discounts the existence of a small but growing population of mixed race Tasmanians in the Bass Straits islands, the offspring of white sealers and Aboriginal women. The story continues into the twentieth century, when the supposedly completely extinct race finally gained recognition by the Australian government, which gave their mixed-race descendants the same rights and services that mainland Aborigines receive (Ryan 1981).

The story also continues in the ongoing controversy about genocide in Australia. In *The Australian* for 18 September 2003, Greg Sheridan declared that 'the cause of Aboriginal welfare and the quality of Australian political culture have been seriously damaged by the moral and linguistic overkill' of those historians who claim that 'genocide' is an accurate term for what happened during the European colonization of that continent. Sheridan was seconding prime minister John Howard, who publicly stated that he wished the historians would stop 'using outrageous words like genocide' (quoted in Henry Reynolds 2001: 2). Sheridan asserted that 'the past mistreatment of Aborigines is the most serious moral failing in our history,' but that it 'never approached genocide or had any relationship to genocide.' Sheridan's article is one of many in the Australian press that have responded to Australia's version of a *Historikerstreit* – that is, of the controversy over the Holocaust among German historians.

The Australian controversy goes back at least to the 1988 bicentenary of the First Fleet, when the official celebrations were countered by Aboriginal protests that declared it 'a year of mourning.' Speaking at a demonstration in Sydney in late January 1988, the Chairman of the New South Wales Aboriginal Land Council, Tiga Bayles, said:

> You think about what White Australia is celebrating today – 200 years of colonisation, the 200 years since they invaded Aboriginal land. And some

of the [white] people seem to expect Aboriginal people . . . to participate in the birthday party. *What bullshit.* That would be like asking the Jewish people to celebrate an anniversary of the Holocaust. (Bayles 1990: 340–1)

For Bayles and other Aborigines, 1788 signifies invasion and two centuries of genocide. But that view of history is 'outrageous' to many – perhaps most – white Australians. The controversy among the historians has heated up since the 2002 publication of Keith Windschuttle's *The Fabrication of Aboriginal History.* Windschuttle denies that the extinction of the Tasmanian Aborigines was genocide. He agrees that the first Tasmanians are extinct, but they had such a 'dysfunctional' culture that they caused their own extinction. Henry Reynolds (2001) concludes that genocide may indeed be an inappropriate label for what happened in Tasmania, but not for the reasons Windschuttle cites. According to the UN Convention on Genocide, if a population defends itself at all vigorously, even its total liquidation technically does not constitute genocide. During the 'Black War' (1826–30), the Tasmanians waged a guerilla war that, Reynolds believes, was the most effective resistance by any Aboriginal group in Australia. Windschuttle thinks the Tasmanians were incapable of doing so; Reynolds credits them with an agency that perhaps means their extinction does not qualify as a genocide, though there were plenty of episodes on the mainland that do.

Those episodes include the five or six decades during which the colonial authorities in Queensland gave at least tacit sanction to gangs of settlers and to the Native Police, an Aboriginal force under white officers trained to gun down other Aborigines (Reynolds 2001: 101–9). As many as 10,000 Aborigines may have been slaughtered during the 'killing times' in Queensland (Palmer 2000: 59). There were numerous 'genocidal massacres' in all of the Australian colonies, though how many and what their death-toll was can only be conjectured. Probably many massacres were never reported.

Prior to the 1940s, even the most sympathetic observers often attributed the demise of the Aborigines throughout Australia partly or wholly to some failing of the Aborigines: the rigidity or savagery of their customs, their mental backwardness, some biological, Darwinian unfitness to survive. In his exercise in genocide denial, Windschuttle resorts to this blaming-the-victim rhetoric as blatantly as any nineteenth-century author. 'It was a tragedy the [Tasmanian] Aborigines adopted such senseless violence,' he writes; 'Their principal victims were themselves' (2002: 130). Their 'violence,' moreover, was criminal, and not 'guerilla warfare' or any other sort of organized resistance to the invasion of their island. According to Windschuttle, the first Tasmanians were a 'dysfunctional' (implicitly, already dying) society, whose reactions to their well-meaning white neighbors were senseless murder and plunder (116–22). The main cause of their downfall was their maltreatment of each other, and especially the abuse of the women by the men, including the apparent eagerness of the men to sell or trade their women to sealers and bushrangers (386). So, delete 'genocide' from Australian history, and blame the victim.

Windschuttle is contradicted by the white observers who had first-hand experience of the Tasmanians, including George Augustus Robinson, who in the early 1830s rounded up the last Aborigines and removed them to a reservation on Flinders Island.[28] Robinson also contradicts *terra nullius* by asserting that the first Tasmanians had a keen attachment to their land: 'Patriotism is a distinguishing trait in the aboriginal character' (21 May 1833; 1966: 725). Moreover, besides the guerilla warfare that they waged in the late 1820s, the Tasmanians were not entirely voiceless. During his round-up Robinson records many of their beliefs and resentments, as in his comment about their 'patriotism.' Though there is a rich and growing body of Aboriginal literature today, and though Tiga Bayles (among many others) can make his views known publicly, in the nineteenth century Aborigines were rarely in a position to become literate in English, and white Australians rarely bothered to learn an Aboriginal language.

In *Writing from the Fringe*, however, Mudrooroo Narogin cites two instances of texts written by Aborigines before 1900. The first is *The Flinders Island Chronicle*, penned by Walter George Arthur and Peter and David Bruny (Robinson gave his Tasmanian charges English names). Narogin quotes a passage as an example of 'Aboriginal protest and a cry of help directed at the white people':

> The brig *Tamar* arrived this morning at Green Island . . . we will hear the news from Hobarton. Let us hope that it will be good news and that something may be done for us poor people they are dying away the bible says some or all shall be saved but I am much afraid none of us will be alive by and by and then as nothing but sick men among us why don't the black fellows pray to the King [William] to get us away from this place. (Narogin 1990: 18–19)

The second example comes from the mainland much later in the century. It, too, is a protest, in which the Koori people petitioned the Aboriginal Protection Board of colonial Victoria about poor conditions at the Aboriginal settlement of Coranderrk. The Board did not believe the petition had been written by the Aborigines, and so hired a detective to investigate. He discovered, however, that the document and others like it were not being forged by white sympathizers, but had been penned by a Koori with the English name of Thomas Dunolly and 'were genuine expressions of the feelings of his people' (Narogin 1990: 19). So a few Aborigines in the 1800s were able to represent themselves and their societies in written form. Further, though they lost far more battles than they won, they also engaged in armed resistance. As the Australian High Court acknowledged in 1992, Aboriginal Australia was never *terra nullius*.

It may be, as Spivak suggests, that many enslaved and colonized people were so thoroughly subjugated they were unable to 'speak' or represent themselves by any means. She wishes to reserve the term 'subaltern' for them. At the same time, besides slave narratives, there were countless slave rebellions, and the one in San Domingo or Haiti turned into a full-fledged revolution leading to independence. Perhaps all colonizing situations produced patterns of resistance among the colonized. British forces were at war in many parts of India and the rest of Asia throughout the nineteenth century. Both the British and the Boers engaged in nearly constant skirmishes and sometimes extended wars against many of the indigenous peoples of southern Africa. In Australia, the Tasmanians and mainland Aborigines also fought back, with tragic consequences, against the white invaders.

Were the Tasmanians 'subalterns' when they waged guerilla warfare in the late 1820s? That depends on how one defines 'subaltern.' It is easy to apply almost any demeaning term to the subjugated. It seems likely, however, that the first Tasmanians viewed themselves as superior to and more authentic than the colonists; at first, they believed white people were ghosts (Narogin 1990). However, Spivak also questions how well the Tasmanians and other colonized peoples have been represented by those who claim to speak on their behalf. In Australia's *Historikerstreit*, they are comparatively well-represented by Henry Reynolds, Lyndall Ryan, and other scholars who grant them the intelligence and agency to resist the invasion of their island. These contemporary scholars echo the nineteenth-century evidence of Robinson, Bonwick, and other first-hand observers. In contrast, the genocide deniers misrepresent both the Aborigines and Australia's history. At least in the nineteenth century, Ann Curthoys notes, white observers 'exhibited an awareness of . . . frontier conflict, and worried over its moral implications' (2001: 3). Yet as Colin Tatz puts it in *With Intent to Destroy: Reflecting on Genocide*, 'Given that there was a widespread assumption that Aborigines were dying out, settlers fulfilled the prophecy by acting to ensure that such was indeed the outcome' (2003: 81). With the advent of white nationalist historiography in the twentieth century, there settled over the continent what anthropologist W. E. H. Stanner in 1968 called 'the great Australian silence' (quoted in Brantlinger 2004: 611). It is only from the 1960s that Curthoys, Reynolds, Ryan, Tatz and other Australian historians and social scientists have reawakened 'awareness of . . . frontier conflict, and worried over its moral implications.'

Notes

1. In *Africa and the Victorians* (1961), Ronald Robinson and John Gallagher contended that the causes of imperial expansion were as much 'excentric' and 'peripheral' as metropolitan. On the frontiers of the Empire, the actions of indigenous leaders such as Col. Arabi in Egypt triggered expansion as much as did leaders in the metropole. 'What *Africa and the Victorians* accomplished . . . was to destroy the European notion of causation – that the springs of British action, for example, lay in Britain alone. Africa and the world at large can no longer be seen as a blank map on which Europeans freely wrote their will' (Louis 1998: 40). The actions by indigenous 'agents' could involve either 'resistance' or 'collaboration.'

2. For a recent example of a work that is mainly celebratory of the British Empire, see Niall Ferguson (2004). Ferguson's notion that the British Empire grew increasingly humane is belied on many fronts – for example, by the brutal repression of the Mau-Maus in Kenya in the 1950s (Elkins 2005; David Anderson 2005). In the introduction, Ferguson fondly remembers his childhood in Kenya shortly after it had gained indepenedence. He mentions without explaining 'the days of White Mischief,' but 'we had our bungalow, our maid, our smattering of Swahili – and our sense of unshakeable security. It was a magical time. . .' (2004: xv). Clearly, he was never thrown into prison like Jomo Kenyatta, much less lynched on a 'White Mischief'gallows. In his main text, Ferguson mentions Kenya only once more, as a former British colony which has not 'managed to sustain free institutions' (308), even though it is today a democracy, albeit a shaky one. He also denies that the British bore any responsibility for the famines that wracked late nineteenth- and twentieth-century India. Compare, however, Mike Davis, *Late Victorian Holocausts* (2001) and also David Fieldhouse, who writes that famines killed '4.3 million in widely spread areas in 1876–78, an additional 1.2 million in the North West Provinces and Kashmir in 1877–78; and, worst of all, over 5 million in a famine that affected a large proportion of India in 1896–97. In 1899–1900 more than a million were thought to have died . . .' (1996: 132).

3. Too often historians treat 'empiricism' like a flag they can wave to suggest that they have command of the facts while postcolonialists just do 'theory.' But 'empiricism' is also a 'theory.' However, rarely do historians subject their notions of 'real events' to any theoretical analysis. In both *The Absent-Minded Imperialists* and *Empire and Superempire*, historian Bernard Porter expresses his aversion to 'theory,' particularly of the postcolonial sort, while also exaggerating the degree to which the Victorians were unaware of the Empire. In the second book, Porter insists that imperialism was never 'a "big deal" for the British people as a whole' (2006: 136). Indeed, 'Britain never turned into a genuinely imperialist society' (33) – an astonishing claim for any historian of the Empire

to make. If Britain 'never' measured up, what does it take to be 'a genuinely imperialist society'? For other historians' reactions to 'theory' and postcolonialism, see Marshall (1993); Kennedy (1996); Peers (2002). I am indebted to David Johnson for e-mailing his essay on the historiography of the Empire.

4. Christopher Bayly comments: 'Writers such as Gholam Hossain-Khan Tabatabai were already denouncing the "drain of wealth" from India almost a century before the foundation of the Indian National Congress' (1999: 56). Bayly adds: 'Indigenous anti-colonial histories in the non-white Empire could trace a much longer pedigree than has been commonly realized. These literary and symbolic resources were, after the 1880s, drawn upon by the first generation of nationalist writers' (57). Burke's emphasis on the 'looting' of India is his version of the economic 'drain.' Even earlier, another Anglo-Irishman, Jonathan Swift, condemned imperialism for being no better than piracy and plunder (Swift 1970: 258). The impoverishment of India by capitalist exploitation is the theme as well of Henry Mayers Hyndman's *The Bankruptcy of India* (1878) and *The Ruin of India by British Rule* (1907). Hyndman also penned *The Indian Famine and the Crisis in India* (1887).

5. Before Lenin, other Marxists–Karl Kautsky, Rudolf Hilferding, and Rosa Luxemburg – offered theories of imperialism. Luxemburg's *The Accumulation of Capital, A Contribution to the Economic Elucidation of Imperialism*, was first published in German in 1913. For Marxist theories of imperialism, see Victor Kiernan (1974) and Brewer (1990).

6. Variations on the theme of the economic causes of imperial expansion include the theory of 'gentlemanly capitalism,' proposed by Peter Cain and Antony Hopkins in *British Imperialism* (1993). They argue that a coalition of landed aristocrats and 'service' sector financiers, based in the City of London, pushed an imperialist agenda for two centuries and more. Imperial expansion had less to do with the Industrial Revolution than other historians have contended. See also Dummett (1999).

7. Howe does not cite either John Mitchel or Gavan Duffy; there is no reference in his index to *The Nation*. He does make a few brief references to Thomas Davis and to Young Ireland.

8. Cannadine's entertaining book echoes Eric Hobsbawm and Terence Ranger's anthology *The Invention of Tradition* (1983) (to which Cannadine was a contributor) and also Benedict Anderson's *Imagined Communities* (1991). These works by historians approximate the Foucauldian emphasis in much postcolonial studies, including Said's *Orientalism*, on the power of discourse to make things happen or to shape reality.

9. See, for example, the quotation from Captain Marryat's *Masterman Ready* on p. 31.

10. *Queen Victoria's Little Wars* is the title of Byron Farwell's book (1972) on the topic; he recounts thirty conflicts between 1837 and 1901.

11. Starting with Marryat's midshipmen novels, there were hordes of boys' adventure novels, many of them treating warfare as a manly sport.

12. By their opponents, New Women were sometimes called 'wild women' (see Linton [1891] and Caird [1892]). In Haggard's fiction, as Laura Chrisman notes, bad things happen because of 'the fatal destructiveness of heterosexuality, and femininity' (2000: 108).

13. Ania Loomba notes that Freud declared the 'sexual life' of women 'a "dark continent" for psychology' (1998: 161).

14. Like his concept of mimicry, 'hybridity' for Bhabha relates mainly to discourse. The languages of both the colonizer and the colonized blur into each other; hybridity is the compromised condition of culture itself (1994: 102–22). 'Partly

because of empire,' writes Edward Said, 'all cultures are involved in one another; none is single and pure, all are hybrid' (1993: xxv). Young argues as well that the nineteenth-century idea and ideal of culture, as in Matthew Arnold's *Culture and Anarchy*, was 'complicit' with racism and imperialism (2001: 62–89).

15. In *War of No Pity* (2008), Christopher Herbert contends that calls for retribution against the Indian rebels were partially balanced by criticism of British activities in and attitudes toward India, including calls for retribution. But the criticisms often contain encomiums to the heroic 'Imperial race' who defeated the rebels.

16. The Blunts have been credited with preserving thoroughbred Arabian horses from extinction.

17. John Rignall agrees with Said, however, in noting that Eliot 'passes over in silence the actual inhabitants of the East and of Palestine in particular. Eliot's blindness to the historical reality of the vaguely defined East is one that she shares with her contemporaries . . . [and] it must qualify any reading of [*Daniel Deronda*] as a critique of imperialism' (2000: 84).

18. 'Discursive formation' comes from Michel Foucault. One criticism of *Orientalism* is that Said tries to combine Foucauldianism with Gramscian Marxism and also with literary humanism (Ahmad 1992). But perhaps his attempt makes *Orientalism* an exemplary work of syncretic or even dialectical cultural criticism and helps to explain why it has been so influential.

19. Nash sees his study of 'counter-Orientalisms' in Urquhart, Palgrave, Blunt, and others as supplementing Said's *Orientalism*, a work which – unlike some of Said's critics such as John MacKenzie, Bernard Porter, and Christopher Herbert – he considers indispensable.

20. Other writers who expressed a reactionary anti-imperialism similar to Blunt's include Hilaire Belloc, whose *The Modern Traveller* satirizes Stanley's exploration journals, and Belloc's friend, G. K. Chesterton (see Carr 2002: 71).

21. In his later writings, including *Culture and Imperialism*, Said answers some of the criticisms of *Orientalism* by including anti-imperialist and nationalist figures such as Gandhi and Frantz Fanon, but he does not return to Blunt and Browne. See also Sprinker (1992) and Ashcroft and Kadhim (2001).

22. Estimates of the Aboriginal population of Australia at the time of the First Fleet (1788) used to be as low as 50,000. According to Stuart Macintyre, however, 'perhaps three-quarters of a million people lived here in 1788' (1999: 14). The population at the end of the 1800s may have been as low as 30,000, though by 1996 it had grown to over 350,000.

23. Brook Miller comments that 'Ideas about British superiority are articulated most emphatically in retrospect to validate confused, muddled, and – in the case of Gordon – failed foreign policy' (2005: 151).

24. The idea of 'the subaltern' was developed by Antonio Gramsci to refer to social classes and groups, including Italian peasants and proletarians, that were subordinate to and yet accepted the 'hegemony' of the rich and the rulers. The idea has been adopted by later historians, including the *Subaltern Studies* collective.

25. African opinions about white colonization were also often represented in missionary accounts, in the press, and even in parliamentary hearings (Magubane 2004: 129–52). In the second half of the nineteenth century, African intellectuals such as Edward Blyden and James Africanus Horton began to voice nationalist opposition to imperialism. Neil Parsons (1998) narrates the 1895 journey of three Africans to Britain to persuade Queen Victoria to secure their territory from the expansion of Rhodesia; their trip resulted in the establishment of Bechuanaland, predecessor of today's Botswana, as a protectorate. Other studies

of African resistance to British imperialism include Les Switzer (1993) and Terence Ranger (1967).

26. This was the same Edward Eyre who later became infamous for brutally repressing the 1865 uprising in Jamaica.

27. Robert Hughes calls the supposed total eradication of the first Tasmanians by 1876 the 'only true genocide in English colonial history' (1986: 120). That assertion is mistaken, not least because it implies that, if the extermination of a race isn't total, then it isn't genocide. On that interpretation, the Nazi Holocaust would not qualify as genocide, because it wasn't total.

28. As the contributors to Robert Manne's *Whitewash* (2003) demonstrate, there is no evidence that the first Tasmanians were 'dysfunctional' in the ways Windschuttle claims.

Chapter 3

Case Studies

Lo, all our pomp of yesterday
Is one with Nineveh and Tyre!

Rudyard Kipling

The case studies in this chapter provide in-depth explorations of imperial themes in several major Victorian literary texts. First, *Jane Eyre* and *Great Expectations* feature characters who come to Britain from the colonies and change the lives of the novels' protagonists. Anticipating imperial Gothic fiction, Brontë and Dickens narrate versions of 'reverse colonization' (Arata 1995: 107–32). Second, Tennyson and Yeats exemplify contrasting uses of Celtic mythology to express antithetical views about the British Empire. Tennyson's *Idylls of the King* is an Empire-boosting work; Yeats's poetry expresses his version of Irish nationalism and resistance to British domination. Third, despite the Indian Rebellion of 1857–8, Kipling's *Kim* and other works about India express a 'desire for the Orient' often represented by 'the Eastern woman,' but often also represented by 'the imperial boy.' Why were there so many 'imperial boys,' and what do they signify? And fourth, adventure stories about Africa mimic explorers' journals, but the journals also mimic adventure fiction. Both journals and fiction narrate quest romances, while raising the question of whether adventure – and therefore romance – would still be possible after the complete mapping and imperial domination of the globe. Both Haggard's *Allan Quatermain* and Conrad's *Heart of Darkness* answer this question negatively.

These case studies represent only a few of the many possibilities for examining imperialism and Victorian literature. From 1837 to 1901, many literary works were published in Britain and its colonies that do not explicitly refer to the Empire, but they were all enabled by it – they all breathe the atmosphere of the power, knowledge, privilege, and readerly leisure that Britain's rule over much of the rest of the world produced.

'Without empire,' writes Edward Said, there would be 'no European novel as we know it' (1993: 69). So dominant was the European imposition on the other continents that Western literature in general, at least since the Renaissance, can be viewed as an 'imperialist project.'[1]

Homecomings

Master and slave, capital and labor, male and female, metropole and periphery: history's language expresses hierarchies of domination and subordination. Taking some of its cues from poststructuralism, postcolonialism seeks to 'deconstruct' or at least interrogate these binary oppositions. Charlotte Brontë's *Jane Eyre* also seeks to deconstruct the hierarchies of gender and class. Because of Jane's encounters with Mr. Rochester and St. John Rivers, slavery and the British presence in India loom in the background; her narrative raises the issue of racial difference, though without directly challenging the racism typical of Victorian culture.

The story of Pip's 'great expectations' challenges conventional ideas about social class if not gender or race. Pip's transformation from blacksmith's apprentice to gentleman is a version of the familiar rags to riches story, minus the basic Victorian ingredient of 'self-help': Pip does nothing to gain his new status. When the source of his 'expectations' proves to be the transported convict Abel Magwitch instead of Miss Havisham, Pip's house of cards tumbles down. That Pip's transformation is due to an ex-convict in New South Wales also brings into question Britain's reliance on the colonies for its prosperity. Both Jane Eyre and Pip react negatively toward the unearned wealth that comes to them from abroad, though for reasons that only implicitly criticize colonization.

A staple of Victorian novels, emigration plots were frequently written in reverse: the colonists or the British soldiers and sailors return to influence the home-bound characters, and sometimes that influence is less than benign. Though not primarily about the colonies, both *Jane Eyre* and *Great Expectations* depict the dramatic alterations of their protagonists' lives caused by characters who return to England from the West Indies and Australia. Further, both novelists utilize the conventions of Gothic romance to render the negative, even nightmarish aspects of the encounters between the main characters and the returnees. The two novels thus anticipate the flourishing of imperial Gothic fiction from the 1880s into the 1900s (see pp. 45–52).

In Brontë's tale, Mr. Rochester returns from Jamaica with his creole wife, Bertha Mason, whom he locks away in the attic of Thornfield Hall as a madwoman. Coming from the tropics, Rochester and Bertha seem to import excessive passion, violence, and sexuality that Jane Eyre must confront and try to tame. They also bring with them a fortune that, like Sir Thomas Bertram's wealth in Jane Austen's *Mansfield Park*, was extracted from slave labor.[2] Bertha is at once the beneficiary of her own family's slave-owning practices and the victim of the predatory colonialism of Rochester's family. Her dark, 'purple face' (Brontë 1996: 328) and Rochester's reference to her mother as 'the Creole' (326) suggest that Bertha is a racial hybrid. Earlier, Jane describes Bertha's 'discoloured face – it was a savage face. I wish I could forget the roll of the red eyes and the fearful blackened inflation of the lineaments!' When Rochester responds that 'ghosts are usually pale,' Jane declares that the face she saw 'was purple: the lips were swelled and dark; the brow furrowed; the black eye-brows widely raised over the blood-shot eyes,' which reminds her of 'the foul German spectre – the Vampyre' (317).

Besides the racial clues in this description, Jane's vampire reference is one of the many Gothic metaphors applied to Bertha, but also to Rochester, Thornfield Hall, and Jane herself. Jane describes Bertha as a 'demoniac' phantom, a monstrous and racially alien 'savage' and 'hyena' (328), 'haunting' Thornfield until she burns the place down, killing herself and blinding her master. Although Jane does not witness it, this conflagration is also an intensely Gothic moment, turning Rochester's mansion into an inferno and liberating both its owner and Jane from the hellish burden of Empire that Rochester has brought to England. According to Gayatri Spivak, in *The Wide Sargasso Sea*, Jean Rhys suggests that Brontë's novel 'can be read as the orchestration and staging of the self-immolation of Bertha Mason as "good wife." The power of that suggestion remains unclear [without knowing] the history of the legal manipulation of widow-sacrifice in the entitlement of the British government in India' (Spivak 1986: 278). That Brontë had *sāti* in mind is evident when Jane tells Rochester she has 'no intention of dying with him.' Jane continues: 'I had as good a right to die when my time came as he had: but I should bide that time, and not be hurried away in a suttee' (Brontë 1996: 306).

Just as the bonfire of Thornfield Hall suggests *sāti*, so Bertha's imprisonment by Rochester as a 'maniac' (328) evokes slavery. But Jane repeatedly applies the term 'slavery' to her own situation rather than Bertha's (of course, she only discovers who Bertha is late in the novel). Thus, Jane likens her rebellious anger toward the Reeds to 'the mood of the revolted slave' (22). Later, Jane condemns Rochester's claim that '"I would not exchange this one little English girl [Jane] for the grand Turk's whole seraglio; gazelle-eyes, houri forms and all!"' (301). '"If you have a fancy for anything in that line,"' Jane retorts, '"away with you, sir, to the bazaars of Stamboul [Istanbul] without delay; and lay out in extensive slave-purchases some of that spare cash you seem at a loss to spend satisfactorily here"' (302). When Rochester asks what she will do with herself while he is bargaining '"for so many tons of flesh and such an assortment of black eyes"' for his harem, Jane replies:

> 'I'll be preparing myself to go out as a missionary to preach liberty to them that are enslaved – your harem inmates amongst the rest. I'll get admitted there, and I'll stir up mutiny; and you, three-tailed bashaw as you are, sir, shall in a trice find yourself fettered amongst our hands: nor will I, for one, consent to cut your bonds till you have signed a charter, the most liberal that despot ever yet conferred.' (302)

This 'liberal' charter would, Jane implies, grant freedom to all of Rochester's fantasy slaves – the Oriental concubines he imagines locking up in his 'seraglio.'

Is Jane's feminist and abolitionist stance compromised by the sacrifice of Bertha or by Jane's marriage to Rochester? Both feminist and postcolonial critics think so (besides Spivak, see, for example, Azim 1993). Joyce Zonana contends that Brontë's 'sultan/slave simile displaces the source of patriarchal oppression onto an "Oriental," "Mahometan" society, enabling British readers to contemplate local problems without questioning their own self-definition as Westerners and Christians' (1993: 593). Perhaps so, but Rochester is the 'sultan' in question. Brontë's deployment of 'feminist orientalism,' Zonana notes, 'is both embedded in and brings into focus a long tradition of Western feminist writing' (593) that often utilizes the discourse of slavery and abolition. At any rate, just because the degree of their subjugation to patriarchy is not so severe as that of women in 'Mahometan' countries, Jane is not claiming that she and other Western women are free.

In her incisive reading of *Jane Eyre*, Susan Meyer unravels the ambiguities of Brontë's analogies between slavery, empire, and patriarchy. Noting that Spivak overlooks Bertha's racial ambiguity, Meyer points out that Bertha appears to grow darker with each of her fleeting appearances, and argues that 'the Jamaican Bertha-become-black is the fiction's incarnation of the desire for revenge on the part of colonized peoples, and Brontë's language suggests that such a desire for revenge is not unwarranted' (1996: 69). As dark (or darkening) outsider, Bertha is to *Jane Eyre* what Heathcliff is to *Wuthering Heights*, except that Heathcliff is able to voice his passion and anger. Yet *Jane Eyre* repeatedly associates 'the qualities of darkness and imperiousness' (Meyer 1996: 79) – after all, Bertha isn't a former slave, but instead comes from a slave-owning family – and thus suggests that 'imperialism brings out both these undesirable qualities in the imperialist, that the British aristocracy in particular [as represented by Rochester] has been sullied, darkened, and made imperious or oppressive by the workings of empire' (79). Thus, the novel's 'opposition to imperialism' stems from Brontë's concern that 'the healthy heart of England,' as Jane calls it, is 'being contaminated by . . . contact with the unjust social systems indigenous to the people with dark skin,' like the sultans of Istanbul or the Jamaicans, whether planters or slaves (81).

For Jane and her author, it isn't just Africans enslaved on Jamaican plantations or Turkish women imprisoned in harems who conjure up the discourse of slavery and rebellion, it is womens' condition in general. In one of the most explicitly feminist passages in the novel, Jane declares that she wishes for a broader scope of action than the quiet routines of governessing (Rochester later refers to her governessing as 'slavery' [Brontë 1996: 303]):

> It is in vain to say human beings ought to be satisfied with tranquillity: they must have action; and they will make it if they cannot find it. Millions are condemned to a stiller doom than mine, and millions are in silent revolt against their lot. Nobody knows how many rebellions besides political rebellions ferment in the masses of life which people earth. Women are supposed to be very calm generally: but women feel just as men feel; they need exercise for their faculties, and a field for their efforts as much as their brothers do; they suffer from too rigid a restraint, too absolute a stagnation, precisely as men would suffer; and it is narrow-minded in their more privileged fellow-creatures to say that they ought to confine themselves to making puddings and knitting stockings, to playing on the piano and embroidering bags. It is thoughtless to condemn them, or laugh at them, if they seek to do more or learn more than custom has pronounced necessary for their sex. (125–6)

If *Jane Eyre* merits attention as a feminist novel, however, one must still ask, with Spivak and Meyer, what are the limitations of its version of feminism, and how does that liberating ideology relate to imperialism and to the racism evident in the portrayal of Bertha Mason? Feminist though she may be, Jane does not question the history of Bertha that Rochester gives her; she does not wonder to what extent Rochester may be responsible for Bertha's lunacy. Both she and the reader feel relieved when Bertha immolates herself, liberating Britain itself, perhaps, from this lunatic, 'savage' burden from the colonies.

For many feminist and postcolonial critics, equally problematic is how *Jane Eyre* portrays St. John Rivers, missionary to India. When Rivers proposes to Jane that she marry him and go with him to India, she refuses. She recognizes he is not doing so because he loves her, but because she would be an expedient aide to him in his proselytizing endeavors, and besides she still loves Rochester. As Diana Rivers tells her,

Jane is '"much too pretty, as well as too good, to be grilled alive in Calcutta"' (462) – perhaps another hint at *sāti*. Yet while St. John Rivers may be 'austere' and 'cold,' he is also determinedly heroic. The novel ends with Jane's praise of his heroism, a conclusion that also endorses the British imperial presence in India:

> A more resolute, indefatigable pioneer never wrought amidst rocks and dangers. Firm, faithful, and devoted; full of energy, and zeal, and truth, he labours for his race: he clears their painful way to improvement, he hews down like a giant the prejudices of creed and caste that encumber it. He may be stern; he may be exacting; he may be ambitious yet; but his is the sternness of the warrior Greatheart, who guards his pilgrim-convoy from the onslaught of Apollyon. His is the exaction of the apostle, who speaks but for Christ . . . (501)[3]

Rochester escapes from the 'hell' of Jamaica and slavery to England, though he comes burdened with his monstrous, scandalous colonial secret. For St. John Rivers, however, 'empire is the active "field" of English exercise and effort' (Perera 1991: 83), which meets entirely with Jane Eyre's and Charlotte Brontë's approval.

Before he departs for India, Rivers helps Jane become a schoolteacher and settle into an independent life, free of the 'slavery' of governessing and of the tribulations of Rochester's attentions. Comparing Rochester's offer that she become his mistress and live at his expense in France to her present independence, Jane asks whether it is 'better . . . to be a slave in a fool's paradise at Marseilles . . . or to be a village schoolmistress, free and honest, in a breezy mountain nook in the healthy heart of England?' (402). Her answer is the obviously patriotic one, affirming, despite all the difficulties she has been through, 'the healthy heart of England.' But she does not end as a school teacher; indeed, as Deirdre David contends, Jane's role will continue to have a bearing on colonial affairs, because that role is the 'reformation of the colonizer rather than the colonized' (1995: 85). Jane Eyre is 'a symbolic governess of empire' (David 1995: 80); Brontë's novel, moreover, 'is about a specific historical moment when women were called upon to be agents in the labor of both reno-vating and expanding Britannic rule' (97) – women including Queen Victoria. In other words, *Jane Eyre* expresses British women's aspirations for greater freedom, agency, and equality with men, even as it also affirms the abolitionist, reforming, and missionary ideals of the British Empire.

When Jane learns that she has inherited £20,000 from her uncle in Madeira, her response is hardly affirmative – this is another problem coming to her from abroad. She tells St. John Rivers that suddenly she is '"gorged with gold I never earned and do not merit"' (Brontë 1996:

432), and she insists on dividing her wealth equally with Rivers and his two sisters (who turn out to be her cousins). Her reaction is similar to Pip's when, in *Great Expectations*, he learns that his wealth and his gentlemanly status are thanks to an ex-convict in New South Wales. But whereas Jane can think of something useful and unselfish to do with her new wealth, Pip rejects the idea of taking any more money from Magwitch, because he feels it is tainted by Magwitch's criminal past. It makes no difference that Magwitch tells him '"what I done is worked out and paid for"' (Dickens 1989: 312).

Pip also seems unimpressed that Magwitch has grown rich through laboring as '"a sheep-farmer, stock-breeder, other trades besides, away in the new world"' (302). Magwitch tells him: '"I lived rough, that you should live smooth; I worked hard that you should be above work"'(304). In rejecting Magwitch's money, however, Pip does not reject the status that Magwitch has elevated him to. Though Pip immediately falls into debt and has creditors hounding him, he does not consider returning to the forge and the work that he had been apprenticed to learn from Joe. This may be mainly because he feels too much guilt for having betrayed Joe and Biddy. But working for his living, as Magwitch did in Australia, seems now beyond Pip's ken – or beneath his new class identity. Apart from trying to get Magwitch out of England, Pip can think of almost nothing useful to do with himself in his gentlemanly condition. He tells Herbert Pocket: '"I know only one thing that I am fit for, and that is, to go for a soldier"' (324), and in a desperate moment 'I actually did start out of bed in the night, and begin to dress myself in my worst clothes, hurriedly intending to leave him there with everything else I possessed, and enlist for India as a private soldier' (319). Soldiering was, of course, both an imperial occupation and one suitable for a gentleman, albeit an impoverished gentleman. Herbert points out that it is not an occupation that will allow Pip to begin '"repaying what you have already had"' (324) from Magwitch. Instead, Herbert suggests that Pip join Clarriker's firm as a clerk, exactly the position that Pip, using Magwitch's money, has secretly secured for Herbert.

Why should Pip feel he must repay what Magwitch has given him, especially if Magwitch has served his time and has earned the money through hard work? Why does the money seem acceptable to him when he believes it has come from Miss Havisham? Either way, like Jane Eyre's inheritance, Pip's new wealth and status are windfalls which he has not had to work for. The idea of a gentleman that both Magwitch and Pip (and apparently Dickens) entertain is of a person elevated above work – perhaps a person who can't work because he has no practical skills. Is

Magwitch's money tainted because he was once a convict, or because he has had to work for it? Miss Havisham did not work to gain her wealth. In becoming a gentleman, Pip has rejected Joe, Biddy, and the forge; in short, he has rejected working-class life. Moreover, Pip's horror of Magwitch seems to have as much to do with his crass manners (eating with his knife, and so forth) as with his criminal past. Pip is also embarrassed by Joe's bumbling manners in Miss Havisham's presence (93–6).

On one level, Pip's reaction to Magwitch is no different from the reaction of 'the colonists' whom Magwitch accuses of treating him like dirt:

> 'The blood horses of them colonists might fling up the dust over me as I was walking; what do I say? I says to myself, "I'm making a better gentleman nor ever *you*'ll be!" When one of 'em says to one another, "He was a convict, a few years ago, and is a ignorant common fellow now, for all he's lucky," what do I say? I says to myself, "If I ain't a gentleman, nor yet ain't got no learning, I'm the owner of such. All on you owns stock and land; which on you owns a brought-up London gentleman?"' (306)

According to Magwitch's thinking, a free 'colonist' riding a 'blood horse' may be his superior in Australia, but 'a brought-up London gentleman' is superior to any 'colonist,' convict or free. And yet in a round-about sense, a London gentleman's status, wealth, and leisure derive from the colonies – that is, from the work and wealth-production that take place in the colonies. After all, what returns to Pip from the colonies is in the first instance money and gentlemanly status; it is only when Magwitch, the colonist from the lower depths, returns to England and locates Pip that these become unacceptable.

It seems just fine to Pip if the source of his 'expectations' is either Miss Havisham or simply unknown: gentlemen don't have to work for their money, or even to know for certain where their money comes from. But when the source of it turns out to be someone who has occupied the lowest, most subaltern rung on the social ladder and who has gained the money in what was at first a penal colony, the nightmare emerges. That New South Wales represents the absolute lowest of the lower depths compared to the metropole is evident when Wemmick, commenting on Jaggers's 'mantrap' brilliance as a criminal lawyer, tells Pip that his employer is '"Deep . . . as Australia." Pointing with his pen at the office floor, to express that Australia was understood . . . to be symmetrically on the opposite spot of the globe. "If there was anything deeper . . . he'd be it,"' perhaps like Lucifer (188).

Of course, Magwitch is personally nightmarish to Pip, who has not forgotten the terror of the opening scene, when the escaped convict grabs him and demands a file and 'wittles.' The threat that Magwitch or the young man he claims is with him will tear out '"your heart and your liver,"' roast, and eat them (3) places Pip's future benefactor on the far side of savagery. Dickens's fascination with cannibalism has been well-documented (Stone 1994). In any case, the melodrama of wealth and social status – London gentleman versus colonists and convicts, getting something for nothing versus working for a living – plays out in an allegorical way that aligns *Great Expectations* with Frantz Fanon's assertion: 'Europe is literally the creation of the Third World. The wealth which smothers her is that which was stolen from the underdeveloped peoples' (1991: 102). To pursue that interpretation of Dickens's novel, one must substitute Australian colonists and particulary convicts for 'the underdeveloped peoples' – those who labor to produce the wealth and leisure consumed by London gentlemen. The threatened cannibalism in the first chapter suggests that substitution, and so does Magwitch's account of how Compeyson '"got me into such nets as made me his black slave"' (Dickens 1989: 331). This interpretation is strengthened as well by perhaps the most obvious Gothic allusion in *Great Expectations*. Pip says that Magwitch sometimes asked him to read in a foreign language:

> not comprehending a single word, [Magwitch] would stand before the fire with the air of an Exhibitor, and I would see him . . . appealing in dumb show to the furniture to take notice of my proficiency. The imaginary student pursued by the misshapen creature he had impiously made, was not more wretched than I, pursued by the creature who had made me, and recoiling from him with a stronger repulsion, the more he admired me and the fonder he was of me. (320)

In this analogy, Pip as Victor Frankenstein becomes the creation; the monster, Magwitch, his creator. Not self-made, the London gentleman is a made man – made in the colonies, that is, and in Pip's case made by an ex-convict. For Pip, nothing could be more nightmarish because more beneath his 'great expectations.'

Though Pip 'softens' toward Magwitch and tries to save him, that effort fails. During the attempt to get the returned convict out of England, Magwitch is injured, but kills his mortal enemy, Compeyson; he is re-arrested, tried, and sentenced to be hung, though he dies of his injuries before the execution. By then, Pip has learned that Estella, the great love of his life, is the child of Magwitch and Molly, a probable murderer, tamed by Mr. Jaggers and working as his servant. Horrified by both of her parents, Pip will nevertheless forever (in both of the endings of the novel) love Estella. He will also maintain his status as a gentleman, though not in London. Instead, like St. John Rivers at the end of *Jane Eyre*, Pip goes to work in the Empire, joining Herbert in Cairo as a clerk for Clarriker and Co.[4] Yes, gentlemen sometimes did have to work for their livings.

Thanks to Magwitch, the social class drama of *Great Expectations* is also a colonial one, with New South Wales serving as one way of measuring the social class hierarchy both at home and abroad. Another way is through Pip's growing sense of guilt: he tries to escape his lowly origins, but he learns he is chained to them by ties of affection and memory, just as he is also inexorably chained to crime, criminals, and the colonies.

Tennyson, Yeats, and Celticism

Reviewing *Poems, Chiefly Lyrical* in 1830, W. J. Fox hailed Tennyson as promising to join the ranks of those poets who 'can blast the laurels of the tyrants, and hallow the memories of the martyrs of patriotism,' acting powerfully 'upon national feelings and character, and consequently upon national happiness' (in Jump 1967: 33). Especially in his role as Poet Laureate from 1850 until his death in 1892, Tennyson often made poetry a medium for the public expression of patriotic and imperialist sentiment, as in 'Ode on the Death of the Duke of Wellington' (1852) and 'Charge of the Light Brigade' (1854). Having read the four parts of *Idylls of the King* that Tennyson published in 1859, future prime minister William Ewart Gladstone called 'the Arthurian Romance' 'highly national,' and yet both Christian and 'universal' in its appeal (Jump 1967: 250).

Begun in the 1830s and completed in 1885, the twelve books of the *Idylls* appear to constitute an epic, the genre that narrates the founding of an empire or a nation. To what extent Tennyson considered the final version of the *Idylls* an epic is unclear, however. After writing 'Morte d'Arthur' in the early 1830s, Tennyson penned 'The Epic' as its companion, apparently to explain why he was not going to write any more Arthurian poems; it expresses his doubt that he (or 'Everard Hall,' the name of the poet in 'The Epic') could produce more than 'faint Homeric echoes, nothing-worth . . .' (Tennyson 1969: 584). In 1858 Tennyson told his American publisher to 'disabuse' himself of 'the fancy that I am about an Epic of King Arthur. I should be crazed to attempt such a thing in the heart of the 19th Century' (638–9). In his *Memoir* of his father, however, Hallam Tennyson writes that after publishing the four 'idylls' in 1859, 'my father's friends begged him to "continue the epic"' (1969: 1:458). The *Memoir* reports that in 1869, after completing 'The Holy Grail,' Tennyson told his son: 'At twenty-four I meant to write an epic or a drama of King Arthur; and I thought that I should take twenty years about the work. They will now say that I have been forty years about it,' suggesting that he did indeed consider it an epic (2:89–90). And Hallam Tennyson has no hesitation in referring to his father's 'great work of the Epic of Arthur' (2:93), though later he quotes Edmund Lushington's advice that the poet substitute the term 'epylls' for 'idylls.' According to Lushington, the separate books 'were little Epics (not Idylls) woven into an Epical unity' (2:130 n. 2).

Besides Lushington, Gladstone disapproved of 'the title of Idylls,' because he thought that Tennyson was gradually producing an epic (Jump 1967: 251). As a generic term 'idylls' is antithetical to 'epic.' It connotes the pastoral mode, local ties versus globalization, peace not war, and rustic innocence versus the scheming and corruption in royal courts, cities, and empires. It is also often placed in opposition to civilization, and yet Tennyson's poem stresses the creation and maintenance of civilization as King Arthur and his knights war against the 'heathen' and slay the 'bandits.' Epic as a genre typically concerns war, with the heroes representing or founding an empire or civilization as they battle the barbarians.

Simon Dentith argues that Tennyson's 'very uncertainty about styling the poem an epic . . . is based not upon modesty about his own powers but about the anachronism of the project' (2006: 76). However, the anachronism of the *Idylls* seems to be part of their point: 'idylls' seems just as anachronistic as 'epic.' If they constitute an epic, then it is one that portrays a dim and distant past, so dim and distant that Tennyson can wrap his own rather vacuous conservatism and religiosity in mystical verbiage and yet turn Arthur and the Round Table into analogues for Prince Albert and the Empire of the Victorian era. As Swinburne sarcastically put it, Tennyson's 'Arthurian idyls' (*sic*) might more properly be called 'the Morte d'Albert' (Jump 1967: 318).

Whatever the poem's generic designation, Tennyson's patriotic and imperialist intentions in writing the *Idylls* are unmistakable. In 'To the Queen' (1873), Tennyson writes:

> The loyal to their crown
> Are loyal to their own far sons, who love
> Our ocean-empire with her boundless homes
> For ever-broadening England, and her throne
> In our vast Orient, and one isle, one isle,
> That knows not her own greatness . . . (1969: 1755)

Like Dilke and Froude, Tennyson hoped the empire would one day form a commonwealth united by race (M. Reynolds 2001: 203). In his 1886 poem 'Opening of the Indian and Colonial Exhibition by the Queen,' Tennyson says about the colonies:

Sharers of our glorious past,
Brothers, must we part at last?
Shall we not through good and ill
Cleave to one another still?
Britain's myriad voices call,
'Sons, be welded each and all,
Into one imperial whole,
One with Britain, heart and soul!
One life, one flag, one fleet, one Throne!
    Britons, hold your own!' (1969: 1358)

The nearly completed *Idylls* (1871), dedicated to Queen Victoria and memorializing Prince 'Albert the Good' as the modern type of King Arthur, form a narrative that comes as close as any poem to being the official epic of the British Empire. Nevertheless, a key problem with using the Arthurian legends found in Malory, Geoffrey of Monmouth, and other early sources is that these are Celtic rather than Anglo-Saxon materials. 'One obvious difficulty in using the Arthurian cycle as the basis of national epic is . . . ultimately insurmountable,' Dentith comments; 'whatever way you tell the story, Arthur's principal enemies are the Saxons . . .' (2006: 70). Dentith quotes J. M. Ludlow from the 1860s:

> We can only make Arthur epical by making him more and more unreal; the only patriotism he appeals to is a microscopic Welsh or Breton patriotism; no religious fervour can be kindled in his favour by making him a Christian hero against certain paynim Saxons, long converted into good Catholics by the time the first minstrel sang of him, in any but a Kymric dialect. (70)[5]

One way around this nationalist or racial difficulty might be termed assimilationist, a version of hybridization. Just as Scott emphasizes the gradual merger of the Saxon and Norman 'races' in *Ivanhoe*, so Bulwer-Lytton in *King Arthur* (1848) stresses the merger of Celts with Saxons:

> . . . the Cymrian's changeless race
> Blent with the Saxon, brother-like; and both
> Saxon and Cymrian from that sovereign [King Arthur] trace
> Their hero line; – sweet flower of age-long growth.
>
>   (qtd. in Simpson 1990: 41)

Bulwer-Lytton fails to explain how the Cymrians could remain 'changeless' by blending with the Saxons. Perhaps 'changeless' means something vague like 'staunch.' Anyway, except for making King Arthur the 'type' of Prince Albert, Tennyson does not suggest a blending of races. On the other hand, he does 'make Arthur epical by making him more and more unreal.' He is the prototype of Albert; he is also a Christian hero whose prototype is Christ. Further, Tennyson's Arthur is characterized more by what he is not or what he does not do than by any positive qualities. 'The blameless King' is so 'unreal' that Queen Guinevere complains, 'He is all fault who hath no fault at all' (1969: 1625).

Arthur is 'Cymrian' or Welsh, but at times he seems very Anglo-Saxon, at least in appearance. Victor Kiernan writes:

> Arthur's expanding kingdom is itself a small empire, subjugating or over-awing less civilized areas and bringing them within the pale of Christian manners. In the same style modern Britain was carrying fire and sword, light and sweetness, into the dark places of Asia and Africa. It may even not be irrelevant that Arthur has an exceptionally fair complexion, as if to typify the White Man ... and one of the latest-written Idylls ('The Last Tournament') gives us a remarkably Nordic vignette of a victorious Arthur on his throne, with golden hair and 'steel-blue eyes.' (1982: 138–9)

In 'The Coming of Arthur,' one of the reasons to doubt that Arthur is Uther's son is that all his relations are 'dark' – Uther is 'wellnigh to black-ness' – while Arthur 'is fair/Beyond the race of Britons and of men' (1969: 1478), glad tidings for white supremacists.[6]

Tennyson also makes Arthur's enemies unreal, or at least as non-spe-cific as he can. They are only vaguely, infrequently identified as Saxon or Germanic invaders; instead, they are 'heathens' or 'pagans,' though Ludlow complains that the actual invaders of Britain had already been converted to Christianity. In 'Guinevere,' the 'brood by Hengist left' is the clearest reference throughout the *Idylls* to the Anglo-Saxons (1726). If those Arthur defeats in the 'twelve great battles' aren't 'the heathen host' who 'swarmed overseas' (1470), then they are Celtic 'kings' feuding among themselves. Arthur and his knights defeat

> Carádos, Urien, Cradlemont of Wales,
> Claudias, and Clariance of Northumberland,
> The King Brandagoras of Latangor,
> With Anguisant of Erin, Morganore,
> And Lot of Orkney. (1473)

'Claudias' sounds Roman, but he probably wasn't; at the end of 'The Coming of Arthur,' the King dismisses the 'great lords from Rome' who demand tribute from him:

> 'The old order changeth, yielding place to new,
> And we that fight for our fair father Christ,
> Seeing that ye be grown too weak and old

To drive the heathen from your Roman wall,
No tribute will we pay.' (1483)

Often the knights' enemies are not 'heathen hordes,' but are instead 'bandits,' 'caitiff rogues,' and 'wrongers of the world' (1529) like the Red Knight in 'The Last Tournament' or Earl Doorm in 'Geraint and Enid.' In that idyll, the 'blameless King' speaks of 'cleans[ing] this common sewer of all my realm' (1574), sounding very much like a Victorian sanitary reformer. At times, too, the poem sounds like the Victorian discourse of colonization, cultivating the wastelands of the world. Arthur

> sent a thousand men
> To till the wastes, and moving everywhere
> Clear'd the dark places and let in the law
> And broke the bandit holds and cleansed the land. (1575)

Kipling might have written those lines about India. At the end of 'Geraint and Enid,' we are told that Geraint dies, far in the future, fighting 'the heathen of the Northern Sea,' but just who 'the heathen' from the North may be is unclear. In 'The Last Tournament,' Arthur says that, forming a sinful counter-Round Table in the North, the Red Knight has gathered

> renegades,
> Thieves, bandits, leavings of confusion, whom
> [My] wholesome realm is purged of otherwise,

who now 'Make their last head like Satan in the North' (1707). Arthur refers to these dregs of the realm as 'heathen,' but making 'their last head' does not indicate that heathenism will be defeated in his time; instead, it is making a come-back like an 'ever-climbing wave' (1707). Tennyson was better at doubt and pessimism than at optimism.

Though *Idylls* is the only reasonable Victorian candidate for an official epic of the British Empire, it is a very strange one, partly because it does not depict 'the twelve great battles' that founded Arthur's realm. It depicts instead only the mopping-up operations, in between love-making and tournaments, that Arthur and his knights undertake after his sovereignty is established. Meanwhile, the realm is declining and falling because of internal failures (mainly adultery). Though Tennyson frames the *Idylls* so that Arthur and the Round Table adumbrate the far greater, purer realm of Victoria's Empire, starting with 'Merlin and Vivien' the narrative no longer depicts the growing strength of Arthur's kingdom but its disintegration, ending with Arthur's death. It is a failed pastoral yet courtly utopia: 'idylls' signals an innocent past, yet Arthur's is a 'civilising mission'; the courtliness of the Round table, however, soon leads to corruption. Vivien's seduction of the old magician Merlin commences the toppling of Camelot from its lofty perch. Most of the *Idylls* are love stories, not war stories, while 'The Holy Grail' depicts a wild goose chase after that visionary symbol, as the realm crumbles. In 'Lancelot and Elaine,' Lancelot summarizes the twelve 'glorious wars' against 'the heathen,' but they are all in the past (1628–9).

Unlike the Germanic sources Tennyson might have used to write an epic about King Alfred, 'the matter of Britain' including Malory and 'some parts of the *Mabinogion*' consisted of stories that were 'already cast in the form of romance' (Dentith 2006: 71), a point that may help to explain why Tennyson called his retellings 'idylls.' Perhaps 'idylls' also suited Tennyson because of the hesitant, piecemeal way he went about composing his narrative; he worked on it through most of his career, starting in the 1830s and not completing it until 1885. Perhaps it refers as well to the relative peace that descends on Arthur's realm after 'the twelve great battles.' Finally, 'idylls' may have something to do, at least unconsciously, with the domestic aspects of the story. Tennyson's poem narrates how Arthur and his knights forged and then tried to maintain their empire through warfare against the 'heathen,' but it also narrates, like countless Victorian novels, how marital infidelity unhinges and ultimately destroys what the heroes have wrought. Arthur's empire-building is undermined especially by the faithlessness of Guinevere; Tennyson's epic reads like another version of that commonplace Victorian melodrama of the 'fallen woman,' and is every bit as moralizing. In 'Guinevere,' the 'blameless King' blames his Queen for the ruination of his kingdom. But did Lancelot and Guinevere actually commit adultery, or were they instead engaged in chivalric courtly love? If only the latter, Tennyson's moralizing subverts the meaning of that highly idealistic form of love-making. Swinburne, who was hardly a prude, complained that the chief love triangle in the *Idylls* was 'rather a case for the divorce court than for poetry' (Jump 1967: 319).

Like Matthew Arnold in 'On the Study of Celtic Literature,' Tennyson delighted in the old, mythic Arthurian materials in romance, song, and history. Also like Arnold, Tennyson took no delight at all in present-day Ireland or the Irish. The Arthurian materials were Celtic, but at least they were 'Cymric,' not Irish. Although Tennyson made three trips to Ireland, including one in 1848 in the midst of the Famine, he detested the Irish 'race.' According to Hallam Tennyson, the great poet left no record of his 1848 visit to Ireland, but the *Memoir* includes an account by Tennyson's host, Anglo-Irish baronet Aubrey de Vere, who writes that Tennyson 'was shocked at the poverty of the peasantry, and the marks of havock [*sic*] wrought through the country by the great potato-famine' (1969: 1:288). Tennyson was apparently even more shocked by what de Vere calls 'that silly attempt at rebellion [by Young Ireland] which put back all [Ireland's] serious interests for a quarter of a century.' De Vere adds: 'Half Europe was in revolt [in 1848] and the prophets of the day averred that England might any day find herself involved in a general war' (1:289). Unlike many other Victorian intellectuals including de Vere, Tennyson had nothing at all to say about the Famine. He spent a few days in Killarney, where he must have witnessed more destitution and starvation. But while there he heard a bugle 'on that loveliest of lakes' which inspired the song in *The Princess*: 'The splendour falls on castle walls' (1:292).

Toward the end of 'In Memoriam,' Tennyson contrasts the English 'love of freedom . . . in her regal seat' to 'The blind hysterics of the Celt. . .' (1969: 962). And in 'Locksley Hall Sixty Years After,' the aging narrator rants: 'Celtic Demos rose a Demon, shrieked and slaked the light with blood' (1362). That may have been Tennyson's reaction to rural violence in Ireland and to Fenianism, but it was apparently also his opinion of Home Rule: 'Celts are all mad furious fools!' (quoted in Edwards 1977: 49). In 'Tennyson and Ireland,' O. D. Edwards concludes: 'Tennyson's view of Ireland was one of naive hostility which became increasingly racialist with age' (50).

Tennyson the English patriot, Poet Laureate, and cheerleader for the British Empire soft-pedaled the Celtic context of the Arthurian legends; but precisely because they were Celtic, Irish poet and nationalist William Butler Yeats found them attractive:

> the legends of Arthur and his Table, and of the Holy Grail, once, it seems, the cauldron of an Irish god, changed the literature of Europe, and, it may be, changed, as it were, the very roots of man's emotions by their influence on the spirit of chivalry and on the spirit of romance. (1961: 185)

Yeats adds that 'of all the fountains of the passions and beliefs of ancient times in Europe, the Slavonic, the Finnish, the Scandinavian, and the Celtic, the Celtic alone has been for centuries close to the main river of European literature' (185). Perhaps noting Tennyson's equivocations about the racial components of the Arthurian stories, while also alert to the anachronistic Victorianness in Tennyson's portrayals of Guinevere, Elaine, and other female characters, Yeats compares *Idylls* unfavorably with Sir Samuel Ferguson's poem *Deirdre*:

> No one will deny excellence to *Idylls of the King*; no one will say that Lord Tennyson's Girton girls do not look well in those old costumes of dead chivalry . . . Yet here [in Ferguson's poem] is that which the *Idylls* do not at

any time contain, beauty at once feminine and heroic. But as Lord Tennyson's ideal women will never find a flawless sympathy outside the upper English middle class, so this Deirdre will never, maybe, win entire credence outside the limits – wide enough they are – of the Irish race. (qtd. in Howes 1996: 26)

Yeats became a nationalist who in the 1880s joined Young Ireland and was influenced by the ideas of Thomas Davis and John O'Leary 'the Fenian, the handsomest old man I had ever seen' (Yeats 1967: 63). Yeats's nationalism was, however, qualified by his Anglo-Irish and Protestant background and by his aristocratic, 'big house' politics. Like W. S. Blunt, he was both anti-modern and anti-democratic; in the 1930s, he flirted with an Irish version of fascism. To some of his critics, these qualifications disqualify Yeats as a nationalist, and perhaps even disqualify him from the canon of late-Victorian and modernist British – or at least Irish – literature (Krause 1996; Longley 1994: 28–30). Yet in 'To Ireland in the Coming Times,' Yeats writes:

Know, that I would accounted be
True brother of a company
That sang, to sweeten Ireland's wrong,
Ballad and story, rann and song . . .

In recent times, Yeats continues, this 'company' includes Young Irelanders:

Nor may I less be counted one
With Davis, Mangan, Ferguson,
Because, to him who ponders well,
My rhymes more than their rhyming tell
Of things discovered in the deep,
Where only body's laid asleep.
For the elemental creatures go
About my table to and fro . . . (1957: 137–8)

Yeats recognizes that his poetical investments in Celtic mythology and in the occult perhaps weaken his claim to be a nationalist on a par with Davis and O'Leary. Cultural nationalism, however, meant more to him than the politics of the moment.

For Yeats, mythology and occultism were not separate categories. According to Jonathan Allison:

There was always an overlap between nationalist and occultist interests, and his attempts at visionary experiences sometimes involved efforts to invoke specifically national spirits or gods. He took from Irish folklore a mass of beliefs involving the supernatural life of Ireland, especially in the remoter parts of the country. Underlying all this was his profound belief in the spiritual superiority of Ireland to godless, industrialized Britain. (2006: 189)

Yeats strove to be both particularist in returning to Celtic origins and cosmopolitan in elevating art over current politics and propaganda. If Irish writers and artists, Yeats believed, could achieve this dual and seemingly contradictory goal, 'The Irish race would have become a chosen race, one of the pillars that uphold the world' (1961: 210):

> I would have Ireland re-create the ancient arts, the arts as they were understood in Judaea, in India, in Scandinavia, in Greece and Rome, in every ancient land; as they were understood when they moved a whole people and not a few people who have grown up in a leisure class and made this understanding their business. (206)

Yeats adds, 'we all hope for arts like these,' and goes on to say that 'I first learned to hope for them myself in Young Ireland Societies, or in reading the essays of [Thomas] Davis' (206).

In 'Easter 1916,' Yeats expresses the tragedy of the uprising that occurred on that date. He disapproves of the violence and also of the fanaticism of the rebels:

> Too long a sacrifice
> Can make a stone of the heart.

Nevertheless, the rebels were martyr-heroes; although the ultimate result of their rebellion was uncertain when Yeats wrote the poem ('Was it needless death after all?'), he celebrates and mourns for the dead much as Tennyson celebrated and mourned the Duke of Wellington:

> MacDonagh and MacBride
> And Connolly and Pearse
> Now and in time to be,
> Wherever green is worn,
> Are changed, changed utterly:
> A terrible beauty is born. (1957: 394)

'With Caribbean and some African writers,' Said writes, Yeats 'expresses the predicament of sharing a language with the colonial overlord, and of course he belongs in many important ways to the Protestant Ascendancy,' so his situation and his politics were extraordinarily complicated (1993: 227). Nevertheless, Yeats agreed with O'Leary that 'All literature and all art is national' (quoted in Allison 2006:190). He expressed his views, including his nationalism, in part through Celtic revivalism, starting with *The Wanderings of Oisin* (1889), *The Countess Cathleen* (1892), and *The Celtic Twilight* (1893). With Lady

Gregory, in 1899 he helped establish the Irish Literary Theatre (later, the Abbey Theatre) to produce Irish plays on Irish themes, including his own plays such as *Cathleen ni Houlihan* (1902) and *On Baile's Strand* (1904). No doubt Tennyson believed that his reconstruction of the legends of Arthur would invigorate Victorian patriotism and imperialism; Yeats certainly believed that Celtic revivalism, redeploying the old stories and fables, was a vital aspect of the nationalist resurrection of Ireland, a country that had to be resurrected because of its devastation by famine, poverty, and emigration. As Declan Kiberd puts it in *Inventing Ireland*, Yeats's 'project' was that of 'inventing a unitary Ireland' through the arts (1995: 124). Many of Yeats's critics and admirers believe that he succeeded.

Yeats, comments Said, was 'a poet writing in English in a turbulently nationalist Ireland': 'Despite Yeats's obvious and . . . settled presence in Ireland, in British culture and literature, and in European modernism, he [was] the indisputably great *national* poet who during a period of anti-imperialist resistance articulates the experiences, the aspirations, and the restorative vision of a people suffering under the dominion of an offshore power' (1993: 220). *Idylls of the King* expresses the political and moral orthodoxies of the Victorian bourgeoisie and aristocracy. It contains much fine poetry, but its message is conventional, conservative, and even trite: Tennyson deplores sin, especially adultery, which he believes can cause empires to topple. His quasi-epic emphasizes the decline and fall of Arthur's realm, which undermines his explicit optimism about Queen Victoria, Prince Albert, and the British Empire. In contrast, although his political views were more complicated, perhaps even more contradictory, than Tennyson's, through his writing Yeats hoped to elevate and liberate Irish culture from British domination. This is evident in *Cathleen ni Houlihan*, in which the title character, written for Maude Gonne to perform, represents Ireland. The play renders subaltern, peasant thought with both simplicity and 'magical realism.'[7] As Michael and his family are preparing for his wedding day, they see a strange Old Woman coming down the lane; they welcome her into their home – though she does not reveal her name to the other characters, she is of course Cathleen. When Bridget, Michael's mother, asks, 'What was it put you astray?' the Old Woman replies: 'Too many strangers in the house,' and adds 'I have had trouble indeed.'

> *Bridget*: What was it put the trouble on you?
> *Old Woman*: My land that was taken from me.
> *Peter* [Michael's father]: Was it much land they took from you?
> *Old Woman*: My four beautiful green fields –

corresponding to the four Irish provinces of Munster, Leinster, Connaught, and Ulster (Yeats 1965: 53). The Old Woman lures Michael away to join the United Irishman's Rebellion of 1798 (during which Michael will in all likelihood join the long list of Ireland's martyr-heroes). His fiancée and his parents try to dissuade him, but as if possessed Michael follows the Old Woman out the door. In the play's last two lines, Peter asks Michael's younger brother Patrick, 'Did you see an old woman going down the path?' and Patrick answers: 'I did not; but I saw a young girl, and she had the walk of a queen' – the image of Ireland reborn.

Oriental Desires and Imperial Boys: Romancing India

'I meet people now who don't care for Walter Scott, or the *Arabian Nights*,' Thackeray wrote in 1863; 'I am sorry for them, unless they in their time have found *their* romancer – their charming Scheherazade' (quoted in Caracciolo 1988: 21). If both Scott's novels and the *Arabian Nights* stand for romance, then the 'charming Scheherazade' embodied it for Thackeray; she, more than any other figure including Lalla Rookh, Cleopatra, and Salomé, served Victorian writers as the representative Oriental woman, a figure of intrigue and desire. Scheherazade is 'both good and physically desirable,' Rana Kabbani notes; she is 'intelligent, pious, learned and dutiful. Yet her innocent nature is in sharp contrast to the bawdiness of her tales' (1994: 50). No doubt Thackeray overlooked the bawdiness; his 'charming Scheherazade' is above all a storyteller rather than a seraglio temptress.

Like the *Arabian Nights* as a whole, however, Scheherazade symbolizes what Ali Bedad calls 'the desire for the Orient' (1994: 15). The 'association between the Orient and sex' was more explicit in works by French than by British authors (Said 1978: 188).[8] With nineteenth-century French literature in mind, Madeleine Dobie comments: 'Like the word "Orient" itself,' the image of the Oriental woman 'triggered a series of associations involving harems and veils, polygamy, eunuchs and political despotism, and perhaps above all, desire intensified by the obstacles placed in its way' (2001: 1). In contrast to the Hindu widows the British believed they were chastely rescuing from *sāti*, 'la femme orientale' of the French writers was a figure of erotic desire to be unveiled and either figuratively or actually possessed, like Gustave Flaubert's Egyptian mistress Kuchiouk-Hanem. Further, by the 1880s, in French culture 'the Oriental woman was such a common figure of artistic representation that it no longer referred to anything beyond art itself and could therefore be marshaled to represent representation' (Dobie 2001: 6). She is just such a figure as well in Oscar Wilde's 1891 play *Salomé* (which Wilde originally wrote in French). As Emily Haddad notes, Wilde and many other writers, both British and French, found in Orientalism the means to celebrate art's freedom both from morality and from the exact representation of nature (2002: 155). 'The Orient's supposedly inherent artfulness,' writes Haddad, 'is the root of the orientalist poetics that points the way towards art for its own sake' (10).

For British writers, the 'desire for the Orient' was tempered or repressed by several factors: evangelicalism; the belief in the general criminality of Indian culture, fueled by the campaigns against *sāti* and *thāgi*; the Rebellion of 1857–8; and the repression of sexuality within Victorian culture–a repression that, however, as Foucault argued in his *History of Sexuality*, was widely acknowledged and debated. As already noted, Rochester openly jokes with Jane Eyre about his not wishing to trade her 'for the grand Turk's whole seraglio; gazelle-eyes, houri forms and all!' (Brontë 1996: 301). Rochester simultaneously expresses and represses the 'desire for the Orient.' Much Victorian writing about the Middle East and India expresses a fascination with 'seraglios.' Ania Loomba notes that 'harem stories' were not just heterosexual, but 'fanned fantasies of lesbianism' (1998: 155). Certainly the *Arabian Nights* 'helped perpetuate the Victorian notion of promiscuous Eastern women,' writes Kabbani, 'and [Richard] Burton's translation in particular gave added substance to the myth. His footnotes and addenda articulated for the West the "carnal" nature of native women' (1994: 51).

Loomba's comment about 'harem stories' and lesbianism suggests that 'the desire for the Orient' was not necessarily heterosexual. As noted in Chapter 2, Burton claimed that, in his travels in India, the Middle East, and Africa, he had discovered a 'Sotadic Zone,' in which male homosexuality was openly and widely practiced. In *Empire and Sexuality*, Ronald Hyam (1990) recounts the homosexual experiences of various Europeans in colonial contexts. The tragedy of Oscar Wilde's trials at the end of nineteenth century demonstrate, however, that it was virtually impossible for any Victorian author to broach the subject of homosexuality except in veiled terms.

Many literary works dealing with the Orient or more generally the Empire are both misogynistic and emphasize the homosocial bonding among male characters, but do not go farther than that. Thus, for example, Edward FitzGerald's *The Rubáiyát of Omar Khayyám* (1859) tamely includes male companionship among Omar's pleasures:

A Book of Verses underneath the Bough,
A Jug of Wine, a Loaf of Bread – and Thou
Beside me singing in the Wilderness –
Oh, Wilderness were Paradise enow!

(in Buckley and Woods 1965: 426)[9]

The homosocial bond between 'the old Tentmaker' and his male disciple is sketchy compared to that between the Teshoo Lama and the eponymous boy-hero of Kipling's *Kim* (1901). At the end of the novel, the Lama, with Kim at his side, 'crossed his hands on his lap and smiled, as a man may who has won Salvation for himself and his beloved' (2004: 288). Earlier, having escaped from his English schooling at St. Xavier's and 'forgetting his white blood,' Kim tells the Lama: ' "I was made wise by thee, Holy One . . ." ' (Kipling 2004: 190). 'The Little Friend of All the World' (5), Kim is also the affectionate disciple of several of the other older men in the novel, including Mahbub Ali, Hurree Babu, Lurgan Sahib, and Colonel Creighton. 'For Kim, who is practically still a child,' writes Eve Sedgwick, 'the exploration of the map of male homosociality, like his many other explorations, is still an exciting pleasure. He is too young for anyone to expect him to route his passionate attachments to older men through a desire for women' (1985: 197–8).

Though Kim avoids becoming romantically involved with the few women in the novel, no other work of British literature more clearly expresses 'the desire for the Orient.' The desire is magnified by Kipling's evident belief that there is no conflict between British rule and all of the diverse Indian cultures Kim samples in his picaresque travels. Conflict comes from outside, in the form of Russian and French meddling on India's northwest frontier. Kim and the other mainly Indian agents working for the British Secret Service easily defeat this rather inconsequential threat. Meanwhile Kim delights in his ability to move easily through all of the many exotic sights and sounds of India; he 'lived in a life wild as that of the Arabian Nights' (Kipling 2004: 5).

If the Oriental woman is an unchanging fetish and sexual fantasy, the 'imperial boy,' whose most famous avatars are Kim and James Barrie's Peter Pan, is also unchanging – he does not need or want to grow up – in part because he is removed from the temptations and tribulations of heterosexuality (Randall 2000; Rose 1992). Further, Kipling's tale is based on the same fantasy of magical omnipotence that informs most imperialist adventure fiction, from Captain Marryat's midshipman stories through Ballantyne's *Coral Island* and Haggard's *King Solomon's Mines* to G. A. Henty's military romances for boys. At the outset of Ballantyne's *The Gorilla Hunters*, Peterkin tells Ralph Rover what he's been doing since their earlier adventures in *The Coral Island*:

> 'I've been fighting with the Caffirs, and the Chinamen, and been punishing the rascally sepoys in India, and been hunting elephants in Ceylon and tiger shooting in the jungles, and harpooning whales in the polar seas, and shooting lions at the Cape; oh, you've no notion where all I've been. It's a perfect marvel I've turned up here alive.' (1861: 13)

But it is not really a marvel for the young heroes of imperialist adventure fiction, whose death-defying adventures anticipate twentieth-century superheroes from Tarzan to Rambo and Indiana Jones. This passage also suggests how British readers were expected to feel about Queen Victoria's 'small wars' – they were not much different from escapades in schoolboy novels like Kipling's *Stalky & Company* (1899). Peterkin also implies that fighting 'Caffirs' and 'Chinamen' is no different from hunting elephants, tigers, and lions, or the gorillas the still boyish heroes proceed to gun down in Africa.

Noting Kim's 'remarkable personal abilities,' John Kucich writes that the sense of his 'sadomasochistic omnipotence . . . can be felt . . . in the novel's famous opening, in which Kim overwhelms several Indian children in a game of king-of-the-castle as they fight for control of an old artillery gun':

> In this scene, Kim seems an unproblematic paragon of British triumphalism—partly because his triumph is the work of a child and partly because he is poor and Irish . . . his victory suggests his indomitable destiny, which depends not on his physical strength but on his seemingly magical powers . . . Kim's abilities are meant to seem superhuman. (2007: 161)

His 'magical powers' are also implicitly identical with those of the British Empire. Kucich cites a number of occasions in which the Lama, Lurgan Sahib, and other characters deem that Kim has something 'genie-like' about him (161). Gautam Chakravarty points out that *Kim* is one of many Anglo-Indian 'romances of surveillance,' starting with Taylor's *Confessions of a Thug*, in which the British protagonists are able to master indigenous 'networks of information' (2005: 159). The fantasy of magical omnipotence suggests one reason why imperialist adventure fiction so often features adolescent (or younger) British protagonists. Except in Gothic romances, magical thinking would be inappropriate for stories about adult protagonists aimed at adult readers. Yet the imperialist belief in the absolute power and unfailing rectitude of British rule is the political corollary of the fantasy of omnipotence.

Said analyzes *Kim* under the rubric of 'the pleasures of imperialism' (1993: 132–62). He points out that in Kipling's 'only successfully sustained and mature piece of long fiction' (132), Kim inhabits what appear to be parallel universes; he is able to maneuver through India with picaresque ease and enjoyment, even as he does so on behalf of the British Secret Service. In his pursuit of the Russian and French agents, Kim travels with the Lama, who is seeking salvation. He accepts the role of the Lama's *chela* or disciple; he also accepts the role of juvenile espionage agent, doing the bidding of Colonel Creighton. The two adult figures – the Lama and the Colonel – represent the two universes, sacred and secular, ancient and modern, Oriental and Western, twinned and yet forever segregated in Kipling's imagination. 'Oh, East is East, and West is West, and never the twain shall meet,' reads the famous line in 'The Ballad of East and West.' Yet they meet all the time in Kipling's fiction and poetry, though without changing in any essential way, a hybridity which forestalls hybridity. With India firmly in British control (the Russian threat never seems very serious, and all of the Indian characters evidently approve of British rule), India can be enjoyed from the inside, as it were; partly because of Kim's exuberance and delight in adventure, the reader gladly goes native, too. The pleasure of doing so seems harmless: like Kim himself, everything and nothing is foreign or particularly dangerous, and all of Kim's 'actions result in victories not defeats' (Said 1993: 157).

With 'Kim's chameleon-like progress dancing in and out of' a colorful, chaotic, and pleasurable India, writes Said, Kipling's novel offers the antithesis of 'the lusterless world of the European bourgeoisie' (158–9). For Kipling, the wishful aspects of *Kim* may also have helped compensate for the disappointments of the Anglo-Boer War of 1899–1902. At any rate, Kim's 'carefree meandering' (159) contrasts starkly with the disillusionments experienced by homebound characters in the novels of Eliot, Gissing, and Hardy, among many others. Kim seems magical in part because he encounters none of the obstacles that, as an Irish orphan, he would undoubtedly have faced in Britain. Kim and the Lama live by begging, but they never go hungry. As do many other imperialist adventure fictions, *Kim* abrogates the reality principle in favor of homosocial pleasure and 'British triumphalism.'

Kim's shape-shifting, trickster character belies the fact that he is as frozen in time as Peter Pan: neither imperial boy progresses toward a clear, satisfactory adulthood. It is true that Kim gets an education of sorts, both from Father Victor and from the Lama; but as the Lama's disciple, he can remain forever childlike, an image of Kipling's ideal self preserved in the amber of a changeless imperial order. Of course the real

Empire was constantly changing and often disappointing as in the case of the Indian Rebellion or the South African war, but one purpose of the imperial boy, in Kipling and in other writers of imperialist adventure fiction, was to forestall or disavow change. Imperial boys are meant to stick their thumbs in the dikes of history.

Like the Oriental woman, the imperial boy is both stereotype and fetish, himself a magical object. *Kim, Peter Pan*, and many other stories featuring imperial boys are antithetical to the bildungsroman or novel of development such as *Jane Eyre* and *Great Expectations*. In Kipling's phantasmagoric India, there is no development, no growing up, only a magical, kaleidoscopic or picaresque redundancy, the forever youthful version of the Lama's Wheel of Life. In *Kipling's Imperial Boy*, Donald Randall comments that Kim,

> still in the care of two partial and incompatible fathers, Mahbub and Teshoo Lama, is left suspended on the brink of an impossible manhood. The predicament implied by Kim's truncated *Bildung*, his insuperable adolescence, mirrors the problem of imperial consolidation, the problem of an empire that has not discovered – that may never discover – its appropriate coming of age. (2000: 158; see also Esty 2007)

Another imperial boy, Conrad's Lord Jim, does come of age, but very abruptly – he experiences no gradual maturation. This is the other, negative outcome for young men in imperialist adventure fiction – growing up entails a courageous confrontation with death. No more than in Kipling's fiction, however, do Conrad's novels solve 'the problem of an empire that has not discovered its appropriate coming of age.' Other imperial boys in the novels of Ballantyne, Kingston, and Henty venture into deserts or jungles, bag incredible numbers of tigers and hostile natives, and return home unscathed and unchanged (Bristow 1991; James 1973; Richards 1989). This is true also of Jim Hawkins in Stevenson's *Treasure Island* and Leo Vincey in Haggard's *She*.

Kim expresses Kipling's nostalgia for the childhood and adolescent years he spent in India. For his first five and a half years, Kipling like Kim absorbed the exotic, colorful world around him through the indulgent tutelage of his ayah, or Indian nurse, and his Hindu 'bearer,' Meeta. In his posthumously published autobiography, *Something of Myself*, Kipling recalls the trips to markets and temples with Meeta, the ayah, 'and my sister in her perambulator':

> In the afternoon heats before we took our sleep, [the ayah] or Meeta would tell us stories and Indian nursery songs all unforgotten, and we were sent into the dining-room after we had been dressed, with the caution 'Speak English

now to Papa and Mamma.' So one spoke 'English,' haltingly translated out of the vernacular idiom that one thought and dreamed in. (1990: 4)

When he was almost six and his sister just three, their parents took them to England and boarded them in what Kipling calls 'the House of Desolation' (7). Abused and neglected, he grew desperately unhappy; six years passed before his parents learned how badly he was being treated. Once they did, they enrolled him in the United Services College, which trained young men for military careers. Kipling wrote about the College in *Stalky & Company*, featuring three imperial boys learning pluck, loyalty, honesty, and a sizable measure of cruelty – all qualities that he associated with imperial mastery and that Kucich analyzes partly in terms of 'sadomasochistic omnipotence.'

When in 1882 Kipling returned to India at age sixteen, he felt he was returning home, and 'my English years fell away, nor ever, I think, came back in full strength' (25). In Lahore and later Allahabad, he worked as a reporter, and many of his early poems and stories appeared in the journals that employed him. He listened to the shoptalk of 'picked men at their definite work – Civilians, Army, Education, Canals, Forestry, Engineering, Irrigation, Railways, Doctors, and Lawyers' (27). He celebrated such servants of India and of the Empire in many of his stories, including 'The Bridge-Builders,' 'William the Conqueror,' and the tales featuring his white subalterns or 'soldiers three': Mulvaney the Irishman, Learoyd the Yorkshireman, and Ortheris the Cockney. Kipling detested those who, often from the safe distance of Britain, criticized the Empire and advocated Indian 'home rule.' A number of his stories express his belief that Indians would never be able to govern themselves ('The Head of the District,' for instance) or become fully rational members of modern civilization ('In the House of Suddhoo' and others).

There is no hint in *Kim* that, while Kipling was writing it, Indian nationalism had emerged as a threat to the Raj – the Indian National Congress was established in 1885 – nor does it express the anxieties aroused by the Anglo-Boer War. As Said notes, 'The conflict between Kim's colonial service and loyalty to his Indian companions is unresolved . . . because for Kipling *there was no conflict*' (1993: 146; his italics). For Kipling, 'it was India's best destiny to be ruled by England' (146); despite or perhaps because of the 'madness' of the Rebellion of 1857–8, 'the Black Year' as it is called in *Kim* (2004: 54), Kipling had trouble even imagining that there might be opposition to British rule. He thus agreed with his friend Haggard, for whom, Wendy Katz comments, the Empire was 'a phenomenon beyond accountability. No one need appeal to any actual concept of justice, peace, or security, because the Empire is, tautologically, justice, peace, and security, and it appeals to nothing greater than itself' (1987: 55).

Most post-Rebellion British writers shared Kipling's views about India and the Empire. In his *Illustrated History of the British Empire in India and the East* (1860), Edward Nolan enthusiastically declares:

> The story of English power and progress in India, and of the wars waged with Persia, China, and other contiguous countries, is probably the most romantic and curious ever unfolded. What deeds of heroism! what unforeseen and unexpected conquests! what striking and singular providences! over what variety and extent of realm the flag of Britain has been unfurled! (1860: 1:viii)

Similarly, Robert Montgomery Martin writes:

> The Anglo-Indian Empire! what do these words represent in the minds of the people of Britain? . . . They speak of dominion over a far-distant sunny land, rich in barbaric gold, precious stones, and architectural beauty, occupying upwards of a million square miles of the most varied, fertile, and interesting portion of this globe, and inhabited by more than one hundred million of the human race. (1858–60: 1:1)

For most British writers, the Indian Rebellion proved beyond doubt that Indians needed the British to tame and civilize them. At the same time, India was a 'jewel in the crown' that every right-thinking Briton wished to retain, perhaps forever.

Dozens of plays and novels dealing with the Indian Rebellion began to appear even while it was taking place (Brantlinger 1988: 199–224; Chakravarty 2005). For their authors, it was unthinkable that the British could or should relinquish control of the subcontinent. To quit India would mean allowing it to revert to the 'barbarism' and 'strife and anarchy' the British supposedly found when they first set up shop there in the 1600s (Martin 1858–60: 1:7).[10] British writers between the Rebellion and independence (1947–8) typically blur together and criminalize all Indian cultures, which they see as sunk in Hindu superstition and Muslim fanaticism (U.P. Mukherjee 2003). The Rebellion itself was just a larger version of 'the fearful audacity with which the Pindarry, Dacoity, and Thug, the trained marauder, thief, and assassin, pursued their murderous avocations, in the blaze of noon as in the darkness of midnight' (Martin 1858–60: 1:7). According to most British commentators, during the Rebellion, India was saved not from the 'feringhee' (the British), but from Indians.

Yet for Indian nationalists, the Rebellion was India's 'first war of independence.' According to Thomas Metcalfe, 'There is widespread agreement that it was something more than a sepoy mutiny, but something less than a national revolt' (1964: 60). V. D. Savarkar's 1909 *The Indian War of Independence of 1857* may have been too keen to attribute nationalistic motives to the rebels, but the Rebellion was far from being merely the superstitious response of Hindu and Muslim soldiers to cartridges greased with taboo animal fat. And it was of enormous consequence to the British. According to Gautam Chakravarty, 'the seventy-odd novels on the rebellion from 1859 to the present day show how more than any other event in the British career in India the rebellion was the single favourite subject for metropolitan and Anglo-Indian novelists' (2005: 3). Until independence in 1947, these novels 'represent the recurring obsessions of the colonial state: surveillance, knowledge and cooptation, which, hardly a surprise, are also the salient concerns of those two canonical Anglo-Indian novels, Taylor's *Confessions of a Thug* and Rudyard Kipling's *Kim*' (7).

Like *Kim*, *Confessions of a Thug* is a novel of the road. That the picaresque adventures of Ameer Ali are criminal does not make them any less exciting and exotic, and indeed links them, in a familiarizing way, with the European picaresque tradition, in which the hero – Lazarillo de Tormes, for example – is a petty thief, albeit not a serial killer. The Gothic version of the tradition, as in Charles Maturin's *Melmoth the Wanderer* (1820), renders the picaro's criminality distinctly diabolical. Taylor refrains, however, from applying Gothic rhetoric to the Thugs, perhaps because he does not need to: their horrific criminality is self-damning. At the same time, the extent, secretiveness, and daring of the crimes of Ameer Ali exercise a fascination over the reader that is both shocking and pleasurable. Like the nearly silent 'Sahib' who listens to and transcribes Ameer Ali's narrative, the reader can take pleasure in knowing that the master Thug is under lock and key, that all the horrible secrets of Thuggee can be revealed to her in the safety of home, and that the British imperial police, including Taylor himself, are stamping it out.[11]

Except for the facts that his deeds include homicide and robbery and that he is very proud of those deeds (he has murdered over seven hundred people and boasts he would have murdered a thousand or more if he hadn't been caught), Ameer Ali has all the attributes of a brave, adventurous hero of romance. 'Glory is of greater import than booty' to Taylor's master Thug, writes Martine van Woerkens, 'and so is risk over comfort. Like Kim, Ameer Ali is driven by adventure, daring, the desire to be unconstrained by rules,' though he, too, adheres to a code of honor (van Woerkens 2002: 250; see also Brantlinger 1988; Majeed 1996). In his own eyes, he is an Indian Robin Hood or knight in shining armor. 'I cannot help looking back with pride and exultation on the many daring feats I have performed,' he says at the beginning of his 'confessions' (Taylor 1998: 15). Through Ameer Ali's proud rather than guilt-stricken narrative, Taylor expresses his views about what was wonderfully beautiful and exciting and yet simultaneously degraded, dangerous, and barbaric about Indian society and culture in the 1820s and '30s. As a documentary crime novel, *Confessions* paints an India that is wildly lawless and desperately in need of British law and order; this was true as well of the many novels written during and after the Rebellion, including Taylor's own 'Mutiny' novel *Seeta*.

Confessions consists almost entirely of the first-person narration of Ameer Ali with very little authorial commentary or intervention by the listening Sahib. While the master Thug's mode may be one of hyperbole, Taylor's – or the Sahib's – mode is the opposite one of understatement: let the confessing criminal hang himself. That Ameer Ali and other Thugs treat what they do as a quotidian activity, simply one more occupation among a myriad ways of making a living, also gives Taylor's novel an air of realistic understatement. The contrast between the nearly silent authority of the Sahib and the Oriental verbosity and perhaps prevarication of Ameer Ali is stark. Yet what motive does Ameer Ali have to exaggerate or lie? He is proud of his leadership, bravery, honor, and accomplishments as a Thug, as well as of his love-life (he is something of an Indian Casanova). Ameer Ali also recounts how, like Kim, he was orphaned at an early age. He was adopted by a Thug leader whose gang had murdered his parents. Instead of being drawn into the British Secret Service, he was initiated into Thuggee, and became in turn the highly successful leader of a band of Thugs. Taylor renders the society of the Thugs as the perverse antithesis of the Raj. Except for its evil deeds, the Thug gang's strict rules, complex division of labor, secret language, and worship of Kali make it a homosocial organization similar to the British Secret Service or the Masons, to which Kim's father belonged. Moreover, the Thugs' control over the lives and deaths of their victims is another version of sadomasochistic omnipotence.

In Taylor's crime novel, there is no mystery in the conventional sense. But there is a mystery about the trustworthiness of Ameer Ali's narrative and also about Thuggee's relationship to Indian culture in general. In one of his infrequent comments, the Sahib remarks how difficult it is to understand someone who, having committed 'so many hundred murders, thinks on the past with satisfaction and pleasure; nay he takes a pride in recalling the events of his life, almost every one of which is a murder . . .' Thuggee is 'a strange and horrible page in the varied record of humanity,' the Sahib continues:

Murderers there have been in every country under heaven, from the time of
Cain to the present . . . but these Thugs are unlike any others. No remorse
seems to possess their souls. In the weariness of perpetual imprisonment one
would think their imaginations and recollections of the past would be insup-
portable to them; but no, they eat, drink, and sleep like others, are solici-
tous about their dress, ever ready to talk over the past, and would, if released
tomorrow, again follow their dreadful profession with a fresh zest. (263)

It is in part the 'zest' that gives to Ameer Ali's narrative its adolescent
energy, as if the Thug anti-hero were the mirror opposite of Kim, oper-
ating on the wrong side of British law and order, and modeling for British
readers a delinquent Oriental society that desperately needed to grow up.

Imperial Boys: Romancing Africa

Another supposedly barbaric, immature area of the world that, even
more than India, needed a jolt from Britain's imperial boys to make it
grow up was Africa. 'The Nile explorers of the 1860s,' Mary Louise Pratt
comments, 'were . . . writing in the relatively innocent decades before the
scramble for Africa unleashed European rivalries in a vicious territorial
scramble' (1992: 215). After the Berlin Conference of 1884–5, the
European powers carved up the entire continent into colonies during the
so-called 'Scramble for Africa.' The Nile explorers include David
Livingstone, Richard Burton, John Haning Speke, James Grant, Verney
Lovett Cameron, and Samuel Baker. When writers of boys' adventure
fiction take their heroes to Africa, they often follow in the footsteps of
these explorers, among whose declared motives were geographical discovery and usually also the eradication of slavery. Thus, the imperial
boys in Robert Ballantyne's *Black Ivory* witness 'the horrible traffic in
human beings' in Africa; Ballantyne cites Livingstone, who claimed that,
regarding the slave trade, '"exaggeration is impossible"' (1873: v). In his
earlier *Gorilla Hunters* (1861), Ballantyne's imperial boys follow the trail
of American explorer Paul du Chaillu, who claimed to have been the first
to discover gorillas.[12] Starting with *Philip Mavor; or, Life amongst
Kaffirs* (1865), W. H. G. Kingston wrote a number of adventure tales set
in Africa, and also published *Great African Travelers from Bruce and
Mungo Park to Livingstone and Stanley* (1874). Among other African
tales, Captain Mayne Reid penned *The Giraffe Hunters* (1867), while Dr.
Gordon Stables contributed *Kidnapped by Cannibals* (1899).[13] And the
American Edgar Rice Burroughs employed Stanley's *In Darkest Africa*
(1890) as a source when in 1912 he began writing his Tarzan stories
(Pettitt 2007: 208).

If the authors of boys' adventure fiction imitated the explorers, the explorers themselves sometimes penned adventure fiction (Low 1996: 2). In 1866 Samuel Baker published an African adventure story, *Cast up by the Sea*. Henry Morton Stanley, the 'discoverer' of Livingstone, wrote *My Kalulu: Prince, King, and Slave* (1889) as an antislavery story for young readers. Joseph Thomson, who explored much of the territory that is now Kenya, penned an ostensibly adult novel, *Ulu: An African Romance* (1888), which flirts, at least, with interracial sex (perhaps its only feature that identifies it as an adult novel). And Sir Harry Johnston, an explorer who became an administrator of British Central Africa, published yet another abolitionist story for young readers, *The History of a Slave* (1889). Finally, du Chaillu wrote a number of boys' adventure stories, including *Lost in the Jungle* (1869), *My Apingi Kingdom* (1870), and *King Mombo* (1902).

These stories and their authors' exploration journals share many features, including the portrayal of Africa as 'the Dark Continent,' an epithet that can simply mean that it is unknown to Europeans, but that obviously also has racist connotations: Africa is a continent populated by childlike, dark-skinned savages who live in the darkness of their superstitions and diabolical customs. In both stories and journals, Africa is frequently portrayed as a hell on earth, the primary locus of slavery, human sacrifice, cannibalism, witchcraft, and fetishism or devil-worship. Through the demonization of 'savagery,' 'the Dark Continent' seemed made to order both for missionaries and for the conventions of imperial Gothic fiction. But savagery could also be posed as an ideal standard against which to measure an enfeebled and effeminate 'civilisation.'

One of the writers of adventure tales who admired certain versions of African savagery and also emulated the pre-Scramble explorers was H. Rider Haggard. Arriving in South Africa in 1875 as a nineteen-year-old unpaid secretary to Sir Henry Bulwer, governor of Natal, Haggard found colonial realities, including conflict between the British and the Boers, discouraging. His major adventure involved neither exploration nor hunting; rather, in 1877 he participated in the nonviolent takeover of the Boer republic of the Transvaal. Haggard traveled to Pretoria with Theophilus Shepstone, who was supposed to work out a defense pact between the British and the Boers against the Zulus. Instead, Shepstone took command of the Transvaal; Haggard was intensely proud of helping to raise the Union Jack in Pretoria. Though Shepstone's action was a betrayal of the Boers, Haggard saw it as a heroic moment for himself and for the British Empire. He claimed that the Boers were less fit for self-government than the Zulus. He also claimed that Britain's 'mission was to conquer and hold in subjection' the inferior peoples of the world (including the Boers), 'not from thirst of conquest but for the sake of law, justice, and order.' He added: 'We alone of all the nations in the world appear to be able to control coloured races without the exercise of cruelty' (1877: 78).

The annexation of the Transvaal was followed by the Anglo–Zulu War of 1879, which commenced in disaster and ended in a pyrrhic victory for the British (Guy 1979). At the battle of Isandhlwana in January 1879, the Zulus destroyed the British force. 'Nobody, either at home or in the colonies,' Haggard declares in his first book *Cetawayo and His White Neighbours* (1882), 'wishes to see another Zulu war, or anything approaching to it' (1). The British defeated Cetywayo's 'impis' later in 1879, but overcoming the Zulus encouraged the Boers to rebel. In this first Anglo–Boer War, Transvaal 'commandos' routed the British at Majuba Hill in 1881, which also ended Haggard's brief experiment as an ostrich farmer. This second disaster brought his South African career to an abrupt close. Gladstone returned the Transvaal to the Boers; Haggard saw this 'retrogression' as a 'great betrayal,' arousing a 'bitterness' in him toward Gladstone and the Liberal Party which 'no lapse of time ever can solace or even alleviate' (1926: 1:194).

Haggard returned to Britain where, while studying law, he began to write fiction. After two little-noticed attempts at writing novels (*Dawn* and *The Witch's Head*, both published in 1884), Haggard penned *King Solomon's Mines* in imitation of Robert Louis Stevenson's *Treasure Island*.[14] Appearing in 1885, it was an immediate success. Haggard's tale is at once a treasure hunt and an exploration narrative, following the British heroes and their sidekick, the noble Zulu warrior Umbopa, into Kukuanaland. Previously unknown to Europeans, this realm of 'darkness' is tyrannically governed by savage and sadistic King Twala and is also oppressed by belief in witchcraft. It turns out that Umbopa is the true ruler of the Kukuanas. After an epic battle in which he, his followers, and the British heroes defeat Twala (the manly and chivalric Sir Henry Curtis kills him in hand-to-hand combat), the British characters make off with a fortune in diamonds, leaving Umbopa to rule his kingdom in peace. Haggard approved of savagery, at least in its Zulu form; his tale does not even hint that Kukuanaland should become civilized or part of the British Empire.

Haggard followed this bestseller with *She* (1887). Though he wrote many other novels, he is famous today mainly because of these two quest romances, both narrating the adventures of British heroes exploring mysterious regions of central Africa. A third romance, *Allan Quatermain*

(1887), has been almost as popular. Along with Stevenson, Andrew Lang, and several other late-Victorian authors, he became one of the champions of romance as opposed to fictional realism. Robert Ballantyne had earlier endowed romance with a religious significance in contrast to realistic fiction: 'we stand up for romance as being the bright staircase that leads childhood to reality . . . and culminates in a vision of God' (quoted in Hannabus 1989: 57). For Haggard, romance meant primarily adventure stories after the pattern of explorers' journals. But the journals, too, often utilized the conventions of romantic fiction, including Gothic romances, darkening 'the Dark Continent' in the process.

The late-Victorian turn to romance stemmed partly from the belief that realism was an exhausted mode. In 1888, critic George Saintsbury explained the exhaustion in Darwinian terms: the realist novel had been 'bred in and in until the inevitable result of feebleness of strain had been reached' (quoted in Arata 1995: 91). The advocates of romance claimed that fiction could be reinvigorated by a return to primitive and boyish forms of storytelling. The purpose of adventure romance, according to Andrew Lang, was to call forth 'the Eternal Boy' in its readers (quoted in Haggard 1926: 2:206). Lang believed that the domestic realism of George Eliot and Henry James was intellectually superior to the romances of Haggard and Stevenson, but romance appealed to aspects of human nature that were both universal and primitive. It brought readers closer to nature, Lang argued, and therefore in his own case closer to 'the natural man within me, the survival of some blue-painted Briton or of some gipsy' that constituted his instinctual, buried self. Romances are 'savage survivals,' Lang explained in 'Realism and Romance,' 'but so is the whole of the poetic way of regarding Nature' (1887: 690). Lang was thus agreeing with anthropologist Edward Burnett Tylor, whose *Primitive Culture* (1872) taught that many aspects of modern culture were 'survivals' from barbarian and savage stages of social evolution. Tylor also declared that 'the mental condition of the lower races is the key to poetry' (1970: 2: 533). Hence, for Lang, Stevenson, and Haggard, adventure romance was the poetry of the natural man – boy, rather – who was also closely related to the savage; romance-writing was a literary way of going native and remaining boyish (Low 1996: 31–5).

Haggard found in romance-writing emotional compensation for the disappointments he experienced in South Africa and also in love. This is especially evident in *She*, an obvious example of what Anne McClintock calls a 'porno-tropic' story (1995: 21–4), starring the most famous *femme fatale* in imperialist adventure fiction, Ayesha or 'She-Who-Must-Be-Obeyed.' Shortly before his departure from England, Haggard fell in love with Lilly Jackson, whom he wished to marry and remembered always as 'the girl with the golden hair and violets in her hand' (Lilias Haggard 1951: 32). Haggard's father prevented their marrying by shipping his son off to Africa. By the time Haggard came home in 1880, Lilly had married another man. He quickly met and married, with Squire Haggard's approval, a woman he did not find particularly attractive. Haggard's wife was a 'good and sensible' woman; but Lilly or 'Lilith' was the woman of his dreams, whom he transformed in his fiction into Ayesha, and Cleopatra, and Sheba. Unattainable and yet eternally ravishing, magical, and dangerous, Ayesha expresses Haggard's misogynistic fetishization of what Freud, with *She* in mind, called 'the eternal feminine' (Freud 1965: 490).

When at the start of *She* Leo Vincey comes of age and opens the mysterious casket his dying father had given to his guardian Holly, they find the shard of Amenartas. Its surface is inscribed in several ancient languages, recounting the love between an Egyptian priest named Kallikrates and the princess Amenartas. Another woman loved Kallikrates, however; jealousy caused her to murder him. The descendant of Kallikrates, Leo is instructed by the writings on the shard to go Africa, to find the murderess and learn the secret of her immortality, and to avenge his ancestor's murder.

In Africa, Leo and Holly discover the domain of the cannibalistic Amahaggers, ruled despotically and magically by She. The light-skinned (perhaps Egyptian, perhaps white) enchantress has lived for two thousand years in her royal necropolis of Kôr, nursing her love for the embalmed Kallikrates. Bathing in a mysterious 'pillar of fire' has kept her and her necrophilia alive; she is just as beautiful and cruel as ever. Both Leo and Holly are bewitched by her beauty; in a chapter alluringly entitled 'Ayesha Unveils,' Holly watches her do a striptease that leads him madly to propose to her.

> She lifted her white and rounded arms – never had I seen such arms before – and slowly, very slowly, withdrew some fastening beneath her hair. Then all of a sudden the long, corpse-like wrappings fell from her to the ground, and my eyes travelled up her form. (Haggard 2001: 158)

and so forth. 'Never before had I guessed what beauty made sublime could be,' says Holly; 'and yet, the sublimity was a dark one – the glory was not all of heaven – though none the less it was glorious' (159). Ayesha's beautiful – or is it sublime? – striptease has been repeated in many later versions, including the 1965 movie starring Ursula Andress. The fantasy of a white or light-skinned woman enthralling university dons, imperial boys, savages, and even beasts has also been often repeated, as in the 1933 movie *King Kong*. Having revealed the 'pillar of fire' to her visitors, and wishing to make Leo also immortal, She steps again into the supposedly immortalizing fire, bidding him to join her. But instead of revivifying her, this time the pillar of fire destroys her, transforming her into an ashen monkey. As She expires, She grows old, like 'a badly-preserved Egyptian mummy,' and shrivels up into a 'hideous little monkey frame, covered with yellow parchment' (292–3). Holly draws the moral that Ayesha, having regained her beloved (in the guise of imperial boy Leo), 'would have revolutionised society, and even perchance have changed the destiny of Mankind' (294), perhaps the way independent women, Haggard feared, were threatening to do in Britain. Therefore 'the finger of Providence' intervened: 'Thus she opposed herself against eternal Law, and, strong though she was, by it was swept back to nothingness – swept back with shame and hideous mockery!' (294). If there is anything more threatening to the imperial boy than growing up, it is a 'strong,' beautiful, independent woman like She.

The identification of romance by Lang and its other defenders with 'the Eternal Boy' and the primitive signals that it is psychologically as well as politically regressive. In the most famous story about going native, *Heart of Darkness*, Conrad explores both versions of regression. Like Haggard, Conrad also found his experience in Africa disillusioning, though with different results. Instead of producing versions of 'African pastoral' (Low 1996: 39) and compensatory romances such as *King Solomon's Mines* and *She*, Conrad wrote two African stories – 'An Outpost of Progress' and *Heart of Darkness* – that can more accurately be called antiromances. The African stories are thus similar to Conrad's Malayan fiction, including *Almayer's Folly* (1895), *An Outcast of the Islands* (1896), and *Lord Jim* (1900), in which the protagonists lose their ways and their lives. Conrad did not reject the values of exploration, adventure, and romance; he believed instead that the era when these were possible was over, superseded by the completion of the Western mapping of the world and the onset of imperialist greed and exploitation. In this respect, he agreed with Haggard, who in 1894 declared: 'Soon the ancient mystery of Africa will have vanished. [Where] will the romance writers of future generations find a safe and secret place, unknown to the pestilent accuracy of the geographer, in which to lay their plots?' (quoted in Etherington 1984: 66). In a passage from *An Outcast of the Islands* that treats the ocean as 'the eternal feminine,' Conrad mourns the disappearance of the romance of sailing; he might almost be writing an epitaph for Haggard's Ayesha:

Like a beautiful and unscrupulous woman, the sea of the past was glorious
. . . It cast a spell . . . its cruelty was redeemed by the charm of its
inscrutable mystery, by the immensity of its promise, by the supreme witch-
ery of its possible favour. Strong men with childlike hearts were faithful to
it, were content to live by its grace–to die by its will. That was the sea before
the time when the French mind set the Egyptian muscle in motion and produced a dismal but profitable ditch [the Suez Canal]. Then a great pall of
smoke sent out by countless steamboats was spread over the restless mirror
of the Infinite. The hand of the engineer tore down the veil of the terrible
beauty in order that greedy and faithless landlubbers might pocket divi-
dends. The mystery was destroyed . . . The sea of the past was an incompa-
rably beautiful mistress . . . The sea of today is a used-up drudge, wrinkled
and defaced by the churned-up wakes of brutal propellers, robbed of the
enslaving charm of its vastness. (1975: 20)

Like the romantic era of sailing, the 'relatively innocent decades' of
African exploration, Conrad believed, were over. The romance and innocence of imperial boyhood had ended abruptly with what Conrad called
'a prosaic newspaper "stunt,"' Stanley's 'discovery' of Livingstone in
1871. When the aging missionary-explorer, already a hero in Europe and
America, had not been heard from for several years, James Gordon
Bennett, publisher of the *New York Herald*, commissioned Stanley to go
find him.[15] The self-aggrandizing Stanley did just that. But there was
a tinge of absurdity about Stanley's trekking into Africa to find
Livingstone. After all, the great missionary-explorer was not a blank
space on the map; nor was he lost – he knew perfectly well where he was,
even if no one beyond central Africa knew. At Zanzibar, Dr. John Kirk,
the British Consul, told Stanley that Livingstone might object to being
discovered: 'I do not think he would like it very well. I know if Burton,
or Grant, or Baker, or any of those fellows were going after him, and he
heard of their coming, Livingstone would put a hundred miles of swamp
. . . between himself and them' (quoted in Stanley 1970: 15). Stanley duly
recorded Kirk's warning, but after finding Livingstone, he concluded that
Kirk had been misleading him. Stanley's journey resulted in the 'Dr.
Livingstone, I presume?' scene, probably the most famous moment in the
history of Victorian exploration: one white man garners fame by discovering another white man in 'the heart of darkness,' and in the process
turns Livingstone into an almost instantaneous mythical hero (Jeal 1973:
337–53; 2007: 117–32). At the same time, that scene became the subject
of countless jokes and satires, like the American Palmer Cox's comic
poem, *That Stanley!* (Pettitt 2007: 13). Tim Jeal, the biographer of both
Livingstone and Stanley, contends that, by promoting Livingstone as

saintly martyr for the cause of eradicating slavery and civilizing Africa, Stanley unwittingly undermined his own claim to have been 'Africa's greatest explorer' (Jeal 2007: 16).

Although Livingstone was apparently glad for the supplies, the letters, and the companionship that Stanley brought him (the journalist idolized his 'discovery,' which Livingstone surely found flattering), the absurdity seems to have registered with at least some of the British and American public. Members of the Royal Geographical Society were miffed because their organization had also sent an expedition to find Livingstone, and Stanley had 'scooped' them. Some of his detractors even suggested that Stanley had never set foot in Africa (Hibbert 1982: 306), while the journalist-explorer himself complained, 'The general opinion is that I am a fraud' (quoted in Jeal 2007: 138). Nevertheless, Stanley's book became a bestseller and he was lionized as another hero of African exploration, almost on a par with Livingstone. The preface to Stanley's next journal, *Through the Dark Continent* (1878), reads like a who's-who of European royalty, politicians, millionaires, and geographical societies.

Much more obviously than Livingstone, Stanley was a self-promoter; it is often easy to see through his self-puffery and self-pity. For example, at the outset of *How I Found Livingstone* (1872), Stanley writes: 'The gladiator meets the sword that is sharpened for his bosom – the flying journalist or roving correspondent meets the command that may send him to his doom' (1970: xvi). In contrast, Livingstone rarely seems to be bragging; perhaps the closest he comes is when he attributes the hospitality he received from the Makolo to his having lived among the Bakwains and earned their respect by his 'tolerably good conduct.' Livingstone adds: 'No one ever gains much influence in this country without purity and uprightness' (1972: 552). Livingstone, moreover, traveled through Africa for the most part peaceably and with minimal aid, while Stanley marched through it like the leader of an army. Although Stanley's trigger-happy version of exploration obviously made him feared, he nevertheless claimed he earned 'the flattering appellation . . . "The white man with the open hand" . . . "Huyu Msungu n'u fungua mikono"' (1969: 1:134).

Stanley's newspaper 'stunt' led to his second journey to central Africa, when the *Daily Telegraph* teamed up with the *New York Herald* to sponsor his expedition 'to complete the discoveries of Speke, Burton, and Livingstone' (1969: 1:3). On his 'new mission' to 'the Dark Continent,' Stanley averred, he might become, 'if God willed it, the next martyr to geographical science, or, if my life was spared,' he would 'clear up not only the secrets of the Great River throughout its course, but also all that remained still problematic and incomplete of the discoveries of Burton and Speke, and Speke and Grant' (1:1). Stanley promised to fill in the 'white blank' on the map of Africa (1:3), but in doing so, Conrad suggests, he helped to turn Africa into 'a place of darkness' (2006: 8). Conrad means, in part, that Stanley helped to bring the relatively innocent, romantic era of exploration to an end.

Like the writers of boys' adventure stories, Stanley also often employs Gothic romance conventions in his depictions of Africa. In contrast to the usually matter-of-fact Livingstone, Africa for Stanley is always 'the Dark Continent.' He may have been less racist than Samuel Baker or Richard Burton, as Jeal claims (2007: 10), but he was nevertheless very much a racist (Pettitt 2007: 46). Despite his antislavery stance, Stanley's use of whip and gun, both against 'natives' and against his own porters, makes it 'difficult to see,' writes Marianna Torgovnick, 'how he differs from the abusive overseer or contemptuous master' of slaves (1990: 32).

Stanley's description in *Through the Dark Continent* of setting sail from Zanzibar as the sun was setting is a clear example of his use of Gothic rhetoric. It would be interesting to know if his expedition really did set sail in the evening rather than in daylight. At any rate, Stanley produces a piece of sublime word-painting for which there is no equivalent in Livingstone, but which resembles nightfall on the Thames at the beginning of *Heart of Darkness*:

> The parting is over! We have said our last words for years, perhaps forever, to kindly men! The sun sinks fast to the western horizon, and gloomy is the twilight that now deepens and darkens. Thick shadows fall upon the distant land and over the silent sea, and oppress our throbbing, regretful hearts, as we glide away through the dying light towards The Dark Continent. (1969: 1:69)

For Stanley, moreover, Africans are like the 'dark continent' they inhabit. At one point, after Stanley's caravan arrived at a village that had perhaps never seen anything so menacing, Stanley writes:

> Then ensued a scene which beggars description. Pandemonium – all its devils armed – raged around us. A forest of spears was levelled; thirty or forty bows were drawn taut; as many barbed arrows seemed already on the wing; thick, knotty clubs waved above our heads; two hundred screaming black demons jostled with each other and struggled for room to vent their fury. (1:229)

As they often did, Stanley and his men shot their way out of this 'Pandemonium' full of 'sreaming black demons.'

While Livingstone's Africans are typically peaceful, hospitable, and amenable to reason, Stanley's are treacherous savages, either indolent and thieving or dangerous and cannibalistic, rendered bloodthirsty by their diabolical superstitions.[16] It is true that Livingstone's outlook toward Africa and Africans 'darkened' during the many years he traveled there. At first, Livingstone distrusted the 'hobgoblin' notion that Africans were often cannibals (Malchow 1996: 53). But, as Howard Malchow notes, he 'was not immune to the attraction of a gothicized rhetoric':

> His *Missionary Travels* . . . contains dark references to unexplained 'depravities' and a detailed account of premature burial – that cliché of nine-teenth-century gothic. And in his last, terrible years of wandering in central Africa, Livingstone, too, came reluctantly to embrace a fully gothicized belief in a savage cannibalism of appetite (of a 'depraved taste' for buried, putrefied human flesh). (1996: 53)

Howard Malchow goes on to note that 'Livingstone's darkening vision must reflect at some level his own failures in the tangled morasses that devoured both his health and his hopes of an African renaissance' (53). Confronting the final days of his life, and although he refused to return to Britain, Livingstone must have looked upon Stanley's arrival at Ujiji as a godsend.

After supposedly polishing off the work of his great predecessors, Stanley went on to participate in the 'Scramble for Africa' that followed the Berlin Conference. 'No longer merely an explorer and commentator on the deficiencies and beauties of Africa,' Daniel Bivona writes, Stanley became after 1878 'the agent of King Leopold assigned the task of "selling" a false vision of a pacified and politically-organized [Congo] Free State to some of the same readers who were presumably entranced by his narratives of the perils of exploration' (1998: 67).[17] Stanley's sub-sequent books on Africa – *The Congo and the Founding of Its Free State* (1885) and *In Darkest Africa; or, The Quest, Rescue and Retreat of Emin, Governor of Equatoria* (1890) – he wrote as Leopold's agent. The first book is an advertisement touting the many benefits that would flow from Leopold's private colony in central Africa. The second book is ironic in part because, like Livingstone and also like Kurtz in *Heart of Darkness*, Emin Pasha did not want to be rescued or to return to civilization.

When Conrad, inspired by Livingstone, went to the Congo in 1890, also as an employee of King Leopold, he was appalled by what he saw. In both his 'Congo Diary' and *Heart of Darkness*, Conrad bears witness to the atrocities that, starting in the late 1880s, grew into an international scandal. However, just as Stanley portrays his journey as an epic har-rowing of hell, demonizing Africans in the process, so Conrad's Marlow likens his journey up the Congo River to a nightmare trip into the under-world. Marlow's Gothic journey also resembles Stanley's search for Livingstone, except that, instead of discovering a saintly missionary,

Marlow discovers Kurtz. And it seems likely that Stanley (but not Livingstone) was one of Conrad's models for Kurtz. 'Conrad does not debunk the myth of the Dark Continent: Africa is the location of his hell on earth. But at the center of that hell is Kurtz, the would-be civilizer, the embodiment of Europe's highest and noblest values, radiating darkness' (Brantlinger 1988: 193).

Conrad reverses the positive and negative poles that Livingstone, Stanley, Haggard, and other imperialist writers affirmed. The white man Stanley found at Ujiji he helped transform into a martyr of missionary endeavor, civilization, progress, and the British Empire. The white man Marlow finds in Conrad's story is the Satan in the lowest circle – the Inner Station – of the Inferno of King Leopold's Congo. So, too, Conrad may have had Haggard's *She* in mind when, instead of a white *femme fatale* dominating an African necropolis, he depicts the 'wild and gorgeous apparition' of an African woman who is apparently Kurtz's mistress and the erotic antithesis of Kurtz's pale-faced, repressed, and deluded 'Intended' (2006: 76). Marlow reinforces the Intended's illusions about Kurtz and his civilizing mission by lying to her, telling her Kurtz's final words were her name, and not 'The horror! The horror!'

Just as the Oriental woman represents 'the desire for the Orient,' both Haggard's She and Conrad's 'barbarous and superb' African woman represent the allure of Africa, including the 'porno-tropic' potential of a release from civilized sexual repression and prudery. They are incarnations of the colonizer's desire for the Other–disavowed, however, by the spectacular death of She in 'the pillar of fire'and by Marlow's lie to Kurtz's Intended. In the last image Marlow gives us of the African woman she is stretching 'tragically her bare arms after us over the sombre and glittering river' (84). Perhaps 'tragically' implies her sorrow at losing Kurtz, but that – like much else in Marlow's dark narrative – is obscure.

Stanley and Leopold claimed that the purpose of colonizing the Congo was philanthropic: the aims were to end the slave trade, to bring civilization and Christianity to the savages, and to add to geographical knowledge about 'the Dark Continent.' Leopold, writes Adam Hochschild, 'so impressed people with his vigorous denunciations of the slave trade that he was elected honorary president of the Aborigines Protection Society, a venerable British human rights organization' (1998: 92). But what Conrad saw in 1890 was slave labor maintained by terror and torture, visited upon Africans by Leopold's agents. During Leopold's private colonization of the Congo, as many as 10,000,000 Africans may have been killed, a genocide on the scale of the Holocaust (Hochschild 1998: 233).

The scandal began to emerge with the 1891–4 war between Leopold's army and Arab slave traders. Conrad probably learned about the war first in the press, but he may also have read Captain Sidney Hinde's 1897 *The Fall of the Congo Arabs*. Hinde and a number of the other Europeans involved in the war are all possible models for Kurtz in *Heart of Darkness*. The fighting involved numerous atrocities; Hinde declared that many of the combatants on both sides were 'cannibals' who indulged in 'disgusting banquets' (1897: 69):

> What struck me most in these expeditions [which Hinde himself helped to lead] was the number of partially cut-up bodies I found in every direction for miles around. Some were minus the hands and feet, and some with steaks cut from the thighs or elsewhere; others had the entrails or the head removed, according to the taste of the individual savage. (131)

Whatever the horrors of the 1891–4 war, they were more than matched by the horrors practiced by Leopold's Force Publique under European officers like Hinde. The Europeans, assisted by African soldiers, organized the slave labor that in 1890 was extracting tons of ivory from the Congo and that, soon after Conrad had been there, began to extract what the Congo Reform Association, under the leadership of Edmund Morel, called 'red rubber.' Writing about 'cruelty in the Congo Free State,' E. J. Glave declared that Leopold's forces had not 'suppressed slavery, but established a monopoly by driving out the Arab and Wangwana competitors':

> Sometimes the natives are so persecuted that they [take revenge] by killing and eating their tormentors. Recently the state post on the Lomami lost two men killed and eaten by the natives. Arabs were sent to punish the natives; many women and children were taken, and twenty-one heads were brought to [Stanley Falls], and have been used by Captain Rom as a decoration round a flower-bed in front of his house. (1897: 706)

Needless to say, Captain Rom must be considered one of the originals of Kurtz, whose Inner Station is also decorated with skulls.

'For Conrad,' writes Felix Driver, 'the romance of exploration led inexorably to disenchantment'; the final triumphs of geographical discovery 'marked the irreversible closure of the epoch of open spaces, the end of an era of unashamed heroism. The modern traveller, he wrote, was "condemned to make his discoveries on beaten tracks"; or worse, to find his romantic dreams shattered by mere opportunists and fortune-hunters' (2000: 4). Driver adds: 'Nostalgia for an age of genuine exploration in unmapped territory was nothing new even in Conrad's time: his distrust of modern tourism in the age of steam travel and popular guidebooks was utterly conventional' (5). What was not conventional was Conrad's transformation of his disenchantment into the masterpiece of imperial Gothic fiction. *Heart of Darkness* is a literary achievement of the highest order not just because its author was a great stylist and a master storyteller, but also because, as Benita Parry writes,

> by revealing the disjunctions between high-sounding rhetoric and sordid ambitions and indicting the purposes and goals of a civilisation dedicated to global . . . hegemony, Conrad's writings [are] more destructive of imperialism's ideological premises than [are] the polemics of his contemporary opponents of empire. (1983: 10)

In contrast to Conrad's, Stanley's reaction to the revelations of atrocities in the Congo was muted, to say the least. He may have been 'privately unhappy' about those revelations, as Clare Pettitt suggests (2007: 199); but he did not publicly denounce Leopold or the bloodletting he knew was happening in 'the Heart of Darkness.' Perhaps Stanley was only an 'unwitting begetter' of the 'crimes against humanity' in the Congo (Jeal 2007: 452) and perhaps he could not have foreseen the full extent of their horror, but once he learned about them, he did not participate in the growing international protest against them. Stanley died in 1904, a year before his friend and admirer, Mark Twain, published his devastating satire, *King Leopold's Soliloquy*, for the Congo Reform Association.

In 'Geography and Some Explorers,' Conrad expresses the thrill he experienced as a youngster daydreaming over the blank spaces on the map of Africa and contrasts it to the disappointment he felt on arriving at Stanley Falls in King Leopold's Congo in 1890: 'A great melancholy descended on me . . . there was . . . no great haunting memory . . . only the unholy recollection of a prosaic newspaper "stunt" and the distasteful knowledge of the vilest scramble for loot that ever disfigured the history of human conscience and geographical exploration. What an end to the idealized realities of a boy's daydreams! I wondered what I was doing there' (1926: 17). Given the centuries of the European and American slave trade, both Stanley and Conrad were late arrivals at the horrific banquet during which the West feasted upon the dark bodies of 'the Dark Continent.' Conrad was at best a reluctant participant in Western imperialism; Stanley was not at all reluctant, and neither was Livingstone: the two explorers both identified the British Empire with civilization and saw themselves as bringing light and salvation to 'the Dark Continent.' In his *Discourse on Colonialism* (1950), Aimé Césaire declared: 'the great historical tragedy of Africa has been not so much that it was too late in making contact with the rest of the world, as the manner in which that contact was brought about; that Europe began to propagate [and emigrate] at a time when it had fallen into the hands of the most unscrupulous financiers and captains of industry' (1972: 23) – men like Cecil Rhodes, King Leopold, and Conrad's Mr. Kurtz. Césaire could have dated the time of contact much earlier, however, to the beginnings of the European version of the slave trade in the fifteenth century.

Coda

'The final scandal of empire,' writes Nicholas Dirks, 'is that empire has not yet been consigned to the past tense once and for all' (2006: 35). On the contrary, since World War II and the era of decolonization, the United States has carried on where Britain supposedly left off. The US has not formally colonized other countries, but it hasn't needed to: because of its economic and military power, the US has imposed its will on much of the rest of the world. The proponents of America's 'new imperialism' frequently claim that it is as benign as its British predecessor, and they often unabashedly cite Kipling's injunction to the US, during the Spanish–American War, to 'take up the white man's burden.' For instance, in *America's Imperial Burden*, Ernest Lefever quotes 'The White Man's Burden' approvingly (while ignoring its racism) in support of his argument that the British Empire was mainly a good thing:

> Conquest, suppression, and racial arrogance aside, the enduring legacy of Britain's long 'dominion over palm and pine' has been civilizing and largely benign. The British brought Christianity, education, medicine, law, and a sense of civic obligation to its colonial subjects – assets that enabled, indeed encouraged, them to demand independence. (1999: 22–3)

So, too, according to Lefever, America may sometimes behave arrogantly toward other countries, but the results of its imperial activities are generally 'benign' and liberating. To arrive at that conclusion, however, Lefever ignores such unpleasant facts as the Philippine–American War or President Nixon's secret bombing campaign in Cambodia. Despite the years of bloodshed and the ultimate defeat of the US, Lefever thinks that the American intervention in Vietnam prevented worse. According to him, when the US withdrew from Vietnam, Pol Pot and the Khmer Rouge arrived, and the Cambodian genocide began (104–5). But this does not take into account the devastating effects of the American bombing campaign on that fragile society, much less US support of Pol Pot's regime (Kiernan 2002: 385).

Also in the Kipling camp, Niall Ferguson argues that 'just like the British Empire before it, the American Empire unfailingly acts in the name of liberty, even when its own self-interest is manifestly uppermost' (2004: 316). Given America's record of subverting democratically elected governments such as Allende's in Chile while supporting dictators such as Pinochet – or for that matter, Sadam Hussein in the 1980s – the notion that it 'unfailingly acts in the name of liberty' is either naive or disingenuous. Lefever, Ferguson, and the other cheerleaders for America's neo-imperialism are using what John Hobson in *Imperialism* (1902) calls 'masked words.' Hobson borrows that phrase from John Ruskin's *Sesame and Lillies* (1864). According to Ruskin:

> There are masked words droning and skulking about us in Europe just now which nobody understands, but which everybody uses and most people will also fight for, live for, or even die for, fancying they mean this or that or the other of things dear to them. There never were creatures of prey so mischievous, never diplomatists so cunning, never poisons so deadly, as these masked words. (quoted in Hobson 1980: 207 n. 1)

Hobson recognizes that the ideology of imperialism in general consists of 'masked words.' He comments that 'imperialism has been floated on a sea of vague, shifty, well-sounding phrases which are seldom tested by close contact with fact' (206). Notions of civilizing the uncivilized, Christianizing the heathen, and bestowing the benefits of free trade too often provide comfort and cover for greed, power, territorial aggrandizement, and genocide.

As this study has demonstrated, nineteenth-century British literature often served as a purveyor of 'masked words' concerning the British Empire. In modern and postmodern literature, film, and other media, imperialism is frequently recollected nostalgically, also in 'masked words,' for instance in the remakes of *King Solomon's Mines* and *She* or in the Indiana Jones movies (Rosaldo 1998). But nineteenth-century authors did not always look favorably on imperialism: from William Blake and Percy Bysshe Shelley to William Morris, Wilfrid Scawen Blunt, and John Hobson, a sizable number of British authors criticized imperialism from various perspectives. Then, too, much Romantic and Victorian writing expressed criticism or ambivalence about specific aspects of the Empire – about the Opium Wars, for example, or the extinction of the indigenous Tasmanians.

It is ironic, however, that Ruskin is the source of the notion of 'masked words.' There was no more avid booster of the British Empire than Ruskin, who in his 1870 Slade lectures at Oxford declared that Britain's 'destiny' was 'the highest ever set before a nation': 'We are still unregenerate in race; a race mingled of the best northern blood. We are not yet dissolute in temper, but still have the firmness to govern, and the grace to obey.' Therefore, Britain must either 'Reign or Die':

> And this is what she must either do, or perish: she must found colonies as fast and as far as she is able, formed of her most energetic and worthiest men; – seizing every piece of fruitful waste ground she can set her foot on, and there teaching these her colonists that their chief virtue is to be fidelity to their country, and that their first aim is to be to advance the power of England by land and sea. (1905: 41)

Many other Victorian writers – Thomas Carlyle, Alfred Tennyson, Charles Kingsley, Robert Ballantyne, James Anthony Froude, Rider Haggard, W. E. Henley, Conan Doyle, Rudyard Kipling, Henry Newbolt – agreed with Ruskin, who fails to recognize his own 'masked words' about race, colonization, and patriotism.

In *Heart of Darkness*, Kurtz provides an example of 'masked words' in the pamphlet he has written for 'the International Society for the Suppression of Savage Customs.' Marlow says that it 'gave me the notion of an exotic Immensity ruled by an august Benevolence. This was the unbounded power of eloquence' in an apparently humanitarian cause. But at the end of the pamphlet Kurtz has scrawled: 'Exterminate all the brutes!' (Conrad 2006: 49–50).

Notes

1. Firdous Azim contends that 'the novel is an imperialist project, based on the forceful eradication and obliteration of the Other' (1993: 37). While the actual 'obliteration of the Other' involved the genocidal extinction of indigenous populations, Azim means the annihilation of the Other in novels that depict the formation of 'a sovereign subject.' In domestic realism, the goal is typically the protagonist's attainment of mature selfhood, signaled by the achievement of economic security and marriage. But there is no such ending for non-European 'Others.' When they appear in domestic novels, they are minor characters to be used, pitied, or laughed at, like the 'Native' in *Dombey and Son*.
2. On the significance of slavery in *Mansfield Park*, see Said (1993: 84–97).
3. Greatheart and Apollyon are references to John Bunyan's *Pilgrim's Progress*.
4. Egypt was not yet part of the British Empire, but it was a staging point for transporting people and goods between Britain and India.
5. It is unclear what Ludlow is saying about the conversion of the Saxons to Christianity, however. If Arthur was fighting them in the early 500s, they were not yet converted.
6. In *The Races of Britain* (1885), John Beddoe offered a pseudo-scientific 'index' of Celtic 'nigrescence,' or blackness, arguing that that race was somehow Africanoid or more primitive than Anglo-Saxons; see Curtis (1968: 66–73).

7. For 'magical realism' see Cuddon (1999: 487–8). Yeats's *Cathleen ni Houlihan* can be usefully compared to George Bernard Shaw's play about Ireland, *John Bull's Other Island* (1904), which offers a non-magical (or simply realistic) depiction of English–Irish relations.

8. Homi Bhabha contends that racial stereotypes are fetishes, expressing both desire and loathing (1994: 66–74). They acknowledge difference yet disavow it through striving to 'fix' or control it in a system of ahistorical essences (black is always inferior to white; the Orient is inherently unprogressive; savages are self-exterminating; and so on). In the case of the fetishized Oriental woman, desire outweighs loathing.

9. *The Rubáiyát* is a creative translation; FitzGerald is usually credited with producing a semi-original work, based on Omar's quatrains (the Persian *rubái* means a four-line verse).

10. In *War of No Pity*, Christopher Herbert (2008) demonstrates that Martin and other commentators on the Rebellion were often critical of British attitudes and activities in India leading up to 1857. That did not prevent Martin or the others from celebrating British heroism or from viewing India, without British rule, as anarchistic and prone to criminality.

11. Caroline Reitz argues that 'the Thug Police became a model for future policing' in Britain 'as well as a benchmark of good government in India' (2004:28). She also accords *Confessions of a Thug* a prominent place in the development of detective fiction, and contends that later detectives – Inspector Bucket in *Bleak House*, Sergeant Cuff in *The Moonstone*, and Sherlock Holmes – are figures of imperial and not just domestic authority.

12. See du Chaillu, *Explorations and Adventures in Central Africa; with Accounts of the . . . Chase of the Gorilla . . .* (1861).

13. Kingston also penned *In the Wilds of Africa; A Tale for Boys* (1871), *Two Supercargoes; or, Adventure in Savage Africa* (1878), and *Hendricks the Hunter; or, The Border Farm: A Tale of Zululand* (1879). Reid wrote *The Bush Boys* (1855) and *The Young Yagers; or, A Narrative of Hunting Adventures in Southern Africa* (1856). Among later writers, Henty emphasized wars in Africa rather than exploration or hunting in *The March to Coomasie* (1874) and *By Sheer Pluck: A Tale of the Ashanti War* (1884).

14. And also in imitation of earlier adventure novels, such as Hugh Walmsley's *The Ruined Cities of Zululand* (1869). See Chrisman (2000: 39).

15. Tim Jeal believes that going to find Livingstone was Stanley's idea, not Bennett's as Stanley claims (2007: 10).

16. Other explorers also painted Africans in diabolical hues. Richard Burton identifies fetishism with devil-worship, as most of them did (1961: 2:326). Burton claimed that Africans were doomed by their 'negro instincts' to remain uncivilized, but they could still labor for the white man to turn Africa into a profitable place for colonization (1967: 311). And Samuel Baker declared that 'the African . . . will assuredly relapse into an idle and savage state, unless specially governed and forced by industry' (1962: 1:211).

17. Perhaps Stanley's touting of the Congo Free State was ingenuous, as Bivona claims; in 1885, Stanley could not have foreseen the horrors of exploitation and extermination that grew from about 1890 on. Jeal's view that Stanley was 'deceived' by Leopold, however, needs to be squared with George Washington Williams's *Open Letter* of 1890, which condemns the fraudulence Stanley used to get Congolese chiefs to sign treaties empowering Leopold (Hochschild 1998: 109–10).

Primary Sources

Allen, Grant [1895] (1975), *The British Barbarians: A Hilltop Novel*, New York: Arno Press.

Baker, Samuel White [1866] (1962), *The Albert N'yanza, Great Basin of the Nile and Exploration of the Nile Sources*, 2 vols, London: Sidgwick and Jackson.

Ballantyne, Robert [1858] (1990), *The Coral Island: A Tale of the Pacific Ocean*, Oxford: Oxford University Press.

——(1861), *The Gorilla Hunters: A Tale of the Wilds of Africa*, London: Nelson.

——(1873), *Black Ivory: A Tale of Adventure among the Slavers of East Africa*, London: James Nisbet.

Belloc, Hilaire (1970), *Complete Verse*, London: Duckworth.

Blunt, Wilfrid Scawen [1914] (1968), *The Poetical Works of Wilfrid Scawen Blunt*, 2 vols, Grosse Point, MI: Scholarly Press.

——[1907] (1922), *Secret History of the English Occupation of Egypt: Being a Personal Narrative of Events*, New York: Knopf.

Bonwick, James [1870] (1970), *The Last of the Tasmanians*, New York: Johnson Reprint Company.

Brontë, Charlotte [1847] (1996), *Jane Eyre*, London: Penguin.

Bulwer-Lytton, Edward (1849), *The Caxtons: A Family Picture*, London: Routledge.

Burton, Richard F. [1855] (1964), *Personal Narrative of a Pilgrimage to Al-Madinah and Meccah*, 2 vols, New York: Dover.

——[1856] (1894), *First Footsteps in East Africa; or, An Exploration of Harar*, 2 vols, London: Tylston and Edwards.

——[1861] (1961), *Lake Regions of Central Africa*, 2 vols, New York: Horizon.

——[1876] (1967), *Two Trips to Gorilla Land and the Cataracts of the Congo*, New York: Johnson Reprints.

——(1886), *The Book of the Thousand Nights and a Night*, 10 vols, London: Burton Club.

Byron, Lord George (1980), *The Complete Poetical Works*, 4 vols, ed. Jerome McGann, Oxford: Oxford University Press.

Caird, Mona (1892), 'A Defense of the so-called "wild women,"' *The Nineteenth Century*, 31 (1892), pp. 811–29.

Callwell, Colonel C. E. [1899] (1996), *Small Wars: Their Principles and Practice*, 3rd edn, Lincoln: University of Nebraska Press.

Carlyle, Thomas [1843] (1965), *Past and Present*, ed. Richard Altick, New York: New York University Press.

——[1849] (1968), 'The nigger question,' *English and Other Critical Essays*, London: Dent, pp. 303-33.

——(1850), *Latter-Day Pamphlets*, London: Chapman and Hall.

——(1964), *Sartor Resartus; On Heroes and Hero-Worship*, London: Dent.

Chambers, Robert [1844] (1969), *Vestiges of the Natural History of Creation*, New York: Humanities Press.

——[1896] (1975), *The Outcast of the Islands*, Harmondsworth: Penguin.

Conrad, Joseph [1899] (2006), *Heart of Darkness*, New York: W. W. Norton.

——[1900] (1989), *Lord Jim*, London: Penguin Books.

——(1926), 'Geography and some explorers,' *Last Essays*, London: Dent, pp. 1–21.

Corelli, Marie [1886] (1973), *A Romance of Two Worlds*, Blauvelt, NY: Rudolf Steiner.

Crèvecoeur, Hector St. John (1986), *Letters of an American Farmer and Sketches of Eighteenth-Century America*, New York: Penguin.

Darwin, Charles (1962), *The Voyage of the Beagle*, Garden City, NY: Doubleday.

De Quincey, Thomas (2001), *The Works of Thomas De Quincey*, vol. 18, ed. Edmund Baxter, London: Pickering and Chatto.

Dickens, Charles [1848a] (1989), *Dombey and Son*, Oxford: Oxford University Press.

——[1848b] (1996), 'Review: *Narrative of Expedition to River Niger*,' *Dickens's Journalism*, 2 vols, ed. Michael Slater, Columbus: Ohio State University Press, vol. 2, pp. 108–26.

——[1850] (1989), *David Copperfield*, Oxford: Oxford University Press.

——[1861] (1989), *Great Expectations*, Oxford: Oxford University Press.

Dilke, Charles Wentworth [1868] (1869), *Greater Britain: A Record of Travel in English-Speaking Countries during 1866 and 1867*, 2 vols, London: Macmillan.

Disraeli, Benjamin [1847] (n.d.), *Tancred; or, the New Crusade*, The Bradenham Edition, vol. 10, New York: Knopf.

Doyle, Arthur Conan [1888] (1909), *The Mystery of Cloomber*, Leipzig: Tauchnitz.

Du Chaillu, Paul (1861), *Explorations and Adventures in Central Africa; with Accounts of the . . . Customs of the People, and of the Chase of the Gorilla,*

London: John Murray.

Duffy, Sir Charles Gavan (1881), *Young Ireland: A Fragment of Irish History, 1840–1850*, New York: D. Appleton.

Eden, Emily [1866] (1937), *Up the Country: Letters Written to Her Sister from the Upper Provinces of India*, ed. Edward Thompson, London: Oxford University Press.

Eliot, George [1876] (1967), *Daniel Deronda*, Harmondsworth: Penguin Books.

——[1879] (1994), *Impressions of Theophrastus Such*, ed. Nancy Henry, Iowa City: University of Iowa Press.

——(1985), *Selections from George Eliot's Letters*, ed. Gordon Haight, New Haven: Yale University Press.

Freud, Sigmund [1899] (1965), *The Interpretation of Dreams*, New York: Avon Books.

Froude, James Anthony (1886), *Oceana, or England and Her Colonies*, London: Longmans, Green.

Glave, E. J. (1897), 'Cruelty in the Congo Free State,' *Century Magazine* 54 (Sept.), pp. 699–715.

Grant, James (1868), *First Love and Last Love: A Tale of the Indian Mutiny*, 3 vols, London: Routledge.

Green, J. R. [1874] (1879), *A Short History of the English People*, New York: Hayser.

Haggard, H. Rider (1877), 'The Transvaal,' *Macmillan's Magazine* 36 (May), pp. 71–9.

——(1882), *Cetywayo and His White Neighbours; or, Remarks on Recent Events in Zululand, Natal, and the Transvaal*, London: Trübner.

——[1885] (2002), *King Solomon's Mines*, Peterborough, Ontario: Broadview.

——[1887] (2001), *She*, London: Penguin.

——(1926), *The Days of My Life*, 2 vols, London: Longmans, Green.

——(1951), *She, King Solomon's Mines, Allan Quatermain*, New York: Dover.

Hemans, Felicia (1914), *The Poetical Works of Felicia Dorothea Hemans*, Oxford: Oxford University Press.

Henty, G. A. (1884), *By Sheer Pluck*, London: Blackie.

Hinde, Captain Sidney L. (1897), *The Fall of the Congo Arabs*, London: Methuen.

Hobson, John A. [1902] (1980), *Imperialism: A Study*, Ann Arbor: University of Michigan Press.

Hyndman, Henry Meyer (1886), *The Bankruptcy of India*, London: Swan Sonnenschein, Lowrey.

James, Henry (1865), 'Miss Braddon,' *The Nation* 1 (9 Nov.), pp. 593–4.

Johnston, Sir Harry H. (1906), *British Central Africa: An Attempt to Give Some Account of a Portion of the Territories under British Influence North of the Zambesi*, 3rd edn, London: Methuen.

Kemble, John Mitchell [1848] (1876), *The Saxons in England. A History of the English Commonwealth till the Period of the Norman Conquest*, 2 vols, London: Bernard Quaritch.

Kendall, Henry (1966), *The Poetical Works of Henry Kendall*, ed. T. T. Reed, Adelaide: Libraries Board of South Australia.

Kingsley, Charles [1855] (1941), *Westward Ho!*, New York: Dodd, Mead.

Kingsley, Henry [1859] (1924), *The Recollections of Geoffrey Hamlyn*, London: Oxford University Press.

Kingston, William Giles Henry [1851] (1906), *Peter the Whaler*, London: J. M. Dent.

Kipling, Rudyard [1901] (2004), *Kim*, New York: Modern Library.

——[1937] (1990), *Something of Myself*, ed. Thomas Pinney, Cambridge: Cambridge University Press.

——(1982), *Kipling: Interviews and Recollections*, ed. Harold Orel, 2 vols, Totowa, NJ: Barnes and Noble.

Knox, Robert [1850] (1969), *The Races of Men: A Fragment*, Miami: Mnemosyne.

Lane, Edward W. [1836] (1963), *Manners and Customs of the Modern Egyptians*, London: Dent.

Lang, Andrew (1887), 'Realism and romance,' *Contemporary Review* 52 (Nov.), pp. 683–93.

Linton, Eliza Lynn (1891), 'The wild women,' *The Nineteenth Century* 30, pp. 79–88.

Livingstone, David [1857] (1972), *Missionary Travels and Researches in South Africa,* Freeport, NY: Books for Libraries Press.

Macaulay, Thomas Babington [1835] (1967), 'Minute on Indian education,' *Macaulay: Prose and Poetry*, ed. G. M. Young, Cambridge, MA: Harvard University Press, pp. 719–30.

——[1840] (1967), 'Lord Clive,' *Macaulay: Prose and Poetry*, pp. 306–73.

MacGregor, John (1852), *The History of the British Empire*, 2 vols, London: Chapman and Hall.

Maning, Frederick Edward ['A Pakeha Maori'] (1906), *Old New Zealand: A Tale of the Good Old Times*, Christchurch, Wellington, and Dunedin, New Zealand: Whitcombe and Tombes.

Marryat, Frederick [1841] (n.d.), *Masterman Ready*, London: Thomas Nelson.

Martin, Robert Montgomery (1858–60), *The Indian Empire*, 4 vols, London: The London Printing and Publishing Company.

Martineau, Harriet [1857] (2004), *British Rule in India: A Historical Sketch*, vol. 5 of *Harriet Martineau's Writing on the British Empire*, ed. Deborah Logan, London: Pickering and Chatto.

Marx, Karl, and Frederick Engels (1972), *On Colonialism: Articles from the New York Tribune and Other Writings*, New York: International Publishers.

Mill, James [1817] (1975), *History of British India*, ed. John Clive, Chicago: University of Chicago Press.

Mill, John Stuart [1848] (1965), *Principles of Political Economy*, 3 vols, ed. J. M. Robson, Toronto: University of Toronto Press.

——[1859] (1982), *On Liberty*, Harmondsworth: Penguin.

Mitchel, John [1854] (1983), *Jail Journal*, London: Sphere Books.

——[1858–9] (2005), *The Last Conquest of Ireland (Perhaps)*, Dublin: University College Dublin Press.

Moore, Thomas (1929), *The Poetical Works of Thomas Moore*, ed. A. D. Godley, London: Oxford University Press.

Morris, William [1890] (2003), *News from Nowhere*, ed. Stephen Arata, Peterborough, Ontario: Broadview Press.

Nolan, Edward Henry (1860), *The Illustrated History of the British Empire in India and the East*, 2 vols, London: James S. Virtue.

Owenson, Sidney (Lady Morgan) [1806] (1981), *The Missionary*, Delmar, NY: Scholars' Facsimiles and Reprints.

Reade, Charles [1856] (1904), *It Is Never Too Late to Mend*, New York: Harper and Brothers.

Robinson, George Augustus, (1966), *Friendly Mission: The Tasmanian Journals and Papers*, 1829–1834, ed. N. J. B. Plomley, Hobart: Tasmanian Historical Reasearch Association.

Roth, H. Ling [1890] (1899), *The Aborigines of Tasmania*, Halifax: F. King.

Rowcroft, Charles (1843), *Tales of the Colonies, or, The Adventures of an Emigrant*, 3 vols, London: Saunders and Otley.

Ruskin, John [1870] (1905), 'Inaugural lecture,' *The Works of John Ruskin*, ed. E. T. Cook and Alexander Wedderburn, London: George Allen, vol. 20, pp. 17–44.

Sale, Lady Florentia [1843] (2002), *A Journal of the First Afghan War*, ed. Patrick Macrory, Oxford: Oxford University Press.

Scott, Sir Walter [1815] (2003), *Guy Mannering*, London: Penguin Books.

——[1827] (2000), *Chronicles of the Canongate*, London: Penguin Books.

Seeley, J. R. [1883] (1971), *The Expansion of England*, Chicago: University of Chicago Press.

Shelley, Percy Bysshe (2003), *The Major Works*, ed. Zachary Leader and Michael O'Neill, Oxford: Oxford University Press.

Smiles, Samuel [1859] (1864), *Self-Help*, Boston: Ticknor and Fields.

Smith, Adam [1776] (1976), *The Wealth of Nations*, 2 vols in one, ed. Edwin Cannan, Chicago: The University of Chicago Press.

Southey, Robert (1878), *The Poetical Works of Robert Southey*, 5 vols, Boston: Houghton, Osgood.

Stanley, Henry Morton [1872] (1970), *How I Found Livingstone*, New York: Arno Press.

Stanley, Henry Morton [1878] (1969), *Through the Dark Continent*, 2 vols, New York: Greenwood Press.

Stevenson, Robert Louis (1996), *South Sea Tales*, ed. Roslyn Jolly, Oxford: Oxford World Classics.

Strachey, Lytton [1918] (1988), *Eminent Victorians*, London: Bloomsbury.

Swift, Jonathan [1726] (1970), *Gulliver's Travels*, New York: Norton.

Taylor, Philip Meadows [1839] (1998), *Confessions of a Thug*, Oxford: Oxford University Press.

Tennyson, Alfred (1969), *The Poems of Tennyson*, ed. Christopher Ricks, London: Longman.

Tennyson, Hallam [1897] (1969), *Alfred Lord Tennyson, A Memoir*, 2 vols, New York: Greenwood Press.

Thackeray, William Makepeace [1844] (n.d.), *Notes of a Journey from Cornhill to Grand Cairo*, Oxford Illustrated Thackeray, vol. 9, Oxford: Humphrey Milford.

——[1848] (1963), *Vanity Fair: A Novel without a Hero*, Boston: Houghton Mifflin.

——[1855] (1962), *The Newcomes*, 2 vols, London: Everyman's Library.

Traill, Catherine Parr (1836), *The Backwoods of Canada; Being Letters from the Wife of an Emigrant Officer*, London: Charles Knight.

Trevelyan, George O. [1866] (1977), *The Competition Wallah*, New York: AMS Press.

Trollope, Anthony [1861] (1989), *Castle Richmond*, Oxford: Oxford University Press.

——[1873] (1968), *Australia and New Zealand*, 2 vols, London: Dawsons.

——[1883] (1968), *An Autobiography*, London: Oxford University Press.

——(1978), *The Tireless Traveler: Twenty–Five Letters to the Liverpool Mercury*, ed. Bradford A. Booth, Berkeley: University of California Press.

[Tucker, James.] [1845] (1929), *Adventures of an Outlaw: The Memoirs of Ralph Rashleigh, A Penal Exile in Australia, 1825–1844*, New York: Jonathan Cape and Harrison Smith.

Tylor, Edward Burnett. [1871] (1970), *Primitive Culture*, 2 vols, New York: Harper and Row.

Victoria, Queen (1908), *The Letters of Queen Victoria*, 3 vols, ed. Arthur Benson and Viscount Esher, London: John Murray.

Waterhouse, Rev. Joseph (1865), *The King and People of Fiji: Containing a Life of Thakombau; with Notices of the Fijians, Their Manners, Customs, and Superstitions, Previous to the Great Religious Reformation in 1854*, London: Wesleyan Conference Office.

Wells, H. G. (1934), *Experiment in Autobiography*, New York: Macmillan, 1934.

Williams, Rev. John (1838), *A Narrative of Missionary Enterprises in the South Sea Islands*, London: Snow.

Williams, Rev. Thomas (1859), *Fiji and the Fijians, part 1: The Islands and Their Inhabitants*, ed. G. S. Rowe, New York: D. Appleton.

Woolf, Virginia [1938] (1966), *Three Guineas*, New York: Harcourt Brace Jovanovich.

Yeats, William Butler (1957), *The Variorum Edition of the Poems of W. B. Yeats*, New York: Macmillan.

——(1961), *Essays and Introductions*, New York: Macmillan.

——(1965), *Collected Plays of W. B. Yeats*, New York: Macmillan.

——(1967), *The Autobiography of William Butler Yeats*, New York: Collier Books.

Yonge, Charlotte [1856] (1876), *The Daisy Chain; or, Aspirations*, London: Macmillan.

Secondary Sources

Ahmad, Aijaz (1992), *In Theory: Classes, Nations, Literatures*, London: Verso.

Aldrich, Robert (2003), *Colonialism and Homosexuality*, New York: Routledge.

Allison, Jonathan (2006), 'Yeats and politics,' *Cambridge Companion to W. B. Yeats*, ed. Howes and Kelly, pp. 185–205.

Altick, Richard (1978), *The Shows of London*, Cambridge, MA: Harvard University Press.

Anderson, Amanda (2001), *The Power of Distance: Cosmopolitanism and the Cultivation of Detachment*, Princeton: Princeton University Press.

Anderson, Benedict (1991), *Imagined Communities: Reflections on the Origin and Spread of Nationalism*, London: Verso.

Anderson, David (2005), *Histories of the Hanged: Britain's Dirty War in Kenya and the End of Empire*, London: Weidenfeld and Nicolson.

Arata, Stephen (1995), *Fictions of Loss in the Victorian Fin de Siècle*, Cambridge: Cambridge University Press.

Armitage, David (2000), *The Ideological Origins of the British Empire*, Cambridge: Cambridge University Press.

Ashcroft, Bill, and Hussein Kadhim (eds) (2001), *Edward Said and the Post-Colonial*, Huntington, NY: Nova Science Publishers.

Auerbach, Jeffrey A. (1999), *The Great Exhibition of 1851: A Nation on Display*, New Haven: Yale University Press.

Azim, Firdous (1993), *The Colonial Rise of the Novel*, New York: Routledge.

Baker, Houston (1982), 'Introduction,' *Narrative of the Life of Frederick Douglass*, New York: Penguin, pp. 7–27.

Bakhtin, Mikhail (1981), *The Dialogical Imagination*, trans. Caryl Emerson and Michael Holquist, Austin: University of Texas Press.

Barrell, John (1991), *The Infection of Thomas De Quincey: A Psychopathology of Imperialism*, New Haven: Yale University Press.

Bartolovich, Crystal, and Neil Lazarus (eds) (2002), *Marxism, Modernity and Postcolonial Studies*, Cambridge: Cambridge University Press.

Bayles, Tiga (1990), 'The year of mourning,' *Paperbark: A Collection of Black Australian Writings*, ed. Jack Davis et al., St. Lucia: University of Queensland Press, pp. 339–42.

Bayly, Christopher A. (1989a), *Atlas of the British Empire: The Rise and Fall of the Greatest Empire the World Has Ever Known*, New York: Facts on File.

——(1989b), *Imperial Meridian: The British Empire and the World, 1780–1830*, London: Longman.

——(1996), *Empire and Information: Intelligence Gathering and Social Communication in India, 1780–1870*, Cambridge: Cambridge University Press.

——(1999), 'The second British Empire,' *Historiography, The Oxford History of the British Empire*, ed. Robin Winks, vol. 5, Oxford: Oxford University Press, pp. 54–72.

Bedad, Ali (1994), *Belated Travelers: Orientalism in the Age of Colonial Dissolution*, Durham: Duke University Press.

Bell, Duncan (2007), *The Idea of Greater Britain*, Princeton: Princeton University Press.

Bell, Morag, Robin Butlin, and Michael Heffernan (1995), 'Introduction: geography and imperialism, 1820–1940,' *Geography and Imperialism, 1820–1940*, Manchester: Manchester University Press, pp. 1–12.

Bell, Morag, and Cheryl McEwan (1996), 'The admission of women fellows to the Royal Geographical Society, 1892–1914; the controversy and the outcome,' *The Geographical Journal* 162:3 (Nov.), pp. 295–312.

Bhabha, Homi K. (ed.) (1990), *Nation and Narration*, New York: Routledge.

——(1994), *The Location of Culture*, New York: Routledge.

Bivona, Daniel (1998), *British Imperial Literature, 1870–1940: Writing and the Administration of Empire*, Cambridge: Cambridge University Press.

Blackburn, Robin (1988), *The Overthrow of Colonial Slavery, 1776–1848*, London: Verso.

Boehmer, Elleke (1995), *Colonial and Postcolonial Literature*, New York: Oxford University Press.

Bolton, Carol (2007), *Writing the Empire: Robert Southey and British Romanticism*, London: Pickering and Chatto.

Bose, Purnima (2003), *Organizing Empire: Individualism, Collective Agency, and India*, Durham, NC: Duke University Press.

Boyd, Kelly (2003), *Manliness and the Boys' Story Paper in Britain: A Cultural History, 1855–1940*, New York: Palgrave Macmillan.

Brantlinger, Patrick (1988), *Rule of Darkness: British Literature and Imperialism, 1830–1914*, Ithaca: Cornell University Press.

——(2003), *Dark Vanishings: Discourse on the Extinction of Primitive Races, 1800–1930*, Ithaca, NY: Cornell University Press.

——(2004), '"Black armband" versus "white blindfold" history in Australia,' *Victorian Studies* 46:4 (Summer), pp. 655–74.

Brantlinger, Patrick (2006), 'Missionaries and cannibals in nineteenth-century Fiji,' *History and Anthropology* 17:1 (March), pp. 21–38.

Bratton, J. S., et al. (1991), *Acts of Supremacy: The British Empire and the Stage, 1790–1930*, Manchester: Manchester University Press.

Brennan, Timothy (1990), 'The national longing for form,' *Nation and Narration*, ed. Homi Bhabha, pp. 44–70.

Brewer, Anthony (1990), *Marxist Theories of Imperialism: A Critical Survey*, 2nd edn, London: Routledge.

Bristow, Joseph (1991), *Empire Boys: Adventures in a Man's World*, London: HarperCollins.

Brooks, Chris, and Peter Faulkner (eds) (1996), *The White Man's Burden: An Anthology of British Poetry of the Empire*, Exeter: University of Exeter Press.

Buckley, Jerome, and George Woods (eds) (1965), *Poetry of the Victorian Period*, Glenview, IL: Scott, Foresman.

Burdett, Carolyn (2001), *Olive Schreiner and the Progress of Feminism: Evolution, Gender, Empire*, Houndmills: Palgrave.

Burns, Wayne (1961), *Charles Reade: A Study in Victorian Authorship*, New York: Bookman Associates.

Burton, Antoinette (1994), *Burdens of History: British Feminists, Indian Women, and Imperial Culture, 1865–1915*, Chapel Hill, NC: University of North Carolina Press.

——(2001), Review of *The Oxford History of the British Empire*, Vols 3 and 5, *Victorian Studies* 44.1, pp. 167–9.

——(2003), 'Introduction: on the inadequacy and the indispensability of the nation,' *After the Imperial Turn: Thinking with and through the Nation*, ed. Antoinette Burton, Durham: Duke University Press, pp. 1–23.

Cain, Peter J., and Antony G. Hopkins (1993), *British Imperialism: Innovation and Expansion, 1688–1914*, London: Longman.

Cannadine, David (2001), *Ornamentalism: How the British Saw Their Empire*, Oxford: Oxford University Press.

Caracciolo, Peter (ed.) (1988), *The Arabian Nights in English Literature*, London: Macmillan.

Carr, Helen (2002), 'Modernism and travel (1880–1940),' *The Cambridge Companion to Travel Writing*, ed. Peter Hulme and Tim Youngs, Cambridge: Cambridge University Press, pp. 70–86.

Césaire, Aimé [1950] (1972), *Discourse on Colonialism*, New York: Monthly Review Press.

Chakrabarty, Dipesh (2000), *Provincializing Europe: Postcolonial Thought and Historical Difference*, Princeton: Princeton University Press.

Chakravarty, Gautam (2005), *The Indian Mutiny and the British Imagination*, Cambridge: Cambridge University Press.

Chamberlain, Muriel (1988), *'Pax Britannica'? British Foreign Policy 1789–1914*, London: Longman.

Chandavarkar, Rajnarayan (2000), '"The making of the working class": E. P. Thompson and Indian history,' *Mapping Subaltern Studies and the Postcolonial*, ed. Vinayak Chaturvedi, London: Verso, pp. 50–71.

Chaudhuri, Rosinka (2002), *Gentlemen Poets in Colonial Bengal: Emergent Nationalism and the Orientalist Project*, Calcutta: Seagull Press.

Chrisman, Laura (2000), *Reading the Imperial Romance: British Imperialism and South African Resistance in Haggard, Schreiner, and Plaatje*, Oxford: Clarendon Press.

Claeys, Gregory (2007), 'The "left" and the critique of empire c. 1865–1900: three roots of humanitarian foreign policy,' *Victorian Visions of Global Order: Empire and International Relations in Nineteenth-Century British Thought*, ed. Duncan Bell, Cambridge: Cambridge University Press, pp. 239–66.

Clancy, Laurie (1992), *A Reader's Guide to Australian Fiction*, Oxford: Oxford University Press.

Clifford, James (1986), 'On ethnographic allegory,' *Writing Culture: The Poetics and Politics of Ethnography*, ed. James Clifford and George Marcus, Berkeley: University of California Press, pp. 98–121.

Colley, Ann C. (2004), *Robert Louis Stevenson and the Colonial Imagination*, Burlington, VT: Ashgate.

Colley, Linda (1992), *Britons*, New Haven: Yale University Press.

——(2002), *Captives*, New York: Pantheon.

Corbett, Mary Jean (2000), *Allegories of Union in Irish and English Writing, 1790–1870: Politics, History, and the Family from Edgeworth to Arnold*, Cambridge: Cambridge University Press.

Cuddon, J. A. (1999), *The Penguin Dictionary of Literary Terms and Literary Theory*, London: Penguin.

Curthoys, Ann (2001), 'Aboriginal history,' *The Oxford Companion to Australian History*, ed. Graeme Davison, John Hirst and Stuart Macintyre, Oxford: Oxford University Press, pp. 3–5.

Curtis, L. P. (1968), *Anglo-Saxons and Celts: A Study of Anti-Irish Prejudice in Victorian England*, Bridgeport, CT: University of Bridgeport, Conference on British Studies.

David, Deirdre (1995), *Rule Britannia: Women, Empire, and Victorian Writing*, Ithaca, NY: Cornell University Press.

Davidson, John (1969), 'Anthony Trollope and the colonies,' *Victorian Studies* 12:3 (March), pp. 305–30.

Davis, Mike (2001), *Late Victorian Holocausts: El Niño Famines and the Making of the Third World*, London: Verso.

Dawson, James (1996), 'Mary Martha Sherwood,' *Dictionary of Literary Biography*, vol. 163; *British Children's Writers, 1800–1880*, ed. Meena Khorama, Detroit: Gale, pp. 267–81.

Deane, Seamus (1997), *Strange Country: Modernity and Nationhood in Irish Writing since 1790*, Oxford: Clarendon Press.

Dentith, Simon (2006), *Epic and Empire in Nineteenth-Century Britain*, Cambridge: Cambridge University Press.

Dirlik, Arif (1997), *The Postcolonial Aura: Third World Criticism in the Age of Global Capitalism*, Boulder, CO: Westview Press.

Dirks, Nicholas (2006), *The Scandal of Empire: India and the Creation of Imperial Britain*, Cambridge, MA: Harvard University Press.

Dobie, Madeleine (2001), *Foreign Bodies: Gender, Language and Culture in French Orientalism*, Stanford: Stanford University Press.

Driver, Felix (2000), *Cultures of Exploration and Empire*, Oxford: Blackwell.

Dummett, Raymond E. (1999), *Gentlemanly Capitalism and British Imperialism: The New Debate on Empire*, London: Longman.

Dunae, Patrick (1989), 'New Grub Street for boys,' *Imperialism and Juvenile Literature*, ed. Jeffrey Richards, pp. 13–33.

Eagleton, Terry (1995), *Heathcliff and the Great Hunger: Studies in Irish Culture*, London: Verso.

Edwards, O. D. (1977), 'Tennyson and Ireland,' *New Edinburgh Review* 38–9, pp. 43–54.

Elkins, Caroline (2005), *Imperial Reckoning: The Untold Story of Britain's Gulag in Kenya*, New York: Henry Holt.

Erdman, David (1969), *Blake: Prophet against Empire*, Princeton: Princeton University Press.

Esty, Jed (2007), 'The colonial bildungsroman: *The Story of an African Farm* and the ghost of Goethe,' *Victorian Studies* 49:3 (Spring), pp. 407–30.

Etherington, Norman (1984), *Rider Haggard*, Boston: Twayne.

Fanon, Frantz [1963] (1991), *The Wretched of the Earth*, trans. Constance Farrington, New York: Grove Press.

Farwell, Byron (1972), *Queen Victoria's Little Wars*, New York: Harper and Row.

Federico, Annette (2000), *Idol of Suburbia: Marie Corelli and Late-Victorian Literary Culture*, Charlottesville: University of Virginia Press.

Ferguson, Moira (1992), *Subject to Others: British Women Writers and Colonial Slavery, 1670–1834*, London: Routledge.

Ferguson, Niall (2004), *Empire: The Rise and Demise of the British World Order and the Lessons for Global Power*, New York: Basic Books.

Ferris, Ina (2002), *The Romantic National Tale and the Question of Ireland*, Cambridge: Cambridge University Press.

Fieldhouse, David (1996), 'For richer, for poorer?' *The Cambridge Illustrated History of the British Empire*, ed. P. J. Marshall, Cambridge: Cambridge University Press, pp. 108–46.

Flanagan, Thomas (1959), *The Irish Novelists, 1800–1850*, New York: Columbia University Press.

Foucault, Michel (1980), *The History of Sexuality: Vol. 1: An Introduction*, New York: Vintage Books.

Gilbert, Helen, and Chris Tiffin (eds) (2008), *Burden or Benefit? Imperial Benevolence and Its Legacies*, Bloomington: Indiana University Press.

Gilroy, Paul (1993), *The Black Atlantic: Modernity and Double Consciousness*, Cambridge, MA: Harvard University Press.

Girouard, Marc (1981), *The Return to Camelot: Chivalry and the English Gentleman*, New Haven: Yale University Press.

Goldie, Terry (2003), 'The guise of friendship,' *Imperial Desire: Dissident Sexualities and Colonial Literature*, ed. Philip Holden and Richard Ruppel, Minneapolis: University of Minnesota Press, pp. 44–62.

Gray, Stephen (1979), *South African Literature: An Introduction*, New York: Harper and Row.

Green, Martin (1979), *Dreams of Adventure, Deeds of Empire*, New York: Basic Books.

Guha, Ranajit, and Gayatri Chakravorty Spivak (eds) (1988), *Selected Subaltern Studies*. Oxford: Oxford University Press.

Guy, Jeff (1979), *The Destruction of the Zulu Kingdom: The Civil War in Zululand, 1879–1884*, London: Longman.

Haddad, Emily (2002), *Orientalist Poetics: The Islamic Middle East in Nineteenth-Century English and French Poetry*, Burlington, VT: Ashgate.

Haggard, Lilias Rider (1951), *The Cloak That I Left: A Biography of the Author Henry Rider Haggard KBE*, London: Hodder and Stoughton.

Hall, Catherine (2002), *Civilising Subjects: Metropole and Colony in the English Imagination, 1830–1867*, Chicago: University of Chicago Press.

Hall, Catherine, and Sonya Rose (eds) (2006), *At Home with the Empire: Metropolitan Culture and the Imperial World*, Cambridge: Cambridge University Press.

Hannabus, Stuart (1989), 'Ballantyne's message of empire,' *Imperialism and Juvenile Literature*, ed. Jeffrey Richards, pp. 53–71.

Hart, Carol (1996), 'Sydney Owenson, Lady Morgan,' *Dictionary of Literary Biography*, vol. 158, *British Reform Writers, 1789–1932*, ed. Gary Kelly, Detroit: Gale, pp. 234–49.

Healy, J. J. (1989), *Literature and the Aborigine in Australia*, St. Lucia: University of Queensland Press.

Hechter, Michael (1975), *Internal Colonialism: The Celtic Fringe in British National Development, 1536–1966*, Berkeley: University of California Press.

Henry, Nancy (2002), *George Eliot and the British Empire*, Cambridge: Cambridge University Press.

Herbert, Christopher (1991), *Culture and Anomie: Ethnographic Imagination in the Nineteenth Century*, Chicago: University of Chicago Press.

——(2008), *War of No Pity: The Indian Mutiny and Victorian Trauma*, Princeton: Princeton University Press.

Hibbert, Christopher (1982), *Africa Explored: Europeans in the Dark Continent, 1769–1889*, Harmondsworth: Penguin Books.

Hill, Christopher (1954), 'The Norman yoke,' *Democracy and the Labour Movement; Essays in Honour of Dona Torr*, ed. John Saville, London: Lawrence and Wishart, pp. 11–66.

Hobsbawm, Eric (1989), *The Age of Empire, 1875–1914*, New York: Vintage Books.

Hobsbawm, Eric and Terence Ranger (eds) (1983), *The Invention of Tradition*, Cambridge: Cambridge University Press.

Hochschild, Adam (1998), *King Leopold's Ghost*, Boston: Houghton Mifflin.

Holden, Philip, and Richard J. Ruppel (eds) (2003), *Imperial Desire: Dissident Sexualities and Colonial Literature*, Minneapolis: University of Minnesota Press.

Howe, Stephen (2000), *Ireland and Empire: Colonial Legacies in Irish History and Culture*, Oxford: Oxford University Press.

——(2001), 'The slow death and strange rebirths of imperial history,' *The Journal of Imperial and Commonwealth History* 29:2 (May), pp. 131–41.

Howes, Marjorie, and John Kelly (eds) (2006), *The Cambridge Companion to W. B. Yeats*, Cambridge: Cambridge University Press.

Howes, Marjorie (1996), *Yeats's Nations: Gender, Class, and Irishness*, Cambridge: Cambridge University Press.

——(2006), 'Yeats and the postcolonial,' *Cambridge Companion to W. B. Yeats*, ed. Howes and Kelly, pp. 206–25.

Hughes, Robert (1986), *The Fatal Shore: The Epic of Australia's Founding*, New York: Vintage.

Hunt, Bruce J. (1997), 'Doing science in a global empire: cable telegraphy and electrical physics in Victorian Britain,' *Victorian Science in Context*, ed. Bernard Lightman, Chicago: University of Chicago Press, pp. 312–33.

Hussein, Abdirahman (2002), *Edward Said: Criticism and Society*, London: Verso.

Hyam, Ronald (1990), *Empire and Sexuality: The British Experience*, Manchester: Manchester University Press.

James, Lawrence (1994), *The Rise and Fall of the British Empire*, New York: St. Martin's Press.

James, Louis (1973), 'Tom Brown's imperialist sons,' *Victorian Studies* 17:1 (September), pp. 89–99.

Jeal, Tim (1973), *Livingstone*, New York: G. P. Putnam.

——(2007), *Stanley: The Impossible Life of Africa's Greatest Explorer*, London: Faber and Faber.

Johnston, Anna (2003), *Missionary Writing and Empire, 1800–1860*, Cambridge: Cambridge University Press.

Judd, Denis (1996), *Empire: The British Imperial Experience from 1765 to the Present*, London: HarperCollins.

Jump, John D. (ed.) (1967), *Tennyson: The Critical Heritage*, London: Routledge and Kegan Paul.

Juneja, Renu (1992), 'The native and the nabob: representations of the Indian experience in eighteenth-century English literature,' *Journal of Commonwealth Literature* 27, pp. 183–200.

Kabbani, Rana (1994), *Imperial Fictions: Europe's Myths of Orient*, London: Pandora.

Katz, Wendy (1987), *Rider Haggard and the Fiction of Empire: A Critical Study of British Imperial Fiction*, Cambridge: Cambridge University Press.

Kelly, Linda (2006), *Ireland's Minstrel: A Life of Tom Moore: Poet, Patriot and Byron's Friend*, London: I. B. Tauris.

Kennedy, Dane (1996), 'Imperial history and postcolonial studies,' *Journal of Imperial and Commonwealth History* 24:3 (September), pp. 9–23.

Khilnani, Sunil (1998), *The Idea of India*, London: Penguin.

Kiberd, Declan (1995), *Inventing Ireland*, London: Jonathan Cape.

Kiernan, Ben (2002), *The Pol Pot Regime: Race, Power, and Genocide in Cambodia under the Khmer Rouge, 1975–79*, 2nd edn, New Haven: Yale University Press.

Kiernan, Victor (1974), *Marxism and Imperialism*, New York: St. Martin's Press.

——(1982), 'Tennyson, King Arthur, and imperialism,' *Culture, Ideology and Politics: Essays for Eric Hobsbawm*, ed. Raphael Samuel and Gareth Stedman Jones, London: Routledge and Kegan Paul, pp. 126–48.

Knapman, Claudia (1986), *White Women in Fiji 1835–1930: The Ruin of Empire*, Sydney and London: Allen and Unwin.

Krause, David (1996), 'The de-Yeatsification cabal,' *Yeats's Political Identities: Selected Essays*, ed. Jonathan Allison, Ann Arbor: University of Michigan Press, pp. 293–307.

Krebs, Paula (1999), *Gender, Race, and the Writing of Empire: Public Discourse and the Boer War*, Cambridge: Cambridge University Press.

Kuchta, Todd (2005), 'Semi-detached empire: suburbia and imperial discourse in Victorian and Edwardian Britain,' *Nineteenth-Century Prose* 32:2 (Fall), pp. 173–208.

Kucich, John (2007), *Imperial Masochism: British Fiction, Fantasy, and Social Class*, Princeton: Princeton University Press.

Lane, Christopher (1995), *The Ruling Passion: British Colonial Allegory and the Paradox of Homosexual Desire*, Durham, NC: Duke University Press.

Lazarus, Neil (2004), 'Introducing postcolonial studies,' *The Cambridge Companion to Postcolonial Literary Studies*, ed. Neil Lazarus, Cambridge: Cambridge University Press, pp. 1–16.

Leask, Nigel (1992), *British Romantic Writers and the East: Anxieties of Empire*, Cambridge: Cambridge University Press.

Lee, Debbie (2002), *Slavery and the Romantic Imagination*, Philadelphia: University of Pennsylvania Press.

Lefever, Ernest (1999), *America's Imperial Burden: Is the Past Prologue?*, Boulder, CO: Westview Press.

Levine, Philippa (2004), *Gender and Empire*, Oxford: Oxford University Press.

——(2007), *The British Empire: From Sunrise to Sunset*, Harlow: Pearson Longman.

Longford, Elizabeth (1964), *Queen Victoria: Born to Succeed*, New York: Harper and Row.

Longley, Edna (1994), *The Living Stream: Literature and Revisionism in Ireland*, Newcastle upon Tyne: Bloodaxe Books.

Loomba, Ania (1998), *Colonialism/ Postcolonialism*, London: Routledge.

Louis, William Roger (1998), 'Introduction,' *Historiography*, vol. 5, *The Oxford History of the British Empire*, ed. Robin W. Winks.

Low, Gail Ching-Liang (1996), *White Skins / Black Masks: Representation and Colonialism*, London and New York: Routledge.

McClintock, Anne (1995), *Imperial Leather: Race, Gender, and Sexuality in the Colonial Contest*, New York: Routledge.

MacDougall, Hugh (1982), *Racial Myth in English History: Trojans, Teutons, and Anglo-Saxons*, Montreal: Harvest House.

McDougall, Russell (2007), 'Henry Ling Roth in Tasmania,' *Writing, Travel, and Empire: In the Margins of Anthropology*, ed. Peter Hulme and Russell McDougall, London: I. B. Tauris, pp. 43–68.

McGregor, Russell (1997), *Imagined Destinies: Aboriginal Australians and the Doomed Race Theory, 1880–1939*, Melbourne: Melbourne University Press.

Macintyre, Stuart (1999), *A Concise History of Australia*, Cambridge: Cambridge University Press.

MacKenzie, John M. (1995), *Orientalism: History, Theory and the Arts*, Manchester: Manchester University Press.

——(1998), 'Empire and metropolitan cultures,' *The Nineteenth Century*, ed. Andrew Porter, Oxford: Oxford University Press, pp. 270–93.

Magubane, Zine (2004), *Bringing the Empire Home: Race, Class, and Gender in Britain and Colonial South Africa*, Chicago: The University of Chicago Press.

Majeed, Javed (1992), *Ungoverned Imaginings: James Mill's The History of British India and Orientalism*, Oxford: Clarendon Press.

——(1996), 'Meadows Taylor's *Confessions of a Thug*: the Anglo-Indian novel as a genre in the making,' *Writing India 1757–1990*, ed. Bart Moore-Gilbert, Manchester: Manchester University Press, pp. 86–110.

Makdisi, Saree (1998), *Romantic Imperialism: Universal Empire and the Culture of Modernity*, Cambridge: Cambridge University Press.

Malchow, Howard (1996), *Gothic Images of Race in Nineteenth-Century Britain*, Stanford: Stanford University Press.

Mana, Lati (1998), *Contentious Traditions: The Debate on Sati in Colonial India*, Berkeley: University of California Press.

Mandler, Peter (2006), *The English National Character: The History of an Idea from Edmund Burke to Tony Blair*, New Haven: Yale University Press.

Manne, Robert (ed.) (2003), *Whitewash: On Keith Windschuttle's Fabrication of Aboriginal History*, Melbourne: Black Inc.

Marshall, P. J. (1993), 'No fatal impact? The elusive history of imperial Britain,' *Times Literary Supplement* 12 March 1993, pp. 8–10.

——(1996), '1783–1870: an expanding Empire,' *The Cambridge Illustrated History of the British Empire*, ed. P. J. Marshall, Cambridge: Cambridge University Press, pp. 24–51.

Masselos, Jim (1985), *Indian Nationalism: An History*, New Delhi: Sterling Publishers.

Maurer, Sara (2005), 'Exporting time immemorial: writing land law reform in India and Ireland,' *Nineteenth-Century Prose* 32:2 (Fall), pp. 48–80.

Mehta, Uday Singh (1999), *Liberalism and Empire: A Study in Nineteenth-Century British Liberal Thought*, Chicago: University of Chicago Press.

Melman, Billie (1992), *Women's Orients: English Women and the Middle East, 1718–1918*, London: Macmillan.

Metcalfe, Thomas (1964), *The Aftermath of Revolt: India, 1857–1870*, Princeton: Princeton University Press.

Meyer, Susan (1996), *Imperialism at Home: Race and Victorian Women's Fiction*, Ithaca, NY: Cornell University Press.

Midgley, Clare (2007), *Feminism and Empire: Women Activists in Imperial Britain, 1790–1865*, Milton Park Abingdon: Routledge.

Miller, Brook (2005), 'Our Abdiel: The British press and the lionization of "Chinese" Gordon,' *Nineteenth-Century Prose* 32:2 (Fall), pp. 127–53.

Mukherjee, Meenakshi (2003), 'The beginnings of the Indian novel,' *A History of Indian Literature in English*, ed. Arvind Krishna Mehrota, New York: Columbia University Press, pp. 92–102.

Mukherjee, Upamanyu Pablo (2003), *Crime and Empire: The Colony in Nineteenth-Century Fictions of Crime*, Oxford: Oxford University Press.

Nairn, Tom (1981), *The Break-Up of Britain: Crisis and Neo-Nationalism*, London: Verso.

Narogin, Mudrooroo (1990), *Writing from the Fringe: A Study of Modern Aboriginal Literature*, Melbourne: Hyland House.

Nash, Geoffrey (2005), *From Empire to Orient: Travellers to the Middle East 1830–1926*, London: I. B. Tauris.

Oppenheim, Janet (1985), *The Other World: Spiritualism and Psychical Research in England, 1850–1914*, Cambridge: Cambridge University Press.

Palmer, Alison (2000), *Colonial Genocide*, Adelaide: Crawford House; London: C. Hurst.

Parry, Benita (1983), *Conrad and Imperialism*, London: Macmillan.

——(2004), *Postcolonial Studies: A Materialist Critique*, London and New York: Routledge.

Parsons, Neil (1998), *King Khama, Emperor Joe and the Great White Queen: Victorian Britain through African Eyes*, Chicago: University of Chicago Press.

Paxton, Nancy (1999), *Writing Under the Raj: Gender, Race and Rape in the British Colonial Imagination, 1830–1947*, New Brunswick, NJ: Rutgers University Press.

Peers, Douglas M. (2002), 'Is Humpty Dumpty back together again? The revival of imperial history and the *Oxford History of the British Empire*,' *Journal of World History* 13:2 (Fall), pp. 451–68.

Perera, Suvendrini (1991), *Reaches of Empire: The English Novel from Edgeworth to Dickens*, New York: Columbia University Press.

Pettitt, Clare (2007), *Dr Livingstone, I Presume? Missionaries, Journalists, Explorers, and Empire*, Cambridge, MA: Harvard University Press.

Pieterse, Jan Nederveen (1989), *Empire and Emancipation: Power and Liberation on a World Scale*, London: Pluto Press.

Porter, Bernard (2004), *The Absent-Minded Imperialists: Empire, Society, and Culture in Britain*, Oxford: Oxford University Press.

——(2006), *Empire and Superempire: Britain, America and the World*, New Haven: Yale University Press.

Pratt, Mary Louise (1992), *Imperial Eyes: Travel Writing and Transculturation*, New York: Routledge.

Punter, David (1980), *The Literature of Terror: A History of Gothic Fictions from 1765 to the Present Day*, London: Longman.

Quayle, Eric (1967), *Ballantyne the Brave: A Victorian Writer and His Family*, London: Rupert Hart-Davis.

Rajan, Balanchandra (1999), *Under Western Eyes: India from Milton to Macaulay*, Durham, NC: Duke University Press.

Randall, Donald (2000), *Kipling's Imperial Boy: Adolescence and Cultural Hybridity*, New York: Palgrave.

Ranger, Terence (1967), *Revolt in Southern Rhodesia, 1896–7; A Study in African Resistance*, Evanston: Northwestern University Press.

Raza, Rosemary (2006), *In Their Own Words: British Women Writers and India 1740–1857*, New Delhi: Oxford University Press.

Reitz, Caroline (2004), *Detecting the Nation: Fictions of Detection and the Imperial Venture*, Columbus: The Ohio State University Press.

Reynolds, Henry (1982), *The Other Side of the Frontier: Aboriginal Resistance to the European Invasion of Australia*, Ringwood: Penguin Australia.

——(1992), *The Law of the Land*, Ringwood: Penguin Australia.

——(1995), *The Fate of a Free People*, Ringwood: Penguin Australia.

——(2001), *An Indelible Stain? The Question of Genocide in Australia's History*, Ringwood, Victoria: Viking Penguin.

Reynolds, Matthew (2001), *The Realms of Verse: English Poetry in a Time of Nation-Building*, Oxford: Oxford University Press.

Richards, Jeffrey (ed.) (1989), *Imperialism and Juvenile Literature*, Manchester: Manchester University Press.

Richardson, LeeAnne M. (2006), *New Woman and Colonial Adventure Fiction in Victorian Britain: Gender, Genre, and Empire*, Gainesville: University of Florida Press.

Rignall, John (ed.) (2000), *Oxford Reader's Companion to George Eliot*, Oxford: Oxford University Press.

Rosaldo, Renato (1998), 'Imperialist nostalgia,' *Representations* 26 (Spring), pp. 107–22.

Rose, Jacqueline (1992), *The Case of Peter Pan, or The Impossibility of Children's Fiction*, London: Macmillan.

Ruddick, Nicholas (1997), 'Grant Allen,' *Dictionary of Literary Biography*, vol. 178, *British Fantasy and Science-Fiction Writers before World War I*, ed. Darren Harris-Fain, Detroit: Gale, pp. 7–16.

Ryan, Lyndall (1981), *The Aboriginal Tasmanians*, Vancouver: University of British Columbia Press.

Said, Edward (1978), *Orientalism*, New York: Random House.

——(1988), 'Foreword,' Guha and Spivak (eds), *Selected Subaltern Studies*, pp. v–x.

——(1993), *Culture and Imperialism*, New York: Knopf.

Schaffer, Talia (2005), 'Taming the tropics: Charlotte Yonge takes on Melanesia,' *Victorian Studies* 47:2 (Winter), pp. 204–14.

Schmitt, Cannon (1997), *Alien Nation: Nineteenth-Century Gothic Fictions and English Nationality*, Philadelphia: University of Pennsylvania Press.

Sedgwick, Eve Kosofsky (1985), *Between Men: English Literature and Male Homosocial Desire*, New York: Columbia University Press.

Semmel, Bernard (1965), *Democracy versus Empire: The Jamaica Riots of 1865 and the Governor Eyre Controversy*, Garden City, NY: Doubleday Anchor.

——(1970), *The Rise of Free Trade Imperialism: Classical Political Economy, the Empire of Free Trade, and Imperialism, 1750–1850*, Cambridge: Cambridge University Press.

Sharpe, Jenny (1993), *Allegories of Empire: The Figure of Woman in the Colonial Text*, Minneapolis: University of Minnesota Press.

Shaw, A. G. L. (1969), 'British attitudes to the colonies, ca. 1820–1850,' *The Journal of British Studies* 9:1, pp. 71–95.

Sheridan, Greg (2003), 'Aborigines victims of irresponsible word games,' *The Australian* 18 September 2003, p. 11.

Simpson, Roger (1990), *Camelot Regained: The Arthurian Revival and Tennyson, 1800–1849*, Cambridge: D. S. Brewer.

Sloan, Barry (1987), *The Pioneers of Anglo-Irish Fiction, 1800–1850*, Gerrards Cross: Colin Smythe.

Spivak, Gayatri Chakravorty (1986), 'Three women's texts and a critique of imperialism,' *'Race,' Writing, and Difference*, ed. Henry Louis Gates, Jr., Chicago: The University of Chicago Press, pp. 262–80.

Spivak, Gayatri Chakravorty (1988a), 'Can the subaltern speak?' *Marxism and the Interpretation of Culture*, ed. Cary Nelson and Lawrence Grossberg, Urbana: University of Illinois Press, pp. 271–313.

——(1988b), 'Introduction,' Guha and Spivak (eds), *Selected Subaltern Studies*, pp. 3–32.

Spivak, Gayatri Chakravorty (1999), *A Critique of Postcolonial Reason: Toward a History of the Vanishing Present*, Cambridge, MA: Harvard University Press.
——(2005), 'Scattered speculations on the subaltern and the popular,' *Postcolonial Studies* 8:4 (November), pp. 475–86.
Sprinker, Michael (ed.) (1992), *Edward Said: A Critical Reader*, Oxford: Blackwell.
Stanner, W. E. H. (1969), *After the Dreaming: Black and White Australians – An Anthropologist's View*, Sydney: The Australian Broadcasting Commission.
Stembridge, Stanley R. (1965), 'Disraeli and the millstones,' *The Journal of British Studies* 5:1 (November), pp. 122–39.
Stocking, George (1987), *Victorian Anthropology*, New York: Free Press.
Stone, Harry (1994), *The Night Side of Dickens: Cannibalism, Passion, Necessity*, Columbus: Ohio State University Press.
Strobel, Margaret (1991), *European Women and the Second British Empire*, Bloomington: Indiana University Press.
Sturgis, James L. (1969), *John Bright and the Empire*, London: The Athlone Press.
Suleri, Sara (1992), *The Rhetoric of English India*, Chicago: The University of Chicago Press.
Switzer, Les (1993), *Power and Resistance in an African Society: The Ciskei Xhosa and the Making of South Africa*, Madison: University of Wisconsin Press.
Tatz, Colin (2003), *With Intent to Destroy: Reflecting on Genocide*, London: Verso.
Thomas, Helen (2000), *Romanticism and Slave Narratives: Transatlantic Testimonies*, Cambridge: Cambridge University Press.
Thompson, Andrew (2005), *The Empire Strikes Back? The Impact of Imperialism on Britain from the Mid-Nineteenth Century*, Harlow: Pearson Longman.
Thorp, Daniel (2003), 'Going native in New Zealand and America: comparing pakeha Maori and white Indians,' *Journal of Imperial and Commonwealth History* 31:3 (September), pp. 1–23.
Tidrick, Kathryn (1981), *Heart-beguiling Araby*, Cambridge: Cambridge University Press.
——(1990), *Empire and the English Character*, London: I. B. Tauris.
Torgovnick, Marianna (1990), *Gone Primitive: Savage Intellects, Modern Lives*, Chicago: University of Chicago Press.
Trumpener, Katie (1997), *Bardic Nationalism: The Romantic Novel and the British Empire*, Princeton: Princeton University Press.
van Woerkens, Martine (2002), *The Strangled Traveler: Colonial Imaginings and the Thugs of India*, Chicago: The University of Chicago Press.
Viswanathan, Gauri (1989), *Masks of Conquest: Literary Study and British Rule in India*, New York: Columbia University Press.

——(1998), *Outside the Fold: Conversion, Modernity, and Belief*, Princeton: Princeton University Press.

Wagar, Warren (1982), *Terminal Visions: The Literature of Last Things*, Bloomington: Indiana University Press.

Ware, Vron (1992), *Beyond the Pale: White Women, Racism and History*, London: Verso.

Washbrook, D. A. (1999), 'India, 1818–1860: the two faces of colonialism,' *The Nineteenth Century*, ed. Andrew Porter, Oxford: Oxford University Press, pp. 395–421.

Webb, Janeen, and Andrew Enstice (1998), *Aliens and Savages: Fiction, Politics and Prejudice in Australia*, Sydney: HarperCollins.

Wilson, Kathleen (ed.) (2004), *A New Imperial History: Culture, Identity and Modernity in Britain and the Empire 1660–1840*, Cambridge: Cambridge University Press.

Winch, Donald (1965), *Classical Political Economy and the Colonies*, London: London School of Economics.

Windschuttle, Keith (2002), *The Fabrication of Aboriginal History*, vol. 1: *Van Diemen's Land 1803–1947*, Sydney: Macleay Press.

Winstone, H. V. F. (2003), *Lady Anne Blunt: A Biography*, London: Barzan Publishing.

Wylie, Dan (2000), *Savage Delight: White Myths of Shaka*, Pietermaritzburg, RSA: University of Natal Press.

Young, Robert (1995), *Colonial Desire: Hybridity in Theory, Culture and Race*, New York: Routledge.

——(2001), *Postcolonialism: An Historical Introduction*, Oxford: Blackwell.

Zonana, Joyce (1993), 'The sultan and the slave: feminist orientalism and the structure of *Jane Eyre*,' *Signs* 18:3 (Spring), pp. 592–617.

Further Reading

Bayly, Christopher (ed.) (1989), *Atlas of the British Empire*, New York: Facts on File. Well-illustrated, thorough, and readable reference work.

Bhabha, Homi K. (1994), *The Location of Culture*, London and New York: Routledge. Contains Bhabha's influential essays on mimicry, hybridity, and stereotypes.

Boehmer, Elleke (1995), *Colonial and Postcolonial Literature*, New York: Oxford University Press. A sensible, wide-ranging survey from the nineteenth-century forward, including some Victorian writers.

Brantlinger, Patrick (1988), *Rule of Darkness: British Literature and Imperialism, 1830–1914*, Ithaca: Cornell University Press. Chapters on India, Australia, Middle-Eastern 'new crusades,' African exploration, and 'imperial Gothic' fiction.

Chakravarty, Gautam (2005), *The Indian Mutiny and the British Imagination*. Cambridge: Cambridge University Press. The best study to date of literary responses to the Indian Rebellion of 1857–8.

Chrisman, Laura, and Patrick Williams (eds) (1994), *Colonial Discourse and Post-colonial Theory*, New York: Columbia University Press. An early and still useful reader.

Colley, Linda (1992), *Captives*, New Haven: Yale University Press. Mostly pre-Victorian, but essential for understanding both 'mimicry' by the colonized and 'going native' by the colonizers.

Dentith, Simon (2006), *Epic and Empire in Nineteenth-Century Britain*, Cambridge: Cambridge University Press. Excellent analysis dealing with Tennyson, among others.

Hobsbawm, Eric (1989), *The Age of Empire, 1875–1914*, New York: Vintage Books. A thorough narrative about all of the European empires in their heyday.

Judd, Denis (1996), *Empire: The British Imperial Experience from 1765 to the Present*, London: HarperCollins. A balanced, readable account.

Lazarus, Neil (ed.) (2004), *The Cambridge Companion to Postcolonial Literary Studies*, Cambridge: Cambridge University Press. Deals with most theoretical issues raised by postcolonialism.

Levine, Philippa (2007), *The British Empire: Sunrise to Sunset*, Harlow: Pearson Longman. A clear, brief account, with a useful chapter on gender.

Loomba, Ania (1998), *Colonialism / Postcolonialism*, London and New York: Routledge. A readable introduction to the major issues.

Marshall, P. J. (ed.) (1996), *The Cambridge Illustrated History of the British Empire*, Cambridge: Cambridge University Press. Like Bayly's *Atlas*, well-illustrated and readable.

Perera, Suvendrini (1991), *Reaches of Empire: The English Novel from Edgeworth to Dickens*, New York: Columbia University Press. Insightful analyses of several novelists.

Porter, Bernard (2004), *The Lion's Share: A Short History of British Imperialism, 1850–2004*, 4th ed., Harlow: Pearson/Longman. Offers a clear, standard account.

Reynolds, Henry (1995), *The Fate of a Free People*, Ringwood: Penguin Australia. The best account of the extinction of the Tasmanian Aborigines. See also Reynolds's other books on Aboriginal–white relations.

Richards, Jeffrey (ed.) (1989), *Imperialism and Juvenile Literature*, Manchester: Manchester University Press. Deals with various aspects of the flourishing of literature for and about 'imperial boys.'

Said, Edward (1993), *Culture and Imperialism*, New York: Knopf. Extends and revises *Orientalism*; covers many nineteenth- and twentieth-century writers.

——*Orientalism* (1978), New York: Random House. A founding work of postcolonial studies, dealing mainly with nineteenth-century British and French representations of 'the Orient.'

Spivak, Gayatri Chakravorty (1988), 'Can the Subaltern Speak?' *Marxism and the Interpretation of Culture*, Cary Nelson and Lawrence Grossberg (eds), Urbana: University of Illinois Press, pp. 271–313. Perhaps the most important of Spivak's many essays on postcolonial topics.

Stocking, George (1987), *Victorian Anthropology*, New York: Free Press. The standard history of the emergence of anthropology in Britain.

Trumpener, Katie (1997), *Bardic Nationalism: The Romantic Novel and the British Empire*, Princeton: Princeton University Press. Analyzes the Romantic 'national tale' and ideas about nationalism in Ireland, Scotland, Canada, and elsewhere.

Young, Robert (2001), *Postcolonialism: An Historical Introduction*, Oxford: Blackwell. Global in scope, this work covers European imperialism and resistance to it from Bartolomé Las Casas in the 1500s to nearly the present.

Index